# The German Way of War on the Eastern Front, 1943–1945

# The German Way of War on the Eastern Front, 1941–1945

## The Decline and Fall of Tactical Management

Jaap Jan Brouwer

Pen & Sword
MILITARY

First published in Great Britain in 2024 by
Pen & Sword Military
An imprint of Pen & Sword Books Limited
Yorkshire – Philadelphia

Copyright © Jaap Jan Brouwer 2024

ISBN 978 1 39903 299 5

The right of Jaap Jan Brouwer to be identified as
Author of this Work has been asserted by him in accordance
with the Copyright, Designs and Patents Act 1988.

A CIP catalogue record for this book is
available from the British Library

Typeset by Mac Style
Printed in the UK by CPI Group (UK) Ltd, Croydon, CR0 4YY.

Pen & Sword Books Limited incorporates the imprints of After the Battle,
Atlas, Archaeology, Aviation, Discovery, Family History, Fiction, History,
Maritime, Military, Military Classics, Politics, Select, Transport, True
Crime, Air World, Frontline Publishing, Leo Cooper, Remember When,
Seaforth Publishing, The Praetorian Press, Wharncliffe Local History,
Wharncliffe Transport, Wharncliffe True Crime and White Owl.

For a complete list of Pen & Sword titles please contact

PEN & SWORD BOOKS LIMITED
47 Church Street, Barnsley, South Yorkshire, S70 2AS, England
E-mail: enquiries@pen-and-sword.co.uk
Website: www.pen-and-sword.co.uk
or
PEN AND SWORD BOOKS
1950 Lawrence Rd, Havertown, PA 19083, USA
E-mail: Uspen-and-sword@casematepublishers.com
Website: www.penandswordbooks.com

# Contents

# Acknowledgements

These two books about the war on the Eastern Front, of which this is the second, can be seen as a logical continuation of my earlier book *The German Way of War. A lesson in tactical management*, which is mainly analytical in nature. Military organizations have fascinated me from my childhood, and I am very pleased that both the literature and my practice as a management consultant still offer new perspectives on them almost every day. Learning is an ongoing process in this area, and that is perhaps one of the most interesting aspects of history. I have tried to translate my fascination into a logical and consistent story that on the one hand offers a clear analytical framework and on the other hand deals sufficiently with the reality of the battlefield.

What I put into words is at this moment reality in the Ukraine, a bitter reminder that forces from the past still can exert power in the present.

A word of thanks to my wife Loes and our children Michiel, Cathelijne and Sophie, who were witnesses to the emergence of this and all my other books on military organizations. They have given me the time and space to dive into books and magazines, whether on holiday or at home, and have been kind enough to listen to all my stories. And to accept as roommate a 1: 8 Tiger tank.

While every effort has been made to trace the copyright holders of illustrations which are not otherwise credited, the publishers and I apologize for any inadvertent omissions.

# Introduction

This is the second of two books devoted to the German way of war on the Eastern Front. The first volume covers the years 1941–1943 and ends with the fall of Stalingrad; this volume then picks up the thread and ends with the fall of Berlin and the aftermath of the war. In order to give the reader an idea of the forces that play a leading role in the following pages, the German and Soviet armies will be analyzed in detail in the first chapter. This is intended to explain why each side reacted in a certain way at a certain moment. After this sketch, the years 1943, 1944 and 1945 will be discussed, and in addition to the historical events, the organizational dimensions of both organizations, their logistics, the security situation behind the front, the fight against the partisans, the production of weapons, and other factors will be described. Finally, there will also be ample room for the story of the individual soldier.

Notes in the text refer to the Bibliography. The first figure is the source's number in the Bibliography, the second is the page number(s).

# Glossary

| German | English |
|---|---|
| Abteilung | Battalion |
| AP grenades | Armour-piercing grenades |
| Auftragstaktik | Decentralized command concept that clearly defines what goal should be reached, but gives freedom in the way of how it should be reached |
| Aussere Führung | Enforced discipline |
| Ausf. (Ausführung) | Mark |
| Befehlstaktik | Centralized command concept that gives no room for own initiative. The team had to follow strict orders or act according to the plan |
| Beweglichkeit | Manoeuvrability |
| Bewegungskrieg | War of manoeuvres |
| Breitkeil | Tank Formation (triangle) with the base of the triangle forward |
| Einheit | Unit but also unity |
| Erfahrungsberichte | Feedback report |
| Ersatz Abteilung | Replacement battalion |
| Ersatzheer | Reserve army |
| Fähnrichsexamen | Ensign exam |
| Fallschirmjäger | Paratrooper |
| Feldersatz Battalion | Replacement battalion at the front |
| Feldgendarmerie | Military police |
| Feldheer | Field army |
| Feldwebel | Non-commissioned officer |
| Flak | Flieger Abwehr Kanon: anti-aircraft gun |
| Flivo: Fliegerverbindungsoffiziere | Liaison officer between army and Luftwaffe |
| Führen durch Aufträge | *See Auftragstaktik* |
| Führung und Gefecht der Verbundenen Waffen | Leading and fighting with combined armed forces |

| | |
|---|---|
| Führen unter der Hand | Leading behind the superior's back |
| General Stab | General staff |
| GROE | Soviet military intelligence service |
| Grundlagen der Erziehung des Heeres | Basics of education of the army |
| HE Grenades | High-explosive grenades |
| Heer | German Army |
| Heeresgruppe | Army group |
| Hilfswillige | Voluntary Russian or Ukraine auxiliary troops |
| Innere Führung | Internalized discipline, self discipline |
| Instandsetzungsabteilung | Logistics battalion |
| Kaiser Heer | Army of the Kaiser |
| Kampfgemeinschaft | Unity in fighting |
| Kampfgruppe | Combat group |
| Kampfstaffel | Mobile combat unit protecting the divisional commander |
| Keil | Tank formation (a triangle) with the tip of the triangle forward |
| Kommandature | Headquarters of the KoRück linked to an Armee |
| KoLuf: Kommandeur der Luftwaffe | Commander of the reconnaissance squadrons at the level of army corps |
| KoRück: Kommandeur Rückwärtiges Heeresgebietes | Commander of an area behind a Heeresgruppe |
| Kriegsakademie | Military academy |
| Kriegsspiel | Wargame |
| Krisenfest | Stress resistant |
| Kriegsschule | Military school |
| Landser | Private |
| Leichter Panzerzug | Light tank platoon (for conducting reconnaissance) |
| Nahkampfführer | Close combat officer (liaison to the Luftwaffe) |
| Nachrichtenzug | Communications unit |
| Oberkommando des Heeres (OKH) | Supreme commander of the army |
| Oberkommando des Wehrmacht (OKW) | Supreme commander of the armed forces |

| | |
|---|---|
| PAK (Panzer Abwehr Kanon) | Anti-tank gun |
| Panzerjäger | Anti-tank units |
| Panzergrenadiere | Armored infantry |
| Panzer Kampfwagen (PzKpfw) | Tank |
| Pionierzug | Engineer platoon |
| Propaganda Kompagnie | Propaganda company |
| Polizeibataillon | Police battalion |
| PVO | Soviet air defence district |
| Reich Kommissariate | Civil administrative regions |
| Reichsarbeitsdienst (RAD) | German state labour force |
| Reichsbahn | German state railway |
| Reichskommissariat | Conquered territory |
| Reichswehr | Army of the Republic |
| Rückwärtiges Heeresgebiet | An area behind a Heeresgruppe |
| Schwere Panzer Abteilungen (sPzAbt) | Heavy tank battalion |
| Sicherungsdivision | Security division |
| Schnelle Kombinationen | Fast combinations |
| Sonder Kraftfahrzeug (SdKfz) | Special vehicle (often a halftrack) |
| Schwerpunkt | Focal point of the attack |
| Stavka | Soviet Supreme Command |
| Stosstrupp | Shock troop |
| StuG (Sturmgeschütz) | Assault gun |
| Truppe | Troops/units |
| Truppenamt | Troop office |
| Verbundene Waffen | Combined arms |
| Wehrkreis | Military district |
| Wehrkreis Prüfung | Examination in the military district |
| Wehrmacht | German armed forces (Heer, Luftwaffe and Kriegsmarine) |
| Werkstatt Kompagnie | Maintenance company |
| Wirtschaftsstab | Organization responsible for the economy in a region |

# Chapter 1

# The Two Armies

## The German Army

The German Army lost two World Wars but is still seen as having been a formidable fighting force. How is this possible? To try to find an answer, we will start with a few quotations from prominent authors to give an idea of what we are discussing in this chapter. An interesting first one is the opinion of Trevor Dupuy, a Colonel in the US Army, who was surprised to find:

> [The] record shows that the Germans consistently outfought the far more numerous Allied armies that eventually defeated them … On a man for man basis the German ground soldiers consistently inflicted casualties at about a 50 per cent higher rate than they incurred from the opposing British and American troops under all circumstances. This was true when they were attacking and when they were defending, when they had a local numerical superiority and when, as was usually the case, they were outnumbered, when they had air superiority and when they did not, when they won and when they lost.

In 1962 Dupuy formed the first of his research companies dedicated to the study and analysis of armed conflict, the Historical Evaluation and Research Organization (HERO). This institute analysed many battles, looking at the relative battlefield performance of the armies and units involved. Some of these analyses are shown in the Appendix.

The relative battlefield performance in the above excerpt relates to the front in the west in the period after the Normandy landings, a theatre in which only a small number of German units fought and were not equipped with the best materiel available. The battlefield advantage of 150 per cent that Dupuy outlines here would have been much higher in the earlier years; on the Eastern Front it could rise to more than 500 per cent. Ultimately, however, history shows that an army can lose a war despite such high battlefield performance, if the enemy can only bring enough men and weapons into the field.

Another interesting analysis is that of Martin Creveld in his book *Fighting Power*. In a few words he describes how we have always been misled:

> Contrary to the widely held clichés about 'blind obedience', *Kadavergehorsamkeit* [slavish loyalty] and Prussian discipline, the German Army had, from the time of Moltke the Elder at the latest, always emphasized the crucial importance of individual initiative and responsibility, even at the lowest levels.

How did the German Army acquire such high battlefield performance? The answer lies in their command concept, *Auftragstaktik*.

## *Auftragstaktik*

In the course of the hundred years before the Second World War, the Germans had put in place a number of important management principles in their military organization. Perhaps the most important of these was *Auftragstaktik*, formulated by von Moltke at the beginning of the nineteenth century. (34: 57)

Evaluation of the German Army after the Battle of Jena in 1806 had shown that it was of little use in battle to operate with plans worked out in detail beforehand; the gunpowder fumes over the battlefield made central control impossible, and only the commanders on the spot could properly assess the local situation. In 1860, von Moltke (1800–1891) introduced the management concept of *Auftragstaktik*: *Führen durch Aufträge* (leading by assignment), as opposed to *Befehlstaktik* (leading by orders) in which central control predominates, the concept used by other armies. The starting point of this new command concept was that planning of combat actions should only take place in outline; local commanders in the field then had the responsibility and authority to adapt their actions according to circumstances. In other words, the context of the operation ('why an objective should be achieved') and the objectives ('what should be achieved by when') were clearly formulated in advance, but the path towards them ('how are we going to achieve these objectives') could largely be decided according to the judgement of the commanders in the field. This separation of 'why' and 'what' on the one hand and 'how' on the other resulted in a flexible organization, with responsibility and authority being exercised at a low level and with a high degree of self-regulation. This resulted in a great independence for individual units, and a high degree of flexibility was expected from commanders in the field in order to respond quickly to actual developments on the battlefield.

This concept, with Blitzkrieg-like characteristics, was well illustrated by the Prussian-Austrian War of 1866 and the Franco-Prussian War of 1870. Both were relatively short conflicts, settled within three months. This also explains the enthusiasm with which the various armies marched off to the First World War, since they believed it would not be long before it became clear who had won. There, however, *Auftragstaktik* came to a complete standstill due to the increased firepower of artillery, which transformed the battlefield into a sea of mud that was difficult to cross.

During and after the First World War, a number of other important principles were added on the basis of the experiences gained, namely:

- The *Schwerpunkt* principle
- The principle of *Verbundene Waffen* (combined arms) and the associated *Einheitsprinzip*.

*Auftragstaktik* was relatively ineffective during the First World War due to the extremely static nature of trench warfare, which offered no room for the type of flexible combat that the Germans had in mind. One of the biggest challenges of trench warfare was how to force and successfully follow up a breakthrough. If a breakthrough was achieved at all, the infantry and artillery were unable to keep up with the rapidly advancing vanguard units; due to the difficulty of the terrain, they simply got bogged down. The advance units thus became isolated and could then easily be neutralized by the enemy. To cope with the problem of breaking through the front, the Germans developed 'Hutier tactics' in the last phase of the First World War: heavily armed units (*Stosstruppen* – stormtroopers) infiltrated through the front line at weak spots (*Schwerpunkte* – key points) and then quickly advanced into the rear areas to disrupt lines of communication and destroy artillery positions. The problem remained, however, that the regular infantry could not support the *Stosstruppen*: the horse-drawn waggons of the infantry and the supply columns could not keep up with the rapid pace of the attack in the muddy and shellhole-pocked

---

**Hutier tactics**
These were named after the Supreme Commander of the German Eighth Army in Russia in 1917, General Oskar von Hutier. The High Command of the German Army ordered him to apply the new tactics developed by the *General Stab* (General Staff) to the fortifications of Riga, which had withstood a two-year siege by the Germans. Optimal application of the concept meant that the fortifications could be taken within two days. From that moment on, the tactic was known in German as *Hutiertaktik*. (15: 172–3 and 41: 2–5)

terrain. This allowed the enemy to regroup and close the gap in the front. The weakness of Hutier tactics was overcome in the Second World War by the use of tanks and armoured tracked vehicles for the transport of infantry, since these could move easily over difficult terrain. (2: 191)

The new offensive doctrine of *Angriff im Stellungskrieg* (attack in trench warfare) fitted in well with the existing concept of *Auftragstaktik*; within a general framework, the various commanders and men in the front line had to act as they saw fit, without waiting for orders from above. This suited the reality of the front in the First World War, where communications – in reality telephone lines – were almost immediately blown to pieces by the artillery during combat. This forced small groups of soldiers to fight independently of each other and to take advantage of opportunities on their own initiative. The German Army was the only organization that recognized and acknowledged the limitations and challenges of the Great War battlefield and responded to them by developing a new doctrine, training their men in it and promoting the key leadership skills that made delegating decision-making to the lowest levels possible. (45: 205–6)

---

**The new soldier**

It is also possible to take a more cynical approach to this change in doctrine. In the hell of trench warfare, 1916 had produced a different type of soldier: a man in a steel helmet, uniform hanging on him, with burning eyes, a closed face, imperturbable, unconcerned at the horrors around him, apathetic but creative, independent and on the edge of insubordination. He had learned to survive as a member of a small group, without leadership and without imposed discipline. His commander's eye was no longer on him; only his own morale and his own assessment of the situation helped him to survive. This type of soldier needed a completely different style of leadership, if he needed any at all. (32: 149)

---

These new tactics led to local successes in 1918, but could do nothing about the strategic reality of a growing preponderance of power on the Allied side, which would eventually lead to the surrender of the German Army later that year.

## The interwar period

After the First World War, the Germans analysed their combat performance very thoroughly at all levels and in all kinds of situations. The experiences were laid down by von Seeckt as a supplement to the doctrine of *Auftragstaktik* in a number of guiding documents, including the *Führung und Gefecht der Verbundenen Waffen* (leading and fighting with combined arms). Part I of this was published in 1921 and Part II in 1923. As the title suggests, a central theme was the cooperation between the various armed forces in integrated units. These documents formed the theoretical framework for the further development of the Reichswehr in the interwar period.

Parallel to this development was the evolution of ideas about the deployment of tanks as offensive weapons. We have already seen that one of the problems after successfully breaking through the front was how to follow up an attack with a second assault wave and the regular infantry. Horse power and the limited motor vehicles available proved insufficient to follow it up quickly and consolidate a breakthrough. So the combination of *Auftragstaktik*, *Verbundene Waffen* and new ideas about the deployment of tanks and motorized infantry laid the basis for the way the Reichswehr would be organized and for its tactical doctrine.

The connecting link in the field of mobility between the two World Wars was to be found in the person of, among others, General Heinz Guderian; he was one of those who linked the aforementioned tactical offensive doctrine to the flexibility and firepower of tanks. This resulted in a new, powerful doctrine, that of the tank offensive, in which the tanks were supported by motorized infantry in armoured vehicles. An important difference with the First World War was that the offensive no longer focused on eliminating artillery, but on eliminating the opponent's C3I (Command, Control, Communications and Intelligence) capability. This can be thought of as the enemy's brain and nervous system. If it could be damaged or destroyed, the enemy front would generally collapse quickly.

Key to the success of this concept was cooperation between the various army branches (infantry, cavalry, artillery, engineers etc.) in the mobile and hectic situation during the attack and after the breakthrough. The principle of *Verbundene Waffen* and that of *Einheit* (unity) played an important role in this: the various arms had to be able to operate as integrated multifunctional combat units, so called *Kampfgruppen*. In other words, cooperation between these different branches always had to run smoothly, looking beyond the traditional divisions between them. Great emphasis was therefore placed on joint training and exercises, so that there would always be intensive and optimal cooperation in combat situations.

The principles of *Auftragstaktik* and *Verbundene Waffen* were combined with the principle of the unity of leadership (*Einheitsprinzip*). The leadership of these multifunctional combat units was in the hands of one ultimately responsible commander, so that there could never be confusion as to who was giving the orders. In accordance with the principle of *Auftragstaktik*, the commander of these multifunctional combat units had maximally decentralized responsibilities and powers. (7: 139) By using a combination of tanks, self-propelled artillery and infantry in armoured personnel carriers (*Verbundene Waffen*), a new dimension was given to Hutier tactics, and German armoured troops were able to employ a highly mobile method of warfare, 'manoeuvre warfare' in the true sense of the term. Guderian, with his background as a liaison officer, also ensured that all units were equipped with sufficient radios and other communication equipment – an absolute prerequisite for maintaining cohesion between units operating over a broad and deep front.

## The Second World War

The combination of *Auftragstaktik*, *Verbundene Waffen*, *Schwerpunkt* and the tank offensive was the basis for the successes of the German Army, especially in the early period of the Second World War. If all the above elements fell into place, this was Blitzkrieg, as seen in the Polish campaign of 1939 and the May Days of 1940, and the evolution of the concept was complete. (39: 51–2)

---

### The philosophy of chaos

It must be understood that the Germans approached the concept of waging war from a fundamentally different philosophical position to their opponents. Almost all other armies faced by the Germans in the wars of the nineteenth and twentieth century saw it as their main challenge to win control of the battlefield. They tried to gain control of the intricate choreography of battle and to direct it along the lines planned by centralized command and control structures. They followed the natural instinct to control one's environment and mould it according to preconceived ideas. In this way, the strategist feels most at home facing a linear and static front, which can be attacked at pre-selected points with a previously calculated number of people and resources. For the Allies in the First and Second World Wars, the ideal battle was a mathematical exercise in which the correct tonnage of shells and an optimal mix of units would physically shatter the enemy at one certain point of the front. However, the more chaotic, fluid and confused the battle, the more the Allies lost their grip on events, and this sometimes led to panic. As a result of the centralized command structure followed to a greater or lesser degree by all Allied commanders, subordinates would often ask their commanding officer, 'What should I do?' in situations that actually offered them opportunities. The responses were often inadequate or passive, because commanders were unfamiliar with the realities of the battlefield.

The Germans, however, accepted chaos as a natural part of warfare and learned to live with it. They often used precisely this confusion and uncertainty ('the fog of war') to gain the initiative on the battlefield, while deliberately unbalancing their opponents by creating as much chaos as possible. By delegating responsibility and decision-making to the lowest echelons, they made it possible for individual commanders to find their own way of reaching predefined goals within an agreed framework. This mobile, fluid, non-linear battlefield was the environment in which the German philosophy and the German Army thrived best. When this philosophy came into full effect in the form of Blitzkrieg during the Second World War, its characteristic elements comprised the following: infiltrations, short, intensive bombardment of communication centres, surprise attacks in the most unexpected places, isolating the opponent's strongpoints, and the unexpected appearance of mobile tank units in the enemy's hinterland which destroyed his logistics and communication structure. (39: 51–2)

In terms of management and organization it is still a very advanced command concept, with quick and independent decision-making at the lowest levels and cooperation between all involved, resulting in a very flexible, agile and resilient organization. Besides this, the Germans could rely on some well-tested weapon systems in the form of their tanks and armoured personnel carriers. With all this the Germans made impressive gains in the Soviet Union in 1941 and the first half of 1942, but the machine faltered in Stalingrad, a battle which would become one of the turning points of the Second World War.

## The Soviet Army

### Looking for a vision
After the First World War and the Bolshevik Revolution the new Soviet Union was looking for a vision for its army while it recovered from the Civil War that had raged for three years. In addition, the Soviet Union had suffered a painful defeat by Poland, after which the March 1921 Soviet-Polish Peace Treaty of Riga had given Poland large areas inhabited by Belarusians and Ukrainians. This had put an end to Soviet ambitions to make Poland a Bolshevik state at an early stage. A new buffer separated the Soviet Union from Germany and Lithuania and would remain in place until 1939. In short, the 'Red Workers and Peasants Army', the official name of the Soviet armed forces, was due for an evaluation of its international role.

In the field of theory, the first publications after the Civil War and the war against Poland focused on the political-ideological character of a possible war. In an article from 1925, M.V. Frunze pointed out that this war would necessarily target the weakest link in the capitalist chain in Europe, so that eventually Soviet regimes could be established everywhere. The Soviets also realized that there was not much that could be learned from the Civil War, because a future war would be so different. According to theorists such as A.M. Zayonchkovski such wars would be fought between groups of states, involving large segments of the civilian population and new technologies which would avoid trench warfare.

Under the leadership of Tukhachevsky, research had been started into the nature of this future war. The conclusion was that the Soviet Army needed much better equipment and more and better training to be able to play a significant role in a future conflict. More specifically, the Soviets needed:

- mechanized infantry machine gun units, supported by large formations of fast tanks and self-propelled artillery
- large cavalry units, which had to be reinforced with armoured units (armoured cars and fast tanks) with great firepower
- large units of attack aircraft

The report also analysed where a capitalist offensive could be expected to come from. Countries such as Great Britain, France, Poland, Italy, the Baltic states and Romania were mentioned as states that could form a coalition and open the attack. Germany and the United States might eventually join such a coalition.

In line with this, preparations for a future conflict were accelerated and a Five Year Plan was drawn up in 1928 to increase the number of tanks in the planning period 1928–1933 from 380 to 7,000, aircraft from 1,232 to 3,332, and guns from 999 to 4,870. Official figures show that by 1933 the planned number of aircraft had indeed been achieved, and more than 10,000 guns were available, but only 1,053 tanks. A great leap forward had been made, despite the number of tanks lagging behind schedule.

In the early 1930s there was much thought in many parts of the Soviet Union about the contours of a future war, the place of new technologies within it and how all these developments could be incorporated into the Red Army as fast as possible. For example, the demoralizing effects of bombing civilian targets were considered long before this was practised in the Spanish civil war at Guernica. As a precaution, the Soviet Union formed special air defence units near cities, the PVOs (the Russian abbreviation for Air Defence). Tukhachevsky, meanwhile, was one of the leading officers in the Red Army and director of the Frunze Military Academy. His ability dominated all other leaders of the Red Army and in 1931 he became Deputy Commissar for Naval and Military Affairs. In the autumn of that year, Tukhachevsky presented to the Politburo his plans for the reorganization of the army, plans that had gained in urgency as a result of developments in Germany. The so-called 'Tukhachevsky plan' was to lead to a number of radical changes within three years, not only in organizational structure, but also in the integration of the Territorial Army into the regular army and the creation of motorized and mechanized units. These last changes were in line with the generally accepted theory in the West that success in a subsequent war would be determined by carrying out a first attack, which should take the spearheads deep into the enemy's hinterland. There they would destroy his entire logistics and C3I system, resulting in the collapse of the enemy's resistance. The Soviet doctrine of deep penetration assumed a breach in the enemy line of defence, followed by an advance of 150–200km deep into the enemy's hinterland. The Soviet units would have to advance in a wide wedge at a rate of between 10km and 32km per day. Tanks, planes and shock armies were central to this concept and they had to be able to advance faster than the 'bourgeois' units. Tukhachevsky assumed that this doctrine required three types of tank:

- to support the infantry in capturing fortifications
- to support the infantry in the open field
- to operate as an independent tank force deep behind enemy lines

The first type should help break through the defence line, the second should support the infantry in exploiting the resulting gap, and the third should advance through the gap at high speed to targets deep in the hinterland. The Air Force meanwhile, would bombard the enemy's supply lines and communications centres, and paratroopers could be deployed against specific targets. By 1936, based on this doctrine, the Soviets had built four mechanized corps, each consisting of 500 tanks and 200 armoured vehicles. In addition, a special organization was set up for the support of ground troops by the Air Force, which served to support these deep penetrations behind the enemy front line. Although the doctrine was still under discussion, the new 1936 officers' handbook, *PU-36*, was built entirely around the doctrine of deep penetration, as was a 'Deep Penetration Instruction' for the military leadership. Themes within *PU-36* included manoeuvring, close coordination between the different weapon systems (the principle of *Verbundene Waffen*/combined arms) and bringing the war into the enemy's territory. According to this manual, 'The infantry, in conjunction with artillery and tanks, will determine the outcome of the battle. For this reason, the other units carry out their mission in support of the infantry.' There was also room for the cavalry ('strategic cavalry able to operate independently under all circumstances'). Tanks could also operate independently, but 'the technical limitations of the materiel' had to be taken into account. With this document Soviet ideas fell into line with the generally accepted doctrines of modern warfare as formulated, for example, by the Reichswehr in 1933 and published in 1936.

The Soviet Union, meanwhile, had produced a series of tanks with a long range and high speed in the early 1930s, the BT (Bystrokhodny Tank, or 'high-velocity' tank), which were initially armed with a 37mm gun, later with 45mm and 76mm guns. There was also a lot of experimentation with other types, including amphibious tanks, and armoured personnel carriers. The Red Army also grew in size. In 1931 there were thirty regular and forty-one territorial divisions, but this number began to grow rapidly in 1934 and the army swelled from 600,000 to 940,000 men. This was made possible by incorporating territorial divisions into the regular army and establishing mechanized and tank brigades and paratroop units. By 1936 about 80 per cent of the territorial divisions had been incorporated into the regular army, which by this time contained no fewer than 1,500,000 men.

Tukhachevsky's reforms also extended to the recruitment, selection and training of recruits and officers. At this time, citizens with a non-proletarian background (the bourgeoisie, nobility, civil servants and rich peasants) could not enlist in the army. This deprived the military not only of part of the possible annual quota of recruits, but also of access to the intellectual and technical knowledge of this group of citizens. The regime tried to remedy this weakness through all kinds of additional courses, but it was clear that it would take more time than had been anticipated. To speed up the process of modernization, reserve officers were mobilized or returned to active service, and the age limit for officers was raised. Tukhachevsky also wanted to build a real officer corps, taking over those training aspects of the Tsarist regime that had proved their worth. As a result, the number of military schools grew from forty-eight to sixty-five, including for the first time schools devoted to armoured warfare. The various armed forces also increasingly studied each other's tactics in order to achieve optimal coordination at the tactical and operational level. In order to improve technical knowledge within the army, 5,000 military technical schools were established within the Red Army by decree in 1932. In addition, Tukhachevsky wanted to re-establish a hierarchy of ranks as in all other armies of the world, despite this being completely contrary to Soviet ideology. After much discussion, the decision to introduce ranks for the senior officers was published on 22 September 1935.

An important breakthrough came with the new constitution of 1936, which made it possible for all citizens to enlist in the army. As a result, the number of potential recruits increased and their technical and intellectual level improved.

All in all, the Soviet army had changed dramatically in the years between 1933 and 1936. The number of men had risen on paper to 1,500,000 (probably 3,000,000 in reality), while mechanized and motorized units and anti-aircraft battalions had made their appearance. Moreover, a new wind was blowing through the army. It was no longer a strictly proletarian force, but one that represented the entire nation. A young, brand new, self-assured officer corps emerged, and the role of the political commissars diminished visibly. The age of the officers was between twenty-five and forty, and there were about 16,000 students in military academies with an annual enrolment of 4,000. Among this young, politically non-aligned officer corps there was also great concern about the forced collectivization carried out by Stalin in the early 1930s. The majority of the men (75 per cent) came from rural areas, where their families were being brutally forced to give up their land. The officers had to deal with men who had been affected by this and who had developed a hatred of the Soviet regime. As a result, the officer corps sometimes openly expressed its resistance to forced collectivization.

These were developments that the hardliners within the Politburo, including Stalin, followed critically.

## The Purges

Oppression was the order of the day while Stalin held sway in the Soviet Union. The Red Army did not escape this fate, and in 1937 Stalin targeted the opposition within it. This opposition had manifested itself first in the undermining of the position of the political commissars, who were linked to the higher level of each division. This was seen by the Politburo as an undermining of the party itself. In no small part, these moves had been initiated by Tukhachevsky, who was seen by Stalin as the leader of the opposition to his rule.

In May 1937 Tukhachevsky published an article about *PU–36* in the army magazine *Red Star* and in the party newspaper *Bolshevik*. One could not have imagined that this article would herald the end of the deep penetration doctrine. But on 10 May, Stalin intervened, and a decree was issued that fully restored the powers of the political commissars. Tukhachevsky was relieved of his post and arrested by the NKVD on 26 May. He was executed on 11 June.

The subsequent purges were mainly directed against former Tsarist officers and veterans of the Civil War. The latter constituted about 20 per cent of the officer corps. Of the approximately 75,000 middle-ranking and senior officers of the Red Army, approximately 30,000 were executed or imprisoned for long periods. About 90 per cent of the generals and 80 per cent of the colonels disappeared, as did three of the five marshals and 75 per cent of the members of the Supreme Military Council. The purges hit the Red Army at a time when it was strong, efficient and looking to a bright future. It was left weak, dazed and disorganized. Young, inexperienced officers were quickly promoted thanks to their supposed loyalty to Stalin.

The disappearance of Tukhachevsky and the group of officers around him marked the end of the creative and progressive school of thought in the army. As tanks, artillery and aircraft continued to pour off the assembly line, they were scattered without a vision across the various army units. New ideas were discouraged and only standard approaches and solutions were accepted. Officers were nervous because each believed he could be next to be purged; they were unsure of their role and position now that professional competence was apparently no longer important and only loyalty to the party mattered.

Tukhachevsky's doctrine was replaced by the views of Pavlov, a tank expert with experience in the Spanish Civil War. In his view, tanks had mainly had an effect on infantry morale; they had not been successful as independent units. In the future, therefore, tanks should only be used to support infantry. In line with this view, independent motorized and mechanized formations were disbanded and tanks were attached the various infantry divisions.

The disappearance of the deep penetration doctrine left a vacuum. The purges had had a devastating effect on the Red Army and left deep scars on the officer corps. The Soviets would therefore encounter major problems in their prologue to the Second World War: the breaking of Finnish resistance during the so-called Winter War from 1939 to 1940.

There were some bright spots: the second Five Year Plan had paid off, and more than 9,000 tanks were available, mainly T-26s and tanks of the BT series. Up to this point, the Soviets had copied British and American tank designs, but now for the first time they were able to develop their own, the T-28, the M-2, the T-34 and the KV-1. In addition, about 2,000 amphibious vehicles, armoured or not, were operational. The number of artillery pieces had grown to 7,000 as planned, the majority of which were pulled by armoured tractors. Also anti-tank and anti-aircraft guns and mortars were either towed by trucks or transported on them. Mechanized artillery pieces that were fully armoured were already being considered. Ideally, these guns, combined with the tank divisions, would move as one armoured force across the battlefield of the future. All in all, a military power had emerged that far surpassed that of countries such as France, Great Britain and the United States. Only Germany could compete to some extent with the Soviet Union.

But despite these impressive numbers, by the end of 1939 the Red Army had inwardly barely recovered from the purges. A few officers had combat experience, but their number was totally insufficient to compensate for the draining of the knowledge and experience of the officers who had fought in the Civil War. And in the years to come, the Soviets would face military challenges of all kinds.

## Time for reorganization

In the two wars to come – the Polish campaign and the Winter War against Finland – the Soviet Army would underperform. During their advance into Poland in 1939, the Soviet units encountered little resistance, especially as the Germans had done all the preparatory work. Yet supply and administrative units lagged far behind, and the Red Army was a ramshackle affair compared to the apparently smooth-running Wehrmacht. The war with Finland was only 'won' by the deployment of a mass of men and machines, and even then Finland only had to cede a small part of its territory. The Soviets were forced to reorganize their army, but in the midst of this reorganization the conflict with Germany erupted. As the German Army initially overran the Soviets, a first improvisation in the structure of the infantry division soon followed in the form of the '7/41' division. This was no more than a horde of soldiers armed with rifles. But there were plenty of men, and a rifle is a simple weapon that anyone using common sense can quickly handle as well as a trained professional. There also appeared the so called rifle brigade, in fact a 'horde of rifles'. These two organizational forms determined the further structure of the Soviet army.

In addition, a rigorous form of specialization was introduced, in the sense that a commander commanded a limited number of different weapons and never more than one major weapon system. In other words, the commander of a rifle company had nothing more under his control than rifles and machine guns. This meant that commanders quickly became good at their 'speciality'. The same was true of the mortar company, the machine gun company, the engineer company, the medical company and the pontoon company. Even larger units such as a rifle battalion only had rifles and machine guns at their disposal. They were supported by specialist battalions such as artillerymen, engineers and communication units, but the presence of these was not essential for the rifle battalion to function. The adage '*In der Beschränkung zeigt sich erst der Meister*' (it is in working within limits that the master reveals himself) aptly expresses what the average commander and his men within the Red Army could handle.

There was also a crisis of leadership, since large Soviet formations were commanded by officers that in other armies would have led smaller units. For example, Soviet brigades were led by lieutenants and captains, and divisions by majors or lieutenant colonels. This, combined with the fact that the commanding levels above them were less professional on the one hand and their men less educated and trained than their opponents on the other hand, resulted in sub-optimal use of forces and very high casualty rates among infantry units. But during 1942 the Soviets gained more and more control over their divisions and were thus able to withstand the Germans more easily and even begin to retake the initiative. Their advantage was that they could always deploy more, many more units and men than the Germans who, despite their much higher battlefield performance, had their hands full keeping the Soviets off their backs. And the Red Army could deploy a number of excellent weapons in large quantities since their production facilities were out of range of German bombers.

All in all, after their first setbacks the Soviets had started to rebuild their forces brick by brick in 1942, finally achieving an army that would eventually take them to Berlin, as we shall see.

## The Eastern Front: situation report January 1943

We now know that Stalingrad, with Midway and El Alamein, was one of the three turning points of the Second World War. But that was by no means clear at the time. Although the Germans had not been able to achieve their ambitions in the east and south of the Soviet Union, and Moscow and Leningrad had still not been captured, they had been able to restore the front line deep in the Soviet Union and were waiting out the winter there and preparing themselves for the year 1943. But there remained the question of whether the Germans were able to keep up with the Soviets in terms of the number of troops available, and with the production capacity of the Soviet Union in this war of destruction. And a war of destruction it was: the Germans would eventually count on this front 1,105,987 dead and 1,108,365 missing or taken prisoner (in total 2,124,352), and 3,498,059 wounded and sick; the Soviets – although there is much uncertainty about this – suffered a total of 8,668,400 dead and 22,326,905 wounded and sick, as well as approximately 20,000,000 civilian deaths, not least because Stalin's regime showed no compassion for its citizens and only focused on its own survival. Both sides had learned, the Germans especially in the field of defensive tactics, while the Soviets were forced to build their forces from the ground up, step by step, adapting to the capabilities of the men. While the Soviets already had the weapons with which they would eventually reach Berlin, the Germans were forced to thoroughly overhaul almost all of their weapon systems, especially the tanks. This rearmament got under way at the end of 1942 and only bore fruit in 1943 and subsequent years; until then the Germans had to rely on their superior tactics and the quality of their men and officers. This was the precarious equilibrium we left the belligerents in at the end of 1942 in *The German Way of War on the Eastern Front 1941–1943*. In *The German Way of War on the Eastern Front 1943– 1945* we will examine the course of the events in the subsequent period.

# Chapter 2

# 1943: A Year Full of Uncertainty

*Stalingrad is often seen as the turning point of the war in the East. It was certainly a crucial confrontation and a blow to the morale of the Germans. Up to that point the Wehrmacht had lost approximately 2,000,000 men in the form of dead, missing or prisoners of war. In May 1943 another 75,000 Germans in North Africa would be marched into captivity. Despite all these losses, the German Army reached its greatest size in 1943 with 5,000,000 men. It was an army that was far from defeated and could face any opponent with confidence. Only in the summer of 1943 would the balance of power in the Soviet Union change definitively. The Soviets would take the initiative and hold it until the end of the war. The experience of 1941 and 1942 had shown that winter was the period of the Soviets, and that in the muddy weather of spring and autumn the Germans took the initiative. The year 1943 was no different.*

Since the year 1943 can be seen as the turning point in the war on the Eastern Front, it is a good time to reflect on the starting position of the two opponents. The structure of the two armed forces at the beginning of 1943 will first be described, specifically the structure of the various units and new weapon systems. In addition, both parties had learned a lot in recent years, which was translated into an adjustment of tactics at all levels in the organizations. After this sketch we will describe the course of the battle in 1943, first the main events and then the experiences of individual units at the front. The chapter will close with the fate of the ordinary Soviet infantryman and civilian, as well as that of German prisoners of war.

## 1. The German Armed Forces

### The Panzerwaffe in 1943

Due to its losses in recent years, the strength of the Panzerwaffe was slowly but surely eroded. In 1942, two new divisions were created, the 26th Division on 15 September and the 27th on 2 October, with the aim of increasing combat power on the Eastern Front. However, the 14th, 16th and 24th Panzer

Divisions went down at Stalingrad in the first months of 1943, and later in the spring the 10th, 15th and 21st were lost in North Africa. In addition, two weak divisions, the 22nd and 27th, were disbanded in the same period. All in all, the size of the Panzerwaffe was reduced by eight divisions in the space of a few months. The Germans managed to replace four of these eight divisions with new ones, built around the core of the survivors and using men destined for other divisions and all the materiel that could be found. Due to these efforts, the Germans were able to deploy thirty-two panzer divisions in the spring of 1943, but mostly below their normal combat strength. Twenty-one divisions of this force, including 4th SS and 2nd Panzer-Grenadiere Divisions, were deployed for the summer offensive of 1943, Operation Zitadelle at Kursk. The fact that only one other armoured division, the 13th with seventy-one tanks, was deployed elsewhere on the Eastern Front is an illustration of the fighting power the Germans concentrated at Kursk.

Four tank divisions were in Sicily and mainland Italy, five others, including three new SS divisions, were in France and one was in the Balkans.

The twenty-one divisions used by the Germans in Operation Zitadelle deployed a total of 1,715 tanks, as well as 147 StuG IIIs, which increasingly became a permanent part of the armoured regiments. Although this was a major achievement, the divisions had without exception less fighting power than in 1941 and 1942, and the strength of German tank divisions began to decline further in the course of 1943. Before Operation Zitadelle, the average tank strength of an armoured division of Von Manstein's *Heeresgruppe Süd* was ninety-five, of which seventy-eight were actually operational, although the nominal tank strength of a German tank division should have been approximately 150. The failure of Operation Zitadelle heralded the final decline of the Panzerwaffe. After almost six months of continuous fighting in the first half of 1943, the strength of the tank divisions would fall to an average of eighty tanks, of which sometimes only twenty were operational; the repair and maintenance system was unable to maintain combat strength, and most of the tanks stood at field workshops or were sometimes literally dragged along during troop movements. One division had only six tanks operational at a certain point. These figures demonstrate the extent to which the Panzerwaffe was rapidly losing its fighting power. Despite the high quality of the materiel and the professionalism of the men and their officers, the shine had begun to come off the Panzerwaffe, and the great successes of Poland, the campaign in the west and the first years on the Eastern Front were never equalled again. From now on, the Panzerwaffe could only contribute to Germany's strategic defence, and would slowly but surely be ground down in the confrontation with the Soviets over the next few years. (41: 67)

### A new generation of tanks

One bright spot came with two tanks of a new generation, the Panther and Tiger. The Tiger tank was first deployed on 29 August 1942 at the front near Leningrad, although this first deployment ended in a fiasco. Four Tiger tanks and one PzKpfw III N of the Schwere Panzer Abteilung (sPzAbt) 502 had to advance down narrow forest paths against well-protected Soviet forces, a situation in which it would have been unwise to deploy tanks in the first place. Their Soviet opponents were battle-hardened units, waiting for the Tiger tanks to get close enough to direct fire at their tracks. And this was successful: the four Tigers got stuck and had to be abandoned by their crews. In the evening the Germans managed to tow away three of the four tanks; the fourth was blown up by engineers. On the positive side, retrospective evaluation showed that the Soviet anti-tank artillery had not been able to penetrate the Tigers' armour, even with 122mm guns. (41: 156)

### Revenge of the Tiger

After its first failed deployment in August 1942, the Tiger was given the opportunity to take revenge during the Soviet Iskra offensive, aimed at the relief of Leningrad.

The help of the same sPzAbt 502 was called in on 12 January to relieve German units that were in danger of being overrun by a Soviet tank brigade. The sPzAbt 502, with four Tiger tanks and eight PzKpfw III Ms, went into battle against the Red Army's twenty-four T-34s and T-60s. And they were successful: half of the Soviet tanks were destroyed and the rest chased back to their lines. In the following weeks, the unit, supplemented by three new Tiger tanks, was continuously deployed and managed to knock out 163 tanks

A Tiger tank at full speed. The Tiger tank had a formidable 88mm gun that had proved its worth over the years.

(T-26s, T-34s, T-60s, and KVs), a quarter (!) of the Soviet losses during the Iskra offensive. The unit itself lost one Tiger, knocked out by an anti-tank shell which hit the less strongly armoured engine compartment. Zhukov, who happened to be visiting the headquarters in the Leningrad sector at the time that this tank was knocked out, demanded that it should be recovered at any cost, and it was. The Russians' study of this tank immediately led to the design of the Su-152 tank destroyer, built around a 152mm howitzer on a KV-chassis. The prototype was developed within twenty-five days and entered production on 1 March. It turned out to be such a potent weapon against the Tiger and Panther tanks that it was soon nicknamed *Zvierboy*, meaning 'animal killer'. (41: 157)

### Tiger tactics

The first three *Schwere Panzer Ersatz Abteilungen* with Tiger tanks received few tactical guidelines and had to fall back on Memorandum Number 87/42 of the *General der Schnellen Truppen* of 10 February 1942. This memorandum simply outlined the capabilities of the tank and did not go into the tactics to be followed. Units made up of PzKpfw IIIs, IVs and Tigers developed the following tactics on the battlefield. In offensive operations, the lighter tanks advanced in front and, as soon as contact was made with enemy tanks, they deflected left and right to allow the Tigers to confront the enemy. In defensive operations, the Tigers took up a well-camouflaged stationary position, their flanks covered by the lighter tanks.

On 20 May 1943 a first revised manual was published, in which the tasks of the Tiger tank were described in more detail. Its main task was to destroy heavy tanks and other heavy armoured vehicles at a great distance. The crews had to actively seek confrontation with these units, and the tanks were not allowed to be used for tasks that could be carried out by lighter tanks or assault guns. In destroying the enemy's heavy tanks they aimed to force a breakthrough and clear the way for the lighter tanks. In other words, the concentrated deployment of Tigers had to ensure a tactical breakthrough, which could be converted into a strategic breakthrough by the lighter tanks. During the phase of penetrating the enemy front, all other units (light tanks, assault guns and infantry) had to support the Tigers. Organizationally, the Tiger battalions were not part of a division, but formed a mobile reserve at Army level. This reserve could be used wherever their deployment could be of decisive importance. However, we will see below that the tank's characteristics in terms of range, maintenance and movement capabilities severely limited its role as a mobile reserve. (57: 36)

## Tiger personnel

The crews of the Tiger tanks came from various units. Chief among them were experienced tank crews who had fought in previous campaigns. Another source was the Schwere Panzer Ersatz Abteilung 500 in Paderborn. Due to the shortage of Tiger tanks, PzKpfw IVs were used for training here. From sPzAbt 503 onward, personnel were drawn from the remnants of tank units that had been greatly reduced in size by combat. Sometimes an existing tank battalion, for example the third battalion of Panzer Regiment 33 of the 9th Panzer Division, was converted in its entirety into a sPzAbt. Without exception, these were battalions with extensive combat experience. Horst Krönke, a tank commander of the sPzAbt 503, tells how, after his additional officer training at the Waffenschule of Ohrdruf/Thüringen, he was in transit in the Soviet Union looking for the 6th Panzer Regiment of the 3rd Panzer Division, but accidentally ended up at sPzAbt 503. 'This [search for his own regiment] turned out to be particularly difficult, because the administrative service at the front did not have accurate information about the exact position of the 3rd Panzer Division. In early January [1944] I arrived at the important railway junction of Zhmerynka. There the administrative department showed me the way to a tank unit in the city. This happened to be the sPzAbt 503.' It turned out that Krönke knew the commander of the unit, Major Graf Kageneck, from the period of the advance in the Caucasus in 1942, when their units had operated jointly. Graf Kageneck arranged with the staff in Berlin that Krönke could stay with him. He needed Panzerkommandante, because a new shipment of Tiger tanks was expected a few days later. (22: 70)

## Tiger repair

The recovery of a Tiger tank after mechanical failure, becoming stuck or stalled by enemy fire was a challenge in itself because a specific recovery tank was missing. The maintenance units had SdKfz 9 FAMO half-tracks at their disposal to recover tanks, and two such half-tracks could tow a Tiger. If the journey was over hilly terrain, a PzKpfw III had to be towed behind the Tiger tank to provide a counterbalance when necessary. Although Tigers could also tow each other, this was officially forbidden, but in practice, especially at the front, it happened regularly. Krönke describes how in February 1944 no fewer than eight Tiger tanks and three FAMO tractors were needed to free a Tiger that was stuck in the mud up to its turret. (22: 72) In another incident, a Tiger towed another Tiger for no less than 150km; the crews wanted at all costs to prevent these tanks from falling into the hands of the Soviets. It was not until 1944 that a suitable salvage tank, the Berge Panther, became available in small numbers. Often, however, due to the lack of sufficient recovery tanks, towing away in combat situations was not possible, and the tank was blown up by its crew. This weakness in the recovery system led to fewer and fewer tanks being available over time. (57: 29)

## Tiger transport

Because the deployment of Tiger battalions could have tactical and even strategic significance, they were often sent in like a kind of fire brigade. Since long trips led to substantial mechanical wear and consumed a lot of fuel, it was preferable to transport the units by rail, especially over greater distances. This was not without problems. In the first place, as the war progressed, movement by rail became increasingly problematic due to air raids and partisan action. Secondly, special transport wagons were required; this required careful planning and coordination of the limited number of available wagons and was time-consuming. Three wagons had to be placed between each wagons carrying tanks, because most bridges in the Soviet Union could not otherwise bear the weight. To enable rail transport, the tanks' 'battle' tracks had to be replaced by narrower 'transport' tracks,

Transporting Tiger tanks by rail was always problematic due to the special wagons required. Here a Tiger tank is safely secured and on its way to the front with its special transport tracks.

as the former were too wide for the rails. All of this, combined with its great maintenance sensitivity, severely limited the Tiger tank's deployability. (57: 30)

## Adjustments in German tactical doctrine

Below is a translation of a German training circular with thirty basic lessons in the field of armour doctrine at the company and platoon level based on the experiences of the Wehrmacht fighting the Soviets. The lessons were written during the war by a company commander and are based on the latest insights from the battlefield. The original text had humorous drawings and stories on one page and combat lessons on the other.

*Panzer Vorwärts! Aber mit Verstand!*

## Preface

The armoured regiment, due to its firepower, mobility and protection, is the main fighting force of the division. Its strength lies in unexpected, concentrated and determined attack, aggressive leadership and daring operations. Fighting in Russia has shown that, in action against the communists, it's not so much about the number of tanks we can deploy, but about the morale and skills of the tank crews. For these reasons alone, German tanks, even in Russia, are victorious. However, combat morale has as little influence on the outcome of the battle as weapons, speed, armour and number of tanks, if these crews are not led by competent officers. Superior tactical leadership in combat is a prerequisite if one aims for few, or even better, no casualties. The purpose of this publication is to collect the experiences of veterans among the officers with combat experience at the front and to communicate these experiences to junior officers in a simple and understandable way.

1. Get to know the terrain before attacking. Use information from other units or study the map carefully. Share this information with the officers you supervise. Precise information and a correct assessment of the terrain can be the difference between victory and defeat.
2. No tank attack is launched so quickly, even under the most urgent situations, that you do not have time to give your subordinate officers a picture of the tactical situation, the mission and anything else that may be of interest for the upcoming mission. Losses due to hasty actions are your responsibility and can jeopardize the success of the mission.
3. Only carefully executed combat reconnaissance can save you from surprises. Protect your flanks and the front. Observation on all sides is the job of every commander. ALWAYS WATCH OUT FOR THE ENEMY!
4. You have to use all your skills to constantly make an accurate assessment of the situation. Only in this way can you make the right decision in the decisive seconds and give short, clear orders without delay. This is the type of leadership you are responsible for.
5. Iron radio discipline is a prerequisite for good leadership, especially when the radio is your only way of communicating. In the case of a platoon in the front of the wedge, the platoons behind should not use the radio, in order to keep the radio net clear for the platoon commander, unless there is an emergency.
6. You must lead with strength. At least two tanks must be positioned in front, and the platoons behind must operate far enough forward to support the leading platoon. The more guns that can be used in the first few minutes, the faster the enemy will be defeated and the fewer losses you will suffer yourself.
7. When you leave cover, do it quickly and all together. The more targets the enemy faces at the same time, the more difficulty he will have in directing and distributing his fire, and the more fire you can aim at the enemy.

8. During the attack, you must drive as fast as possible. At low speed you can see and aim only a fraction better than at high speed, and the chance of getting hit is much higher. Only two speeds are important for a tank: half speed (to shoot!) and full speed forward. This is the basic principle of tank combat!

9. When anti-tank guns are deployed at long or medium range, you must first return fire and then manoeuvre. First stop to get a shot, then manoeuvre with the entire company to take out the enemy, while one platoon continues to fire at the enemy.

10. When anti-tank guns are deployed at close range, stopping is suicide. Only an immediate attack at the highest speed and firing with all weapons will succeed and limit losses.

11. In combat with anti-tank weapons, you must never – even under cover of a strong screen of fire – allow a platoon to attack alone. Anti-tank guns never operate alone. Remember – a tank alone in Russia is lost!

12. You must continuously ensure that there is sufficient distance between the vehicles. This forces the enemy to divide his fire and makes it more difficult for him to direct the fire. Short gaps must be avoided at all times, especially in critical situations, or the number of losses will increase.

13. When encountering an impossible obstacle, such as a minefield or an anti-tank ditch, you must immediately and without hesitation give the order to withdraw to the nearest cover. Standing still, in the crosshairs of the enemy, and trying to continue the attack is pointless in these circumstances and will only cost you losses. Your consideration of how to make a new start can best be done in cover.

14. If during the attack you may need to pass enemy tank positions, for example at the edge of a forest, you must stay as close to their minimum range as possible, or stay far enough away that you are beyond their maximum effective range.

15. Enemy tanks should not be attacked immediately as they will see you and know your strength before you can take them out. Better to avoid them until you get into a good firing position and can surprise them from behind or on the flank. Repulsed enemy tank attacks must be followed up aggressively.

16. If possible, attack enemy strongholds, for example a small village or an artillery position, from multiple points at the same time to distribute the enemy fire and mislead them as to the true position and direction of the attack. This way you can break through more easily and you will suffer fewer losses.

17. Always maintain dug-in positions and camouflage against potential air or artillery attacks. Apologies afterwards do not make up for the losses from these actions.

18. You don't always have to be economical with ammunition. At decisive moments, if you can avoid casualties, you may expend ammunition at a rapid rate (e.g. in case of an emergency attack).

19. Never split your attacking power; that is, never deploy the company's units in such a way that they cannot support each other. If your attack has two objectives, you must first use all weapons to reach one objective and then the second objective. In this way you will capture the two targets and suffer a small loss.

20. Dive-bomber and artillery support must be followed up immediately, i.e. at the moment the bombs or shells hit the target. When the bombardment has stopped it will be too late. You must realize that such a bombardment usually only suppresses the enemy's actions, it does not destroy him. It is better to risk a grenade or bomb from your own troops than to ride into an active anti-tank defence.

21. Other weapons and units attached to you must not be misused. Do not use them for purposes other than what they are intended for; for example, do not use tank destroyers as assault guns, Panzergrenadiere as tanks, or reconnaissance or engineer units as regular infantry.

22. Unarmoured or lightly armoured units attached to you must be protected against unnecessary losses. They have non-combat duties, which is why they are attached to your unit.

23. Units attached to you are not your servants, but your guests. You are responsible for their supplies and must share everything with them. Don't use them for standby duty! This way they will do a better job and be more loyal to you when you need them. And that will often be the case!

24. In combined actions with the infantry or the Panzergrenadiere, you must ensure that everyone works well together. Only then can you help each other and achieve success. Which of the two is the leader within the whole is of secondary importance. What you need to know is that it is the opponent's intention to separate the groups and you must avoid that at all costs. Your war cry must be 'Protect the infantry!' and their war cry must be 'Protect the tanks!'

25. You and your men must always concentrate on your mission, for example capturing a bridge, and you must not be distracted by enemy actions, for example in your flank, unless this threatens the achievement of your mission. Then you have to attack and destroy the enemy.

26. After a successful action, for example capturing a bridge or occupying a village, you 'keep the helmets on'. This means: prepare for a counter-attack, for it will certainly come, sometimes in a place where you don't expect it.

27. In defensive positions, place your tanks so that not only can their firepower be deployed, but they can move into action quickly. And also, only place a limited number of tanks in stationary firing positions, keep the majority in cover as a mobile reserve. Tanks must defend aggressively.

28. Against a strong enemy defence it is useless to continue the attack. Each repulsed attack only costs more casualties. Your efforts should always focus on stopping the enemy with a small force, attacking the enemy in another weaker place with the bulk of the units, in order to force a breakthrough and destroying the enemy by a surprise attack in the flank or rearguard.

29. Always remember that the men are not yours, but Germany's. Pursuit of personal glory and senseless heroic behaviour lead to success only in exceptional cases, but always cost blood. In the fight against the Soviets you must combine your courage with your assessment of the situation, your guts, your instincts and your tactical insight. Only then will you have created the preconditions to be

successful in battle, and your men will not only be loyal to you but will always be at your side, ready to fight.

30. The armoured division in modern war today takes the place of the cavalry as the decisive weapon. Armoured officers are to carry on the cavalry tradition, representing an aggressive attitude on behalf of the Panzerwaffe. But pay close attention to the basic combat principle of Marshal Blücher's motto: 'FORWARD AND THROUGH!' (but keep thinking!).

## Motorization

We have already seen that the German Army's motorization was very limited. And motorization was of great importance because it implies mobility, which was central to the concept of the Germans. This mobility had made it possible in the preceding campaigns to defeat much stronger opponents in a short period of time. In 1939 only 14 per cent of the 93 divisions available to the Germans were motorized. By 1940 the number of divisions had grown to 138, but the degree of motorization had fallen to 10 per cent. This then grew to 18 per cent in 1941 and fluctuated between 18.5 in 1942, 18 in 1943 and 22 per cent in 1944. The efforts of Speer and German war industry clearly paid off in the last years, but it was not just a problem of prioritization; German industry was simply unable to produce enough vehicles.

At the start of Operation Barbarossa, the Germans had 322,000 vehicles at their disposal. Of this number, 44 per cent were found in the infantry divisions, where they were mainly used for supplies, and another 22 per cent were with administrative and other units. In other words, relatively few vehicles were directly linked to combat units, and the fact that the infantry divisions had many vehicles had little effect on their marching speed; in general, they could only advance as fast as they could walk. It is estimated that the German Army would have needed about 170,000 extra vehicles in 1941 to achieve an acceptable degree of motorization. Had they had these numbers, they would have been able to advance faster and deeper into the Soviet Union, and the course of the war might have been different. The Germans could have requisitioned these vehicles in the occupied territories in the spring of 1941 before Barbarossa, but decided not to because they assumed that the Soviets would then smell trouble. They did proceed to requisition them in 1942, when it became clear that 50,000 vehicles had been lost in the preceding period and the end of the war was not yet in sight. The lost vehicles had mainly been deployed at the front lines, and their destruction severely limited mobility. In the following years, a total of approximately 290,000 vehicles changed hands as part of the claims in occupied territories.

Incidentally, these were for the most part anything but suitable for military purposes, let alone for use in the Soviet Union. The shortage of vehicles became all the more acute as, later in 1942, nearly 100,000 vehicles were lost at the Battle of Stalingrad alone. One of the difficult side-effects of these requisitions was an almost unmanageable number of vehicle types, each with specific maintenance and spare-parts requirements, a nightmare for those responsible. Including the materiel of the Allies, eventually 2,000 different types of vehicle were deployed, including 170 types of artillery, 73 of tanks and armoured vehicles and 52 of anti-aircraft guns. (32: 202)

---

**Logistic efficiency**
The effects of being forced to switch from trucks to horse traction may become clear from the figures below. A truck is capable of transporting 6 tons per day over a distance of at least 150km. A horse and cart can transport a maximum of 1 ton over 30km. A truck is therefore almost thirty times more efficient than a horse and cart. Moreover, a horse and cart is simply not physically capable of covering the same distance per day as a truck; it will arrive eventually, but only after five days. In addition, horses eat more hay in weight than a truck needs petrol. The loss of part of a division's vehicles therefore had major effects. It greatly limited mobility and actually reduced the maximum distance to be covered per day to 30km.

---

In 1941, German industry was still largely focused on civilian production and produced only 67,000 military vehicles. The year 1942 was not much better, with only 96,000 military vehicles produced; as we have seen, this annual production corresponds to the losses at Stalingrad. It was not until 1943 that pressure was applied to drastically increase the number of vehicles. By the end of 1943 more than 600,000 were available, many of which were to be used for the campaigns in France and Italy, while others were deployed on the Eastern Front. In other words, motorization of the combat units was and remained limited. The efforts of Speer and the war industry eventually translated into a degree of motorization, at 22 per cent in 1944. But in that year a staggering 399,000 vehicles would be lost. This definitely meant the end of genuine mobility for the German Army: horse and cart would again become the most common form of transport.

The growth in production illustrates the fact that until the end of 1941 German industry was primarily focused on civilian production and only slowly switched to war production and a war economy. It was only through Speer's intervention that the necessary steps towards mass production were taken. But by then it was already too late; the chance of winning the war on the Eastern Front through a Blitzkrieg-like approach had been lost. For the Soviets, this

> **Transport capacity**
> A German division needed about 300 to 350 tons of supplies per day for everyday use, about 10,000 tons per month. If a major offensive was being prepared, this tonnage would be much greater. The Germans calculated that to transport these supplies over a distance of 450km they would need thirty-nine columns of thirty-two 2-ton Opel Blitz trucks each, a total of about 1,200 trucks per division. With over 130 divisions at the start of Barbarossa, it would have taken about 156,000 vehicles to advance deep into the Soviet Union. In addition, it must be taken into account that not all these trucks were operational and that some would be destroyed by the enemy. Hence a minimum number of 170,000 would be a low but realistic estimate.

problem was much less of an issue. Their concept of war was not based on mobile warfare, so their need for vehicles was much less. In any case, most of the vehicles they had were lost in the first months of the war. But this was not a problem for them; they were able to keep mass production going and supply their units with sufficient material at all times.

> **Unknown, but loved**
> What the Opel Blitz meant to the Germans, the legendary 'Polutorka' Gaz-AA truck was to the Soviets. This truck was one of the most commonly produced vehicles in the Soviet Union; more than 1,000,000 units were manufactured between 1930 and 1950. The Gaz-AA was used in all kinds of roles: commercial transport, ammunition transport, as a tanker, an ambulance, a radio car and mobile workshop, a mobile anti-aircraft gun platform. The truck ran on a variety of fuels, including, if the outside temperature allowed, kerosene. The load weight was around 1.7 tons and it had a top speed of 75kph.

In addition, the Soviets received 400,000 trucks (!) from the Allies as part of Lend-Lease from 1942 onwards. This stream of vehicles arrived just in time to give the Red Army the necessary mobility as their offensives got under way in 1943.

## Mobile anti-aircraft guns

In the course of 1943, the focus of anti-aircraft defence shifted more and more to Western Europe, and in particular to Germany itself. The pressure from Bomber Command and the US Eighth Air Force slowly but surely became so great that all kinds of Luftwaffe units and 88mm Flak guns were transferred from the east. This had immediate consequences for the fight on the ground on the Eastern Front: the Germans would have to manage with many fewer

An SdKfz 7 with a 37mm Flak gun near Belgorod in August 1943. The camouflage scheme on the tractor, gun and ammunition trailer consists of sand-coloured spots on the dark factory-applied base colour.

anti-aircraft guns in the future to protect themselves against the growing strength of the Soviet Air Force. As a temporary solution, they developed mobile anti-aircraft guns in the form of a 20mm or 30mm Flak gun on the chassis of the outdated PzKpfw 38(t). The first examples reached the front in the course of 1943. Anti-aircraft guns were also placed on the various types of half-tracks such as the SdKfz 251: this configuration could consist of a single 20mm or 30mm Flak cannon or a 20mm quadruple Flak combination.

All these solutions offered only partial relief against attacks by the Soviet Air Force. And, perhaps more importantly, in 1943 the Luftwaffe was less and less able to provide ground support. This gave the Soviet units ever greater room for manoeuvre, their logistical movements were less often disrupted and they were able to build up reserves deeper behind the front.

### Guderian and Speer: the hope for Germany

On 1 March, Guderian was reinstated by Hitler; the setbacks at Stalingrad and in North Africa demanded a man of his calibre. He was given the position of Inspector General of the Panzerwaffe with far-reaching powers in the fields of management, organization, equipment and training. His functional rank was that of Commander of an Army; in practice, he was answerable only to Hitler and he had only to consult Zeitler, Chief of the General Staff. His powers extended not only to all tank units and mechanized infantry units of the Heer, but also to those of the Luftwaffe and the Waffen SS. The only exception to this was the armoured units of the *Sturmartillerie*, which had the prized StuG assault guns. The reason for this was that these units did their job so well at an operational and tactical level that outside influence was considered undesirable by everyone, including Guderian himself. They therefore remained under the command of the artillery. Ironically, it was precisely these assault guns that would play an increasingly important role in the future as a replacement for tanks, which would be in ever shorter supply.

Guderian was faced with the task of getting the Panzerwaffe back on its feet after the traumatic year of 1942. He first turned his attention to the production side of the problem. On closer inspection, he found that there was a discussion raging within the General Staff in early 1943 that almost led to tank production being limited to the production of Tigers. If this trend had continued, total German tank production would have fallen to just twenty-five Tigers per month. By the fall of 1942, production of the PzKpfw III had ceased; only chassis of this tank were produced, which served as platforms for various anti-tank and artillery guns. In addition, in view of the production capacity needed for the new medium-heavy Panther tank, it was also considered whether to discontinue production of the PzKpfw IV, with the exception of the chassis of this tank for further construction. The General Staff changed its mind at the right moment, but it is illustrative of the gap that had developed

One of Hitler's fantasies was the *Sturmtiger*, a heavy mortar on the chassis of a Tiger tank, specially developed for combat in cities. The tank weighed 68 tons, and only eighteen were built.

The magazine *Signal* discussed the successful tests of the new Panther tank in detail. It passed with flying colours a comparison test with a Sherman tank captured in North Africa.

between the realities of the battlefield and the opinions of decision-makers in Berlin. The PzKpfw IV ultimately remained in production until the end of the war and would continue to form the backbone of German armour, along with the many surviving examples of the PzKpfw III. Tanks like the Tiger and the Panther, however impressive in terms of performance, were able to force local dominance, but had little influence on the eventual course of the war.

Guderian immediately recognized the dangers of the aforementioned suggestions and advised Hitler to take into account that the new Panther tank would not be operational before July or August 1943. In his view, all efforts should be aimed at increasing production of the PzKpfw IV F2 with the 75mm L/43 or L/48 anti-tank gun. In addition, there was an urgent need for a second generation of tank destroyers. For the Panzergrenadiere, a simplified version of the SdKfz 251 had to be produced in large quantities. The reconnaissance units also had to be re-equipped with the four-wheeled SdKfz 221, although it was clear that these units actually needed the fast, well-armed, eight-wheeled SdKfz 234. These orders for German industry came in addition to the existing production programme which, as well as relatively standard products, was characterized by an almost infinite number of modifications and adjustments, resulting in an unclear and often unpredictable need for spare parts and associated logistics for all fronts. The fact that German industry did not completely collapse under these demands was largely due to Speer, who was appointed by Hitler in February 1942 as head of the *Reichsministerium für Bewaffnung und Munition* (from September 1943, *Reichsministerium für Rüstung und Kriegsproduktion*). He initiated a policy that was characterized by:

- standardization of all kinds of weapon systems
- simplification of all kinds of weapon systems
- rationalization of production processes.

While building on organizational changes that had already been introduced by his predecessors, he managed to improve both the breadth and depth of German war industry and ensured that production increased by leaps and bounds. In doing so, he had to overcome much resistance within the existing military- industrial complex to prevent German industry from continuing to focus on the achieving best quality rather than the necessary quantity. Production increased spectacularly in 1943.

**Production figures 1943**

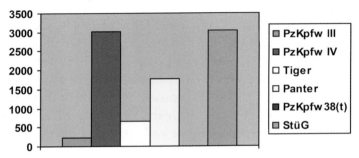

In 1943 the first StuG IVs became available to units at the front. This one is being scrutinized by a number of senior officers.

From the table we see that production of the PzKpfw III and the PzKpfw 38(t) had been reduced and stopped respectively. The newcomer was the Panther, while production of the Tiger tank increased from 84 to 647 and production of the PzKpfw IV increased from 994 to 3,013; all these tanks had the 75mm L/43 or L/48 gun. The combined production of the StuG III and the new StuG IV increased from 789 to 3,042, while total tank production increased from 4,475 to 8,705, a 94 per cent increase.

## 2.  The Soviet Armed Forces

### Soviet infantry

Until 1943, the infantry was the central element of the Soviets' concept of warfare, and Soviet tanks played a secondary role given their losses in the preceding years. The Soviets were well aware that the deployment of infantry en masse was the only answer to the German technique of mobile warfare. In line with this, by the end of 1943, as the Red Army increasingly took the initiative from the Germans, only 320,000 of the 4,000,000 troops deployed were stationed in units that could properly be called mobile. That represents a meagre 8 per cent, while at that time the Germans, even though they had seen better days, could classify 14 per cent of their units as mobile. Despite the fact that the Soviet infantry, certainly in the early stages of the war, had suffered the greatest defeats and the greatest number of casualties, as in all other belligerent countries it recruited the least able men. The motorized and mechanized armed forces, such as the air force, artillery and navy, could look forward to a large influx of relatively highly trained recruits. In this way in the Soviet Union, as in Germany, the motorized units became the elite of the ground forces. They were given the best men, the best training and the best and most powerful weapons. They were often the decisive element in battle and, if necessary, formed the last line of defence – at least in the later years of the war, because until early 1943 it was the Soviet infantry that managed to hold out heroically against the Germans. (11: 91)

   The Soviet infantry was not entirely forced to move on foot and had some armoured vehicles at its disposal. In June 1941, for example, approximately 60 per cent of the 10,000 available armoured vehicles were assigned to infantry divisions. However, these were generally light or obsolete vehicles, which did not survive the first months of battle. By 1942, all of these vehicles had disappeared and were replaced by newer models already in mass production. The Soviets in their unparalleled way managed to produce 4,700 armoured vehicles in the first three months of 1942, compared to the Germans' 6,189 units in the whole year. Moreover, only 30 per cent of the Soviet production consisted of the T-34 and KV-tanks, classified as medium by the Soviets but which the Germans at the front already had their hands full with; the rest were heavy tanks. As a result, the Soviets were never short of vehicles at any point during the war.

As part of their 'combined arms' doctrine, the Germans placed approximately 25 per cent of their tanks in infantry divisions. As the war progressed, they increasingly dispersed their tank units among these infantry divisions, often in the form of assault guns or anti-tank units. This reinforcement was necessary in view of the enormously long front that had to be held by the infantry divisions; an infantry division was generally responsible for about 20km of front, and such a long front line could not be covered by artillery alone. In 1942, 12 per cent of all tanks, mainly assault guns, could be found in infantry divisions, and this percentage rose to 31 in 1943 and 47 in 1944. In dispersing the materiel in this way, the original ideas about the structure, deployment and strength of the Panzerwaffe slowly but surely evaporated during the course of the war.

**The Soviet mobile forces**

At the beginning of the war, the Soviet army had seventy-eight tank and mechanized brigades at its disposal. The brigades were one-sided in structure and contained no infantry. With most of the original units largely wiped out by 1941, the Soviets were forced to form completely new tank brigades. Despite their losses, they were able to build large numbers of excellent tanks in the months and years after the German invasion. These found their way to infantry units, which slowly but surely evolved into tank brigades. Due to this organic growth, the new brigades had a balanced composition and consisted of twenty-one tanks and supporting infantry, a total of approximately 1,300 men. The infantry served to protect the tanks during combat, avoiding one of the pitfalls of tank unit composition: too many tanks and not enough infantry. Part of these tank brigades managed to survive the harsh conditions of the battlefield, and in the course of 1942 the Soviets were able to combine them into tank corps. These corps were the Soviet equivalent of the German Panzer Divisions. They consisted of three tank brigades (battalions), three battalions of motorized infantry and additional units such as artillery and engineers. These tank corps formed the basis for the Soviet variant of mobile warfare and they eventually managed to achieve results that the Germans had thought impossible.

The Soviet tank corps in 1943 thus corresponded to the ideal composition of a tank division as seen by all belligerents based on the experience of the preceding war years. A Soviet tank corps was well-balanced and consisted of about 30 per cent infantry almost entirely armed with semi-automatic machine guns; it therefore had excellent firepower. In addition, a Soviet tank corps had no fewer than 240 armoured vehicles, including the necessary tanks. A weak point was the lack of artillery; for practical reasons, the tank corps did not have any, although it could rely on the support of independent artillery brigades or *Sturmovik* fighter-bombers. Given the communication and coordination problems within the Soviet army, this was not exactly an ideal solution. It meant that if a tank corps encountered strong resistance during an offensive it had three alternatives: to try to fight its way through (which was a risky undertaking), to move around it (which put too much strain on its communications and coordination capabilities), or to call in artillery and infantry support. Since the latter was usually delayed, the offensive often came to an end quickly. Another weakness was the lack of an efficient supply system, especially motorized supply units. At best, a Soviet offensive had a range of two full tanks of diesel: the full tank at the start of the offensive and the extra barrels of diesel that the tanks carried on their rear deck. This considerably limited the depth to which an offensive could penetrate. Moreover, captured fuel could not be used, because the Germans used petrol for their tanks and other vehicles. For the Soviets this was a structural organizational problem; for the Germans the problem was mainly a lack of vehicles. We have seen in that context that the lack of sufficient motorized supply units was one of the reasons why the Germans had not succeeded in 1941 in defeating the Soviet army a single campaign. In addition, independent tank brigades always were kept in reserve; they were used to reinforce infantry divisions for a limited period of time, for example during offensives. In the fall of 1942 the Soviets were able to form the first tank corps from tank brigades, and by the end of 1943 they were able to deploy twenty-six of these corps against twenty-five German tank divisions. During this period the Soviets also overtook the Germans in armoured vehicles: 5,628 Soviet vehicles to 5,400 German. The tank corps continued to evolve. If we compare the German Panzer division from 1944 with a Soviet tank corps, the following picture emerges.

|  | Panzer Division | Soviet Tank Corps |
|---|---|---|
| Total size | 14,727 | 11,115 |
| Infantry | 8,684 | 6,340* |
| Tanks | 174 | 278 |
| Armoured vehicles | 359 | 412 |
| Artillery | 213 | 215 |

* All armed with semi-automatic rifles

The main difference between a German Panzer division and a Soviet tank corps was that the latter had 60 per cent (!) more tanks: compared to the nominal strength of 174 tanks of a German Panzer division in 1944, the Soviets could field 278 tanks, often of superior design. Moreover, the strength on the German side was often theoretical, given that only a limited number of the tanks was operational. The Soviet tank corps had as much artillery as the German Panzer division, although the Soviet artillery was less effective, as we shall see below. Either way, these tank corps, whether or not combined into tank armies, would become the main formations of the Red Army and take it to Berlin.

### The Mechanized Corps

The Soviets also used their tanks and armoured vehicles in combination with other units, as the Germans did with their Panzergrenadiere Divisions. The Soviet counterpart was the mechanized corps, which was in fact little more than a motorized infantry division. These were specialized units of large size which had many armoured vehicles at their disposal. There were never many such divisions in action due to the lack of experienced men and specialized units to fully exploit their potential. The Soviet mechanized corps numbered 18,000 troops, consisting of 40 per cent infantry, 300 pieces of artillery, and 250 tanks and armoured vehicles. The Soviet mechanized corps specialized in advancing behind the German lines as quickly as possible after breaking through the front in order to dig in or entrench themselves behind the enemy, preferably taking over the Germans' important logistic and communication hubs. Thanks to the abundance of infantry, artillery and armoured vehicles, they were generally very capable of repelling all German counter-attacks in situations where a Soviet tank corps, for example, would have easily lost out. Fortunately for the Germans, a lack of experienced men and specialized units meant that the Soviets were rarely able to field more than half a dozen such units.

### Artillery

Next to the mobile armoured units, artillery was the main weapon system of the Soviets. The importance attached to artillery by the Red Army is evidenced by the fact that as early as 1943 the Soviet artillery forces had 2.4 times as many men as the mobile forces and three times as many guns as the tanks. By the end of 1944, little had changed: the artillery forces had three times as many men and twice as many artillery pieces as the mobile forces had men and tanks. Here we have to take into account the Soviet definition of artillery: everything with a calibre larger than 45mm. The importance of this weapon should not be underestimated. Artillery fire caused the most casualties among all belligerents in the First World War, and in the Second World War on the Western Front things were little different: artillery fire was responsible for 90 per cent of the casualties on the German side and 70–80 per cent of the Allied casualties. In the Soviet Union, however, artillery fire accounted for 50 per cent of the casualties on the German side, but by far the largest share of the casualties on the Soviet side. This indicates that however abundantly the Soviet army was equipped with artillery, it was considerably less effective than its German counterpart. The Germans, on the other hand, lost many men to (machine) gun fire, hand grenades, mines, etc. These differences are all the more striking when we realize that after 1942 the Soviets on the Eastern Front had more and better artillery than the Germans; the way the artillery was deployed was clearly more important than its quantity and quality. Consequently, the Germans were always able to win artillery duels with the Soviets, unless they were overwhelmed by a massive Soviet deployment or were fatally short of ammunition. The reason for the low effectiveness of Soviet artillery was simply that they had insufficient qualified personnel. As a result, the Soviet artillery functioned at 1918 levels in terms of fire control. All belligerents had managed to elevate the use of artillery in the First World War to a true art, but not in mobile warfare. As the number of guns grew, the shortage of sufficiently qualified personnel became more acute. The Soviets tried to solve this by specialization; they did not spread the guns over the various units, but concentrated them in large units the size of brigades, divisions and even corps. These units were preferably only used in attacks, the so-called 'artillery offensives'.

---

**Flying artillery**

The Soviets had flying artillery at their disposal in the form of the excellent IL-2 *Sturmovik*, which was often compared to a flying tank. The entire front part of the aircraft was covered with a layer of 14mm steel. The cockpit, engine and gas tank were bulletproof, and the cockpit glass was made of 65mm bulletproof glass. The aircraft had four machine guns in the wings, which were replaced by heavier weapons later in the war. However, the *Sturmovik* was poorly protected at the rear, from where German fighters preferred to attack and managed to shoot many *Sturmoviks* down. The Soviets solved this by installing a tail gunner with a 25mm machine gun in the IL-2M version. Although the *Sturmovik* was one of the most successful aircraft of the Second World War, German and Finnish fighter pilots were not impressed by its qualities. This does not alter the fact that the Soviets successfully continued to deploy this aircraft until they reached Berlin. In total, more than 30,000 *Sturmoviks* were produced.

However, these artillery units were not capable of mobile actions because these were technically too complicated in terms of direction, coordination and fire control. Defensively, they also often suffered, and direct confrontations with German artillery were avoided. Only towards the end of the war did the Soviet artillery achieve some success in duels against German defensive artillery positions, due to the then poor condition of the German artillery.

Despite the limited effectiveness of the Soviet artillery, it must be said that 50 per cent of German casualties, more than 1,000,000 men (!), were accounted for by Soviet guns and that the 'artillery offensive' was often the basis of successful Soviet attacks.

These 'artillery offensives' were a logical consequence of the relatively backward fire control techniques. During such offensives, up to 20,000 artillery pieces were deployed, about 200 to 300 per kilometre of front. Their role was to systematically destroy the German fortifications at the front and positions behind it from stationary positions. The procedures were extremely simple and inflexible. Before the offensive could start, the artillery had first to calibrate its fire. In other words, the units had to determine where they themselves were and where the German positions were, so that they knew for sure who and what they were firing at. This calibrating procedure could take up to three days and, in addition to performing the necessary calculations and actually firing, consisted of building up the necessary communication network with adjacent units, in order to prevent these units from coming under friendly fire. In addition, of course, extensive ammunition dumps had to be built up. The German artillery could be deployed much more quickly due to the superior training of their gunners and infantry, in particular due to the emphasis on cooperation, better means and implementation of communication and logistics. The Germans were usually able to make their artillery function optimally after just one day.

Even if the Soviet artillery had had sufficient technically trained personnel, its efficiency might not have been much higher due to its poor fire control technology and cumbersome procedures. But that did not matter to the Soviets; the successes of the Red Army's offensives in 1943 and 1944 were due in no small part to the massive deployment of artillery, however inefficient it was. The only way to avoid the destructive power of the Soviet artillery offensive was to pull back at the right moment – which the Germans usually did. Not all Soviet artillery was so inefficient, of course: there were units that were not inferior to those of the Germans, and their numbers would grow in the course of the war.

Not every gun was classified as artillery. For example, the Soviets did not regard anti-tank guns as such. These differed from other guns in two respects.

In the first place, due to their high muzzle velocity, the wear on the barrels was much greater than in field artillery. Secondly, much heavier shells had to be used to absorb the force generated by the high muzzle velocity. This meant that less explosive charge could be used. Against tanks and armoured vehicles, the high kinetic energy of the anti-tank shells provided the desired armour-piercing effect, while shells with a high explosive charge were required for classic artillery fire. (11: 142)

## 3. Battlefield practice

### The offensive doctrine of the Soviets

How did the above work in practice? In theory, both German and Soviet attacks were carefully planned actions, with infantry, tanks, artillery and engineers working closely together. In reality, only the Germans were able to carry out attacks under clear direction and coordination; Soviet attacks were generally poorly managed affairs. One of the reasons was that the most qualified personnel in the Soviet army were in the tank, artillery and engineering ranks. The infantry, which bore the lion's share of the work, came off much worse. As we have seen, the artillery was often effective but not really efficient; engineering was good, especially at clearing minefields; and the Soviet tank forces were excellent, some of this being due to the superior quality of the Soviet tanks. While the Germans had a well-balanced and proven offensive doctrine, after 1941 the Soviets had to build their offensive doctrine from the ground up. The main aim of their offensives, including towards the end of the war, was to break through the German defensive positions and allow motorized units to advance through them. It was the Soviet artillery that had to blow a hole in the defensive positions, since the infantry would not be able to break through on their own. The German defence was too flexible for that, and the coordination between the German artillery and infantry was too good. These had to be destroyed if a Soviet offensive was to have any chance of success.

A typical Soviet attack was heralded by increased patrol activity on the Soviet side in the weeks leading up to the offensive. About three days before the offensive, the artillery took over and began calibrating by firing at German positions. As we have seen, the artillery acted as a crowbar to punch holes in the German front. An attack often started with the well-known 'artillery offensive' lasting two to three hours. The guns then shifted their fire to positions further behind the front to support the infantry. However, the Germans entrenched in fortifications generally survived the artillery bombardment, so the Soviets had to deploy tanks in addition to infantry to force a breakthrough. After breaking through the first line, however, the battle was not yet over; the Germans often built defensive lines with a depth of 6–8km. This necessitated the use of tanks combined with infantry, since by the time the Soviets broke through, they were beyond the range of their own artillery. In addition, the Germans laid anti-tank and anti-personnel minefields throughout their defence lines and around their artillery positions. This necessitated the deployment of engineers. All this placed high demands on the coordination capabilities of the Soviets which were by no means always well developed.

A separate phenomenon that the Soviets had to take into account were the German machine-gun nests. One well-placed machine gun, if well protected, with a good field of fire (a special point of attention) and sufficient ammunition, could hold up the Soviet infantry over a one-kilometre front for extended periods of time. The Germans had thirty-two to sixty-five machine guns per kilometre of front, and machine guns that had survived the artillery bombardment could thus halt a Soviet offensive over a wide front. Tanks or mechanized artillery had to take out these pockets of resistance as quickly as possible. The anti-tank guns in these defensive positions were, however, relatively vulnerable to artillery fire. The Germans had three to six anti-tank guns per kilometre of front, in addition to ten to twenty Panzerfausten. One gun was capable of knocking out an average of three tanks before itself being destroyed; a Panzerfaust could account for one tank. However, the anti-tank guns were difficult to protect against the destructive power of the artillery bombardment and many of them were knocked out before the battle really started. (11: 140)

## Soviet tank doctrine

Tanks were a decisive weapon on the Eastern Front. The Soviets had paid a high price for gaining experience with tank units in the early years of the conflict, but not in vain, for by 1943 they were increasingly able to manoeuvre their tank armies. Tank armies in this period generally consisted of two tank corps and one mechanized corps, the corps being the equivalent of a German Panzer Division. Control and coordination at the operational level during combat, however, remained a constant problem, and much depended on the practice and repetition of tactical manoeuvres. In general, the first phase of the attack consisted of the artillery offensive described earlier. This bombardment was followed by a heavy tank attack in a first wave and T-34s with mounted infantry in a second wave. Should a breakthrough be achieved, more T-34s, T-60s, T-70s and infantry would follow. Tactically, Soviet tank commanders were not yet able to act independently to respond to the possibilities offered by an actual battlefield situation, so they followed standard patterns of attack.

If the breakthrough did not succeed, an attack would follow the next day at the same place and in the same manner. This was continued until one of the belligerents had run out of men or materiel. This tactical doctrine was not changed or modified during the Second World War and led to unimaginably high losses against the experienced German units.

The Germans, in turn, tried to separate Soviet infantry and tanks during such attacks, so that they could not support each other. In general, this was not a problem, since the infantry, who had insufficient armoured personnel carriers, rode on top of the tanks and were thus easy prey to German machine-gun fire. The tanks were then intercepted using the 'sword and shield' tactic: a front of anti-tank guns stopped the enemy tanks, which were then attacked from the flanks by the panzers.

The Germans developed a number of other tactics which led to heavy losses being inflicted on the Soviets. But there was no lack of men and materiel on the Soviet side: in 1943 alone 20,000 T-34s were produced (!), in addition to tens of thousands of other tanks and artillery pieces. Furthermore, the Soviets proved to be motivated, tenacious and disciplined fighters, capable of surprising the Germans in all sorts of ways, as we shall see below. Moreover, the call for revenge on the invader grew ever stronger, now that large parts of the Soviet Union were liberated for the first time and it became clear what carnage the Gestapo and the Allgemeine SS had wreaked on the civilian population. The liberation of the rest of the Soviet Union was a cause for which the Soviet soldier would willingly give his life (41: 169), quite apart from the fact that any deviance from the party line would lead to the death of the man involved and probably his family too.

### The offensive doctrine of the Germans

The Germans had a proven offensive doctrine. In the years 1941 and 1942 they had learned many valuable tactical lessons from the harsh experience of the battlefield. Earlier in this chapter, we discussed the changes in the field of tank tactics in detail. This continuous learning process at all levels and in the various weapon systems was essential to the Germans, whose battlefield advantage depended on their superior training and command. It was a question of 'learn or perish'. A kind of 'Eastern school' emerged in the field of tactics, and some of its maxims are described below:

- It was not necessary to cover the entire line or sector, as the Soviets were not inclined to conduct outflanking manoeuvres on the relatively open flanks of the Germans.

- Soviet anti-tank positions could not be breached by tanks alone; infantry had to advance with the tanks and take on most of the work, supported by the tanks.
- Although a rapid advance during offensive operations was one of the specialities of the Germans, a few hours of preparation (or days for larger actions) paid for themselves in the form of fewer casualties. Soviet defensive positions were often well built, but relatively easy to break through with proper preparation.
- Tanks had to attack in successive waves. This allowed them to support each other and made direction and coordination easier. Infantry-reinforced tank regiments attacked over a one-kilometre front, tank divisions over a front of between two and three kilometres. Once a gap had been created in the defence lines, other units would penetrate the enemy's hinterland and advance quickly to targets located behind the front.
- Infantry riding on tanks or armoured vehicles had to leave them only at the last moment in order to maintain the momentum of the attack. All vehicles, armoured or not, had to advance in groups from cover to cover.
- Artillery had to lay down a smokescreen and use concentrated fire to protect the flanks of the advancing units against enemy attacks.

---

**German combined tank and infantry tactics**

Grossjohan describes the capture of the Russian city of Tikhonova in a combined action of tanks and infantry. 'For me and my men, the attack on Tikhonova was an exact copy of the attack on Luka. We led the tanks through the mud and darkness of the night with our green-capped flashlights to the city's boundaries. Then it started. After the Panther tanks lined up, they first shelled the city with machine-gun fire. Their tracer ammunition set many buildings on fire. The burning buildings clearly illuminated our targets. As the targets became visible against the light of the blazing fires, the Panthers' 75mm guns began to sow death and destruction among the stunned Soviet defenders. By the time we infantry entered the city, the Soviets were almost unable to put up a coordinated resistance. We had virtually no casualties and captured many Soviets before night gave way to day.' (19: 102)

---

The *Erfahrungsberichte* (post-action reports) system enabled the Germans to continuously adapt to new situations. This meant that in the field of management and organization they were able to compensate to a certain extent over a considerable period of time for the effect of the Soviets' superior forces.

## German defensive doctrine

The traditional German 'defence in depth' was virtually impossible on the Eastern Front due to its vast extent; in mid-1942, the front was 1,800km long. It had to be defended by 140 infantry divisions (out of a total of 205), in other words an average of about 13km of front per division. Normally a division in a defensive position was responsible for twice the width of front as in offensive operations. In practice, this amounted to 5km of front for offensive operations and 10km for defence. Two regiments of the division were deployed to the front and one was kept in reserve; alternatively, three regiments were deployed to the front with one battalion of each in reserve. So of every three units (company, battalion, regiment) one was always in reserve. This was theoretically 'defence in depth'. In practice in the Soviet Union, units were generally spread thinly over long distances, in extreme cases over 40km of front, and only at divisional level there was a reserve in the form of anti-tank units and engineers.

This was only the position on the front line itself, for the division was in fact responsible for an entire defensive zone in front of and behind it. This zone extended from the outposts 5km ahead of the front line to the artillery positions of the division 5km behind it: in total, an area 10km deep. The fortified outposts had to be able to hold off enemy patrols and direct the fire of the division's 105mm and 150mm artillery pieces in the event of a large-scale enemy attack. The front line itself and the area in front of it were reinforced with minefields, fortifications and trenches. We have described above how this line was fortified, including the use of machine-gun nests and anti-tank positions.

All this served to win time during an enemy attack: defence in depth meant that there had to be enough time for mobile reserves to absorb the attack and, ideally, proceed to an offensive. In practice, the Germans used a combination of defensive and offensive actions. A well-coordinated, mobile offensive was a powerful defensive tool against the massive but clumsy and inflexible Soviet offensives, a good example of the formula 'mass times speed equals thrust', by which a smaller, mobile force can defeat a larger slow-moving attacker. Therefore, both defensively and offensively, the Germans were able to make the Soviets bite the dust again and again. Occasionally, the Germans were forced to switch to real mobile defence, and in such cases, motorized units had to be able to be deployed quickly at various locations in a large area.

## Soviet defensive doctrine

There was a big difference in defensive doctrine between the two sides. Due to their greater flexibility, the Germans could afford a mobile form of defence, whereas the Soviets were forced to limit themselves to positional defence. This was no problem for the Soviets: they had ample numbers of infantry at their disposal (at the beginning of the war twice as many as the Germans, later three to five times as many). They could therefore afford stationary-position defence and to seal a large part of the front with sufficient troops. They kept about 10 per cent of their units behind the front in reserve. In addition, for obvious reasons, the Soviets had great difficulty developing a flexible, mobile method of defence. Soviet defences could delay but not stop a determined German attack. The Germans did not have the manpower and equipment for such an offensive in mid-1943, otherwise their advance would simply have been unstoppable.

The Soviets recognized the importance of slowing down German offensive actions and pinning down the German units, but they realized that they had little chance of doing this in the open field. Standard Soviet defence consisted of a so-called basic defence line with mobile reserves on hand for emergencies. Defence in depth consisted either of a coherent system of fortifications (centralized defence) or isolated fortifications (decentralized defence). When cornered by the Germans and forced to give up their positions, the survivors retreated to the next line of defence. A division could thus slowly but surely 'burn out' in the course of an offensive, and was then replaced by a fresh one.

Soviet defensive operations were unimaginative affairs. Standard procedure was to hold the position for as long as possible. That this was possible was partly due to the bravery of the Russian soldiers, and partly to the fact that anyone found behind the front for no good reason was mercilessly shot by the secret police, who patrolled the area behind the front. The Germans therefore assumed that the Soviets would remain where they were, fighting on or not, waiting for the tide to turn. It was an important step forward for the Soviets that in 1942 and 1943, unlike in 1941, they were able to escape the German encirclement attempts. For example, during their summer offensive of 1942, the Germans pursued the Soviets in an attempt to encircle them, but failed to do so. Much to Hitler's anger, the Soviets managed to stay ahead of the Germans and to keep their force intact.

While the Soviets did not have time to learn or refine their doctrine, they did accumulate tremendous experience during the war. In addition, their numbers grew and they were increasingly supported defensively by mobile units. This, combined with the tough fighting mentality of the Soviet soldier, made it increasingly difficult for the Germans to break through Soviet positions as the war progressed. In the end, they no longer had the strength to do so and could only hope to slow down the Soviet offensives. It was less because of German defensive action and more because of the lack of a sufficiently equipped logistics system on the Soviet side that these offensives became stuck. As the war progressed, fighting took on more and more the character of a battle of attrition, so feared by the Germans, and the focus was on the quantity rather than the quality of the armies involved.

Later in the war, the differences between German and Soviet defensive doctrine would diminish as the Germans became less mobile and the Soviets more so. The trucks, but also the radio equipment, which were supplied by Great Britain and America in the course of 1942 under Lend-Lease, made a great contribution to this enhanced mobility.

## Lend-Lease

During 1942/43, substantial supplies under the Lend-Lease programme began to reach the Soviet Union. Soviet figures always suggested a limited contribution of up to 4 per cent of the total Soviet production, but these do not reflect reality. The United States and Great Britain supplied large quantities of aluminum, magnesium, coal and other raw materials, things to which the Soviet Union no longer had access due to the advance of the Germans. This enabled them to maintain their own war production. In addition, the Allies supplied some 24 million uniforms, 14.5 million pairs of shoes, 4.2 million tons of food, 11,800 wagons and locomotives and a very large number of trucks.

These Lend-Lease trucks in particular were of importance to the Red Army. At the end of the war, 66 per cent (!) of the Soviet truck fleet consisted of Lend-Lease equipment. In all, the Soviets had 400,000 trucks and 47,000 Willys jeeps at their disposal. These enabled the Red Army to re-supply their more forward mobile units during the advance and continue to support them once they had broken through the German lines. Without these trucks, any Soviet offensive in the period 1942–1945 would have come to a halt after only a limited distance, allowing the Germans to surround the advancing Soviet troops. The Soviets were less satisfied with other Lend-Lease items. For example, the Valentine and Mathilde tanks fuelled the Soviets' suspicion that they were being given second-rate equipment. These tanks could only accommodate a gun of up to 40mm in their turrets, a calibre that was completely insufficient to match the German tanks. They therefore described these as light tanks, and Soviet commanders rightly complained that they could in no way stand comparison with, for example, the T-34. The Sherman tank was more appealing, but its narrow tracks significantly limited its mobility in the muddy Russian terrain. That the width of the tank, and therefore of its tracks, was dictated by cargo requirements for sea transport and the dimensions of American engineering bridges did not, justifiably, interest the Soviets.

The same applied to the aircraft delivered. The transport aircraft were appreciated, but the fighters were considered to be of inferior quality. At the front in the Soviet Union, the Soviets needed ground support and fighter aircraft that could operate at low altitudes. The Allies' focus, on the other hand, was on long-range bombers and interceptor fighters. As a result, the Soviets received aircraft types such as the P-39 Aircobra, the P-40 Warhawk and early types of Hurricane, aircraft that had previously proved their worth on other fronts under different circumstances but did not meet the harsh requirements of the Eastern Front. Things were complicated by the fact that the Soviets refused to let the Allies train their pilots and mechanics. Yet Soviet aces like A.I. Pokryshkin and G.A. Rechkalov owed their victories to their P-39s, and these types of aircraft gave the Soviets convincing air superiority over the Kuban bridgehead for the first time in the spring of 1943. (16: 150–1)

### *Maskirovka* (deception)

As the war progressed, the Soviets became more aware of the benefits of deception, or *maskirovka* as they called it, and learned to use it more and more. They defined *maskirovka* as a set of measures designed to mislead the enemy about the presence and positioning of military units, their objectives, their size, combat power and command structure. *Maskirovka* was supposed to contribute to achieving surprise in conducting military actions, so that one's own combat power was preserved as long as possible. After a hesitant start in 1941 and 1942, the Soviets perfected *maskirovka* by 1943 and applied it on a strategic, tactical and operational level. In the first months after the start of Barbarossa, the Soviet military was focused on survival and showed little interest in proper security measures. For example, the lack of sufficiently secure radio traffic during this period meant that the German intercepting units had no problem in acquiring a good picture of the intentions and actions of the Soviets at a tactical level. But at a strategic level, German intelligence services failed barely six months later, when they did not detect the presence of three newly arrived armies near Moscow. While it is unclear whether this was due to *maskirovka* or chance, it did make the Soviets aware of the importance of deception. The Germans, in turn, managed to trick the Soviets into believing that their summer offensive of 1942 would target Moscow by distributing maps of the Moscow region to their men, holding talks about the offensive and interrogating PoWs specifically about the area. When the Soviets launched an attack on Kharkov to relieve the expected pressure on Moscow, they ended up in the middle of the area where the Germans were building up their forces for Fall Blau and suffered heavy losses.

In the course of 1942, the application of *maskirovka* was further professionalized and became part of every plan. A special *maskirovka* staff was also set up at the front, and instructions were given at the operational level on how to make dummy tanks, artillery and other equipment. During the battle for Stalingrad, the Soviets reaped the first fruits of this. While Chief of Staff Zeitzler declared in November that 'the Russians no longer have any sizeable reserves and are incapable of mounting a full-scale attack', the Soviets actually were preparing two major counter-offensives, Saturn and Uranus, which led to the encirclement of Stalingrad and eventually the downfall of the German Sixth Army.

Based on the experience gained, the Soviets formulated the following principles for *maskirovka*:

• The purpose of the operation should only be known to a limited number of staff officers.
• Verbal orders may only be given to the lower echelons as 'U-hour' approaches.
• The units must be well camouflaged at night; no movements may take place during the day.
• Unauthorized visitors/passers-by are not allowed to enter the area where the operation will take place.
• Reconnaissance actions may only be performed by units already in the front line.
• There should be radio silence from arriving units, especially tank units.
• Engineers' moves and preparatory actions may only take place at night
• The artillery may not fire.

The Soviets would perfect their *maskirovka* techniques in the run-up to their summer offensive in 1944. We will discuss this further in the next chapter. (1: 56–61)

After having sketched the background, we will now move on to the course of the battle in 1943.

## 4. The course of the battle in 1943

### Crimea

After the Soviet offensive had died down in early 1943, the German Seventeenth Army found itself in the Kuban region. Hitler considered this a good starting point for the offensive he envisioned for 1943; Stalin on the other hand intended to encircle the Seventeenth Army as he had done with the Sixth in Stalingrad. The Seventeenth Army consisted of six corps with a total of 400,000 men, who had taken up defensive positions behind the Gothic line. To encircle these units, Stalin wanted to cut off their retreat across the Kerch Strait to the Taman Peninsula. He envisaged an attack along three axes:

- The Fourteenth and Eighteenth Armies would attack towards Krasnodar and Slavyansk
- The Forty-seventh Army would advance towards Novorossiysk
- A spectacular amphibious landing on the Taman Peninsula, behind the German positions.

The Soviets assumed that the coastal strip would be less well defended than positions further inland.

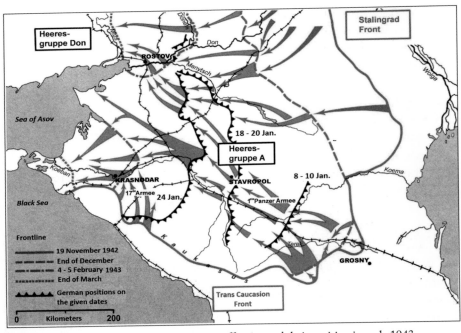

The advance of the Soviets during the winter offensive and their position in early 1943.

What the Soviets did not know was that the Germans had been closely monitoring Soviet radio traffic for quite some time and on that basis considered an action in the region of the Taman Peninsula, through the Kerch Strait or even in Crimea itself very likely. They therefore held exercises in the Bay of Ozereyka, which happened to be the very place where the Soviets had planned to launch their main attack. The Germans were thus much better prepared than might have been expected, although their troop strength in that location was clearly lower than on the rest of the front. As a consequence, when the Soviets landed in Ozereyka Bay on 4 February they were met by heavy German artillery fire. After that, problems followed each other in rapid succession. First of all, during the amphibious landings, the tanks intended to force a breakthrough disembarked too early, filling their engine inlets with water and stalling. Subsequently, the naval ships, which should have provided artillery support, withdrew too early and left the transports heading to the beaches without cover. As a result, the Soviet units on the beach were unable to move forward or backward and only had the choice of fighting to the death or surrendering.

The landings in the Bay of Novorossiysk, on the other hand, intended as a diversionary tactic, succeeded. While the Germans were unhurriedly planning a counter-offensive for 7 February, the Soviets rapidly expanded the bridgehead and dug in. When the Germans finally launched their offensive they were unable to drive the Soviets out of their positions. The Soviets, in turn, were unable to break through the encirclement, and a stalemate was the result. On the mainland, meanwhile, the Soviet offensive continued on a wide front. The Germans fell back to the positions of the Gothic line as planned, and on 12 February Krasnodar was abandoned. Von Manstein's subsequent surrender of Rostov on 14 February was of great strategic importance: his units had held the city long enough to allow the entire First Panzer Army to escape from the Caucasus, averting a disaster.

Stalin wanted to round off the success of the offensives of recent months by encircling the German units on the east bank of the Dnieper. The idea was to

Camouflage became increasingly important to the Germans due to the threat of the Soviet Air Force. Here a well-camouflaged SdKfz 7 tractor with a 150mm howitzer drives over a bridge built by the engineers.

advance across the Donets via Kharkov into the Germans' rear area and isolate them. Von Manstein recognized the danger and asked Hitler for permission to conduct a tactical retreat. Hitler initially refused to give up the Donets basin, but eventually gave in to pressure from Von Manstein, and the German units were allowed to build a defence line behind the River Mius.

### The Germans take the initiative

Von Manstein sent the units of Army Abteilung Hollidt to the River Mius to form a front, with the First Panzer Army on the north wing and the Fourth Panzer Army on the south. Meanwhile, Hitler had decreed that Kharkov should be held at all costs. Hausser with his newly formed SS Panzer Corps was responsible for the defence of Kharkov. However, the Soviets did not sit still, and by 14 February the encirclement of the city was almost complete and a new Stalingrad threatened for Hausser's units. Despite pleas, Hitler refused to authorize a retreat. On 15 February Hausser took matters into his own hands and ordered his units to break out. Hitler was furious, but Hausser escaped the usual court martial because Hitler eventually realized that he had made the right decision, and the Führer could not afford the loss of Hausser's SS divisions.

During the same period, Hollidt had settled on the Mius and held out despite pressure from three Soviet armies. Hollidt was only concerned about the northern flank, because the First Panzer Army had still not built up a real defence line. And this was precisely the area on which part of a Soviet tank

Kampfgruppe Peiper on the move. StuG IIIs together with SdKfz half-tracks form the protective shield for the sixty ambulances and other vehicles that brought the wounded of the trapped units of the 298th and 320th Infantry Divisions to safety.

**Joachim Peiper's armoured ambulances**

During and after the battle for Stalingrad, the Germans transported entire divisions by train from Western Europe to the east in order to fill gaps and build new lines of defence. One of the most spectacular 'power projections' was the deployment in February 1943 of the 2nd SS Panzer Corps, comprising the SS Division Das Reich and SS Division Hohenstaufen, under Paul Hausser. Their goal was Kharkov and the stabilization of the front by forming a defence line. The objective was to prevent a further advance of Soviet units to the west after the fall of Stalingrad and to guide as many German units as possible to safety through the 'no-man's-land' several hundred kilometres wide.

Immediately after their arrival by rail the end of January 1943, the 2nd Corps had spread across the snow-covered plains to make contact with the troops of the 298th and 320th Infantry Divisions and guide them to safety. The latter had been retreating in small groups towards Kharkov following the Battle of Stalingrad, and during this harrowing journey many were captured by Soviet units. In some cases, German prisoners of war were liberated by Waffen SS reconnaissance units, who attacked Soviet positions deep in the hinterland. Units of the SS Leibstandarte Adolf Hitler Division succeeded in forcing a temporary corridor for the survivors of the 320th Division, but this was cut on 12 February. Surrounded, and with 1,500 wounded in their ranks, they had to be pulled out as soon as possible. A Kampfgruppe led by SS-Sturmbannführer Joachim Peiper, at that time the commander of the 2nd Panzer Grenadiere Battalion, which was equipped with half-tracks, was ordered to save these units. Peiper's battalion, strengthened with a unit of StuG III assault guns and sixty ambulances, managed to punch a hole in the Soviet lines, destroy several Soviet tanks and advance almost 50km behind the Soviet lines to find the remains of the division. After the wounded had been loaded into the ambulances, Peiper's forces and the remaining men from the rescued divisions discovered that Soviet troops had cut their retreat by destroying the only bridge over the River Udy. The Waffen SS unit attacked the Soviets and, after close and heavy fighting managed to retake the bridge and provisionally repair it. Although the column of ambulances was able to cross to the German lines on the safe bank of the river, the heavy StuGs and half-tracks could not, requiring Peiper to seek other ways to cross the river. After a reconnaissance behind Soviet lines, another crossing point was discovered, enabling Peiper to return with his units and escort the rescued infantrymen back to the safe lines of the Division. Peiper's losses were limited to a few dozen dead and injured. This incident was thus a perfect illustration of *Auftragstaktik*, the doctrine of deep penetration in the hinterland, and the use of a Kampfgruppe, as well as leadership, courage, decision-making power, perseverance and determination of all those involved.

corps, consisting of 150 tanks led by Popov, had set its sights. His objective was to advance south towards the Sea of Azov and isolate the German units. North of Popov, the Soviet Sixth Army advanced into the gap that still existed between the First Panzer Army and the units of Army Abteilung Lanz. The

25th Soviet Tank Corps had meanwhile, in a third breakthrough, captured a railway junction important for the supply of Hollidt's units. Von Manstein wanted to isolate these three advanced Soviet spearheads and throw them back across the Donets. First of all, Popov's units were dealt with by the SS Division Viking. Although the latter were not yet at full strength, they caused alarm to Popov, who feared that he would face a much stronger force than expected. While Popov was reconsidering his position, his forward units were cut off from their supplies in a combined action by the 11th Panzer Division and the 333rd Infantry Division. Radio communication indicated that Popov was running out of fuel, and in a classic example of mobile warfare, German panzers pushed Popov's units back, leaving the elimination of the fuel-less tanks to the infantry. Requests from Popov to withdraw were met with orders to advance further.

On 19 February, the Soviet Sixth Army suffered the same fate. Hausser and his SS Panzer Corps attacked this army in the northern flank, while the 48th Corps took over the southern flank. The two units met at Pavlograd on 23 February and isolated the most advanced Soviet elements. Again, the commander of the Soviet Sixth Army was ordered to advance further, because aerial reconnaissance had indicated that the Germans were still retreating. On 28 February the curtain fell on both Popov's units and the Sixth Army: both forces were surrounded by the Germans before they could reach the Donets. Although the number of prisoners was fewer than expected due to the encirclement not being impermeable, most of the Soviet materiel fell into German hands.

Von Manstein now scented success and sent Hausser's units north again towards Kharkov. The cold weather meant hard ground, which enabled a rapid advance. Hausser brushed aside the 3rd Tank Corps en route to Kharkov and advanced rapidly towards the city, which he reached just before the onset of the thaw. On 8 March his forces seized the access roads to Kharkov and the city was sealed off from the rest of the world. The Germans then entered the city and were back in control on 15 March, a month after Hausser had disobeyed Hitler's order and left. The Germans now maintained their momentum and advanced north to recapture Kursk. The Sixty-Ninth Army, lying on Hausser's route and already badly battered in previous fighting, was unable to put up any serious resistance and was pushed aside. On 17 March Hausser reached the outskirts of Belgorod and took the city the next day.

The end result of the rapid German advance was that west of Kursk there was now a large bulge in the line that contained six Soviet armies. Von Manstein's plan was to cut off these units by having Heeresgruppe Mitte attack them from the north and his own forces from the south. He knew that

A PzKpfw IV-F2 and Panzergrenadiere engaged in street fighting in Kharkov.

the Soviets could do nothing against this, but von Kluge, commander-in-chief of Heeresgruppe Mitte, was still building up his own front and refused to give up units for this operation. In addition, the onset of the thaw, bringing with it the inevitable mud, brought the German advance slowly but surely to a halt. With this, the Germans had missed an excellent opportunity, one that could have changed the outcome of the war. When they finally launched an attack on the bulge at Kursk four months later, Operation Zitadelle, the situation had changed to the Germans' disadvantage.

## Leningrad

In the north, meanwhile, the siege of Leningrad entered its second year. The population was suffering under an almost complete blockade, and only those who could fight were given rations; the rest had to survive as best they could. In January, the Soviets did their best to establish a corridor along Lake Ladoga. They succeeded on 20 January, quickly building a railway line on the swampy bottom of this six-mile-wide corridor. On 6 February, the first train carrying food arrived in the city. The Soviets tried to widen the corridor in the following months, but a first attempt on 10 February failed, at the cost of 11,000 men, when the allies of the Germans stationed there, including the

Spanish Azul division, managed to stop them. On 19 March they made a second attempt, which was repulsed by the Flemish Legion.

During this period the Germans also focused on further shortening the front line. For example, in the north there was the bulge around Demyansk containing the German II Corps. This bulge was connected to the German lines by a narrow, 10km-wide corridor and attracted great interest from Timoshenko. On 28 November 1942 and again on 23 January 1943, the Soviets tried unsuccessfully to cut through this corridor, but it was clear that the position of II Corps was untenable in the longer term. On 23 January, Hitler therefore gave permission for a retreat, which he believed should take seventy days. German units started this operation on 17

Panzergrenadiere and an accompanying tank advance in the woods near Leningrad in August 1943.

February, but it soon became clear that the pace had to be increased, otherwise the units would be overrun by the advancing Soviets. The the evacuation was duly accelerated, and on 27 February the last men reached the German lines; although the forward positions had been lost, II Corps had been saved.

Now only one bulge remained, near Rzhev. This area held large numbers of men and much equipment from the Fourth and Ninth Armies. Hitler had once intended to relaunch the offensive on Moscow from these positions, but on 6 February he gave permission for the straightening of the front here. The withdrawal began on 1 March, before the onset of the mud period. The Germans had created an ingenious system of mines and booby traps to delay the advance of the Soviet units as long as possible, and this operation was also completed successfully on 22 March.

Although the Soviet winter offensive of 1942/43 had forced the Germans on to the defensive and they had lost an entire army in addition to much ground at Stalingrad, Von Manstein's tactical ingenuity had successfully stabilized the situation in the south. The German units had withstood the various Soviet offensives well, and the front line was considerably shorter and more defensible than before. The Germans were still able to repel any attack

A PzKpfw IV and a StuG III operate together here in the vast landscape of the Soviet Union.

by Soviet units of a similar size. Now that they had come through the Russian winter reasonably well, they were preparing for the summer. And there was no reason to believe that they would be less successful this year than they had been in the previous one.

## Kursk

After the shortening of the front line in the spring, a number of imperfections remained in the central part of the front. The northernmost of these was an eastern bulge containing Germans at Orel, with to the south a western bulge containing Soviets at Kursk. The latter, with a length of 160km and a diameter of 112km, attracted more interest from the Germans, who were already anticipating another major encirclement. Hitler viewed the offensive at Kursk as a stepping stone to his summer offensive of 1943. Von Manstein, in turn, was all too aware of the danger of a similar Soviet action aimed at cutting off the German units in the eastern bulge at Orel. A successful offensive at Kursk, on the other hand, would greatly reduce the danger of a Soviet offensive at Orel. During the planning sessions in April it was assumed that ten to twelve tank divisions would be sufficient to make the offensive a success, but Hitler felt it was necessary to deploy more units. In addition, he was keen on deploying the new Tiger tank in large numbers for the first time at Kursk, combined with the new Panther, which was now also coming off the production line in large numbers. However, the labour-intensive production of these two tanks had not got off to a good start; only fifty Panthers and twenty-five Tigers were being produced per month.

The final plan was clear: the Germans would attack on a limited front and concentrate their forces on the weak spots. Heeresgruppe Mitte would try to force a breakthrough from the north from Belgorod, and Heeresgruppe Süd from the south from the Oka River area. The spearheads of the armoured

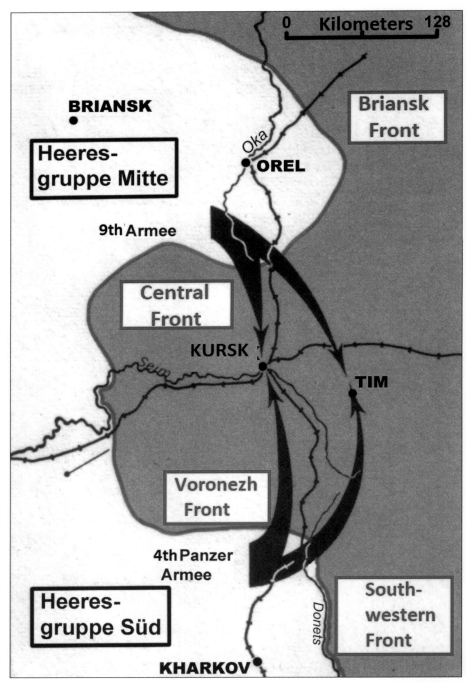

The outlines of the German plan of attack at Kursk.

troops could focus all their attention on advancing as quickly and far east as possible, their flanks covered by other units. The units involved were given a maximum of six days to prepare, and the offensive could start from 28 April. The actual launch date depended on a number of circumstances, including the arrival of more new Tiger and Panther tanks, which postponed the date first to 12 June and later to July. The Soviets, in turn, were all too aware of their vulnerability. With a new German offensive towards the Caucasus or the Volga no longer likely, Zhukov advised Stalin on 8 April to consider a possible attack on Moscow. On the road to Moscow lay Kursk, once again underlining the importance of the area. Zhukov also advised not to plan offensive actions immediately, but to let the Germans advance against strong defences. Only then should the Soviets take the initiative and launch their summer offensive. Despite some initial resistance, Stalin agreed to this plan, and the Soviets began to strengthen their defensive positions in the Kursk bulge.

In the Kursk region, the Soviets were able to deploy a large number of units. Heeresgruppe Mitte, operating from the north, faced the Central Front under Rokossovsky. This consisted of five infantry armies, a tank army and an Air Force army and enjoyed superiority in men, tanks and artillery on all points. Von Manstein in the south faced the Voronezh Front under Vatutin, which had the same structure and superiority in numbers as the Central Front. Behind Vatutin was the Reserve Front under Koniev, with four infantry armies, a tank army and an Air Force army.

The Soviets' defence was based on a system of three fortified zones with strongpoints surrounded by minefields. Each strongpoint contained three to five artillery pieces, sometimes anti-tank guns, mortars, engineer units and a machine-gun position. The strongpoints at crucial positions sometimes had twelve anti-tank guns. The defence system was at some points 150km deep and made up of six defensive belts. In addition to the 20,000 guns, one third of which were anti-tank guns, the strongpoints were surrounded by minefields with 1,800 anti-tank mines and 2,000 anti-personnel mines per linear kilometre of front.

In the run-up to the confrontation, the German rear areas were increasingly rendered unsafe by partisans under the direction and coordination of the Red Army. The backbone of this movement was formed by Soviet soldiers and officers who had become isolated and had retreated into the woods during the rapid advance of the Germans in 1941. They had trained and now led the growing partisan movement, and tied down the Sicherungsivisionen and other security units which had to guard logistic and communication lines,.

Although the date for the offensive was initially set for 12 June, the surrender of the German and Italian units in North Africa made Hitler and the army

Soviet soldiers with their 76.2mm guns in action during one of the many bitter battles for cities. The same type of gun could be found in many Soviet tanks.

leadership aware of the danger of landings in southern Europe. Hitler wanted to prevent the offensive in the east from attracting all the military's attention. In addition, it had become clear to Von Manstein that the Soviets had built up a solid line of defence. Hitler's solution was to deploy more Tiger and Panther tanks, but waiting for these, many of which had yet to leave the factories, gave the Soviets the opportunity to strengthen and refine their defences. In the end, Hitler decided on a three-week postponement, moving the start date to mid-July, and the Germans adjusted their tactics accordingly. They decided to concentrate their tank units one after the other in a number of spearheads in the hope of being able to break through the defence lines at a number of crucial points (the well-known *Schwerpunkte*) and then, in accordance with their philosophy, to advance quickly to take the key communication and logistics points.

On 2 July, Hitler determined that 5 July would be the final date. The Ninth Army under Model would attack from the north and several units of Heeresgruppe Süd under Von Manstein from the south. In the north, Model would concentrate on the use of infantry to infiltrate and break through the Soviet defence line; Von Manstein, given the composition of his force, concentrated on the use of tanks. He had fewer infantry divisions than Model, and if he deployed them in the same way, his units would advance too slowly. Opposing the forty-two German divisions were fifty-four Soviet

The Germans tried to deploy as many new Tiger tanks as possible at Kursk. Here a unit is on its way to its positions. The original plan was to equip one Company of each Panzer Division with twenty Tigers. Eventually, they were placed in independent *Abteilungen* at corps level.

infantry divisions, twelve tank corps and sixteen mechanized brigades. The Germans had slightly fewer tanks than the number they had started Operation Barbarossa with in 1941. In addition, the Panthers turned out to be plagued by a large number of mechanical defects in the run-up to the fighting, ranging from engine fires to gearbox problems. This confirmed Guderian's fears that this tank was being deployed too quickly. After the first days of fighting, the number of operational Panthers had fallen from a theoretical 200 to no more than forty.

At 1500 hrs on 4 July, the Germans launched their offensive: the Fourth Panzer Army under Hoth in the south attacked to capture the higher ground in front of their lines. By evening, the Germans were past the Soviet positions and preparing to launch the offensive in full force the next morning. In addition to the fifty-four Tiger tanks of the three companies of the sPzAbt 503, Hoth could deploy the Tiger-equipped companies of the SS Panzer Grenadiere Divisions, a total of 101 Model E Tigers.

**Composition of the German forces**

| Heeresgruppe Süd | |
|---|---|
| Fourth Panzer Army (under Hoth) | *SS Panzer Korps:*<br>• 1st Panzer Division Leibstandarte SS Adolf Hitler<br>• 2nd Panzer Division Das Reich<br>• 3rd Panzer Division Totenkopf<br>*XLVIII Panzer Korps:*<br>• 1st Panzer Division<br>• 11th Panzer Division<br>• Panzer Grenadiere Division Grossdeutschland |
| Army Abteilung Kempf | *III Panzer Korps:*<br>• 6th Panzer Division<br>• 7th Panzer Division<br>• 19th Panzer Division |
| | sPzAbt 503 (three companies of Tiger tanks) |
| **Heeresgruppe Nord** | |
| Ninth Army (under Model) | *XLVII Korps:*<br>• 2nd Panzer Division<br>• 9th Panzer Division<br>• 20th Panzer Division |
| | *LI Panzer Korps:*<br>• 18th Panzer Division<br>• sPzAbt 653 eand 654 (with Elefant tanks) |
| | sPzAbt 505 (two companies of Tiger tanks) |

In the north, units of the Ninth Army manoeuvred into their starting positions. On 5 July the Germans tried to break through the defence lines from the north and south, but were unable to make any significant territorial gains. Model had expected such resistance, but he realized all too well that after breaking through the first line, his units would still have to fight their way through a 10–15km-deep defensive belt. The Soviets were already concentrating troops in that area to launch counter-attacks.

In the south, the armoured units of the Germans and the Soviets confronted each other. On 6 July, units of the 2nd Panzer Division attempted to seize the higher ground north of Kashara, but were halted by the Soviet defences. These in turn began to deploy their armoured units, and the confrontation eventually developed into the largest tank battle in history. In the area between Ponyri and Soborovka, about 15km wide, the two opponents eventually deployed between 1,000 and 1,200 tanks and assault guns, supported by twice as many artillery pieces. The battle raged for four days. The aim of both sides was to gain control of the higher ground around Olkhovatka, which would offer the Germans a good overview of the area controlled by the Soviets. On 9 July they reached the outskirts of Ponyri and the battle swung to and fro for three days. The Soviets were unable to drive the Germans out of their positions; the Germans in turn could make only slight progress.

## The power balance at Kursk

| Germans | Soviets |
|---|---|
| 900,000 men | 1,337,000 men |
| 2,700 tanks and assault guns | 3300 tanks and assault guns |
| 10,000 artillery pieces | 20,000 artillery pieces |
| 2,500 planes | 2,650 planes |

The plan of Hoth, commander of the Fourth Panzer Army, was not to advance directly to the centre of the bulge immediately, but to head first to the north-east towards Prokhorovka and then to swing north. The Soviets did not expect such a manoeuvre and built up their strongest defensive positions to face a northern attack. The climax would be reached here on 12 July in a tank battle, the 700 tanks of the Fourth Panzer Army facing the 850 tanks of the Fifth Guards Tank Army.

The first phase of the attack by Hoth's units did not go smoothly: his new Panther tanks got stuck in a minefield and had to be helped back onto their way by engineer units. In contrast, the Gross Deutschland Division, operating on the right flank, had succeeded in advancing 8km into enemy territory and reaching its first objective, the village of Tsjerkassy. Hausser's SS Panzer Korps had also been successful with the new tactic of simultaneous shelling and bombardment of enemy lines. He had managed to break through the positions of the Sixth Guards Army and had advanced 30km inside the Soviet lines. It seemed as if a classic breakthrough had been achieved as his tanks rolled forward at a rapid pace. Hausser's flank was covered on the right by Army Abteilung Kempf.

In May 1943 these T-34s are on their way to Kursk. Infantry are riding on the tanks towards their positions.

These units advanced quickly to the east, where the defences were less strong, to attack the Soviets from the rear in an outflanking, northward movement. Kempf was unable to keep up with Hausser's pace, and as the latter advanced, his right flank became more vulnerable. It seemed, though, that the Germans could achieve the necessary broad penetration as the XLVIII Panzer Corps on Hausser's left flank also made ever greater territorial gains. This corps was to take Oboyan and secure the bridges over the Psel River, before turning east and advancing with Hausser's units towards Prokhorova to destroy the Soviet strategic reserves. But in the end these flanking units, held up by Soviets who put up tough resistance from their trenches, could not keep up with Hausser. The Soviets saw both the threat posed by Hausser and the vulnerability of his flanks, and they deployed the 2nd Guards Tank Corps from Konev's strategic reserve to attack Hausser's flank. Unlucky enough to be spotted from the air, this Corps was the first to have to deal with Henschel-129 ground support aircraft equipped with anti-tank guns in an air-to-ground duel. The Henschels succeeded in taking out no fewer than fifty tanks. With this, the counter-attack on Hausser's flanks, who incidentally had completely missed this event, was nipped in the bud.

Hausser advanced rapidly towards Prokhorova, and Konev tried with all his might to stop his advance by deploying the Fifth Guards Army with the 17th and 29th Tank Corps. On 11 July, these units arrived in the area Hausser was heading for, and the Soviets decided not to regroup the units before the attack but to deploy them immediately, worried that Army Abteilung Kempf would soon join Hausser. On 12 July the Battle of Prokhorova began, the crucial tank encounter of the offensive. Within this battle, the possession of the town of

Built on the chassis of Ferdinand Porsche's design for a heavy tank, the Ferdinand was the first German tank destroyer developed specifically for this purpose. The tank was later named 'Elefant'. (*Model by S. Nair*)

Rzhavets played a crucial role: if the Germans could take the town they could unbalance the Soviet defences and achieve victory. The battle was fierce, and the Soviets tried to position their tanks as close to the Germans as possible to offset the much better German aiming equipment. In order to finally break through the Soviet lines, the Germans applied a tactic of deception: a tank column led by a few captured T-34s managed to pass the Soviet positions unimpeded on the night of 11/12 July, to take the town the next day. The way was now open for the Germans to launch the decisive thrust. However, they had paid a high price, leaving 300 tanks on the battlefield at Prokhorova, including seventy Tigers; in all, the Soviets had lost more than half of their 850 tanks. The question was therefore whether the Germans still had the strength to continue the offensive after such terrible losses.

---

**The Soviet version of roadside assistance on the battlefield**
The Soviets also got better and better at repairing tanks on the battlefield. When the Fifth Guards Tank Army, part of the Reserve Front, had to cover more than 200km from the rear to the front in 48 hours, it was accompanied by trucks full of tools and spare parts. The accompanying troops from the workshops performed miracles, and almost all tanks reached the battlefield. Though the Fifth Guards Tank Army lost almost 400 tanks during two days of heavy fighting, 112 of them were able to be redeployed within hours thanks to the efforts of the field workshops. (40: 212)

---

In the north, meanwhile, Model had made progress and was about to break through the Soviet lines at Teploye. If he succeeded, Kursk would be within reach. He set 12 July as the day for the final attack. But despite all the progress the Germans had made, two events would determine the outcome of Operation Zitadelle.

First of all, the Soviets in the north had turned their attention to the German bulge at Orel. On 12 July, the Eleventh Guards Army attacked the positions of the Second Panzer Army of Heeresgruppe Mitte and advanced towards Orel. Model now had to take into account the positions of his rearguard. These developments came on top of the Allied landings in Sicily on 10 July, after which the entire geopolitical and strategic landscape changed instantly. Consequently, Hitler delayed Operation Zitadelle and announced that units from the Eastern Front were to be moved to Western Europe. Von Manstein urged Hitler to be allowed to press on, because victory was within reach. Hitler authorized Von Manstein to advance further, but forbade Model to continue the attack because his rear was threatened. The Fourth Panzer Army under Hoth then pressed on and surrounded the Soviet Sixty-Ninth Army and two tank corps between Rzhavets, Belenikhono and Gostishchevo.

This unit of T-34 tanks equipped with the new 85mm gun preparing to face the German tanks at Kursk.

Despite these successes, on 17 July the curtain finally fell on Operation Zitadelle: Hitler ordered that two panzer divisions be transferred from Heeresgruppe Süd to Heeresgruppe Mitte in order to defuse the Orel crisis. In addition, Hausser's entire SS Panzer Corps was transferred to France to face a possible Allied invasion. Little did they know at the time that this would not take place for another eleven months. All in all, the offensive slowly but surely died down. Despite having had victory within reach, the Germans had to surrender the initiative to the Soviets. They did not miss this opportunity.

---

**Battlefield performance**

Kursk, the Obeyan sector from 5 to 11 July 1943. Much has been said about the superior battlefield performance of the German units. Below is an example from one of Kursk's sectors.

|  | Soviets | Germans |
| --- | --- | --- |
| Fighting strength at the beginning of the battle | 98,000 | 62,000 |
| Number of dead | 22,000 | 13,600 |
| Losses with equal combat strength | 34,750 | 13,600 |
| Absolute combat effectiveness ratio per man per man | 1.00 | 2.55 |
| Relative combat effectiveness ratio per man | 1.00 | 4.08 |

**Explanation**

The Soviets began the battle with 98,000 men versus 62,000 on the German side, a factor of 1.58 to their advantage. If there had been as many Germans as Soviets, then the Soviet losses would have been correspondingly higher. The number of deaths when compared with each other produces the absolute combat effectiveness ratio of 2.55. In other words, 2.55 Soviets were killed for every German. The relative combat effectiveness ratio is 1.6 higher at 4.08, because the Soviets were in entrenched positions and thus enjoyed an advantage. But however great the difference in combat effectiveness, the less effective side, if it can compensate by throwing more men into battle, will still win in the end – as will be seen.

At the end of the fighting, both sides had lost more than 1,500 tanks. For the Soviets, the consequences were less serious because they were able to replenish the losses at any time. Guderian and Speer were saddened to note that all their efforts to restore the Panzerwaffe to its former level had been in vain; strategically, the Battle of Kursk had far-reaching consequences for the future of the Panzerwaffe.

In addition, the fighting at Kursk had demanded the utmost from the Luftwaffe, and its inability to definitively gain air superiority and support a decisive breakthrough was one of the factors that led to the suicide of Luftwaffe Chief of Staff Colonel General Hans Jeschonnek. He had always been a staunch proponent of a ground support role for the Luftwaffe. His successor, General Günther Korsten, saw as his priority the defence of the homeland against Allied air raids. This led to the large-scale transfer of Luftwaffe units from the Eastern Front to Germany and meant that the German Army could rely less and less on air support. Thousands of valuable 88mm flak guns were also transferred back home, depriving units on the ground of their most potent anti-tank and anti-aircraft weapons. As a consequence, the power of the Soviet Air Force grew and the Germans were forced to move more and more at night and to pay great attention to camouflage techniques. We have seen that these developments led to the production of the first generation of mobile anti-aircraft guns as late as 1943.

Even more than Stalingrad, the fighting in this six-week period can be seen as the turning point of the war on the Eastern Front. The Germans had thrown everything they had against the Soviets, but the Soviets soaked up the pressure and then went on the offensive themselves.

Zhukov had shown that his wait-and-see strategy had paid off. Although the Germans had almost broken through the bulge at Kursk, they had paid a heavy price. The Red Army, in turn, was now ready to go on the offensive all along the front. The focus of the Soviets was on the area of Heeresgruppen Mitte and Süd, with the previously described offensive at the bulge around Orel being no more than a diversionary action. On the one hand, the Soviet forces at Kursk were in a dire situation and the Germans were still able to advance. On the other hand, Operation Zitadelle concentrated so many German units in one area that the Soviets were free to choose the location for their future offensive.

**The Soviet counter-offensive**

The offensive at Orel consisted of a three-axis attack. The left wing of the West Front and the central units of the Bryansk and Central Front were to attack the Second Panzer Army and the Ninth Army. The Western Front would advance along the first axis to the south towards Orel, while the Bryansk Front would also attack towards Orel along a second axis to the west with the aim of splitting the German units in the bulge. At a later date, the Central Front would support the other two fronts from the bulge at Kursk along a third axis. The Soviets assumed that the Germans had properly fortified their bulge, and indeed they had, albeit to a lesser extent than the Soviets. On 13 July, the Eleventh Guards Army broke through the German lines and advanced 20km. Other units were less successful, but the objective was achieved: the Germans could not advance much further at Kursk without endangering their rear. In the second half of July, under pressure from the Central Front, the Germans were forced to give up the territory they had conquered with so much effort. At the beginning of August, Orel itself was threatened, and when the Soviets reached the outskirts of the city on the night of 3/4 August they immediately went on the offensive; by 5 August the city was in their hands. Model, meanwhile, had successfully let his units fall back to the Hagen Line, a line of defences at the western base of the bulge. Despite heavy fighting, the Soviets failed to isolate parts of Model's force or create a second Stalingrad, something they fervently hoped for. The reason was that Hitler had allowed Model to withdraw, not so much because of his strategic acumen, but more because the Führer wanted to deploy these units in Italy. The result was a resounding victory for the Soviets: by mid-August the bulge at Orel had been completely cleared of Germans. In the months that followed, Heeresgruppe Mitte would be forced further and further west beyond Smolensk, finally taking up positions west of Berezina in November. The strength of Heeresgruppe Mitte also gradually declined during this period as their losses were not compensated for by replacements. For example, the Third Panzer Army lost a third of its strength during this period and its divisions became each responsible for more than 40km of front. The fact that the divisions were able to hold the line was mainly due to the smart deployment of a combination of assault guns and anti-tank units and the flexible deployment of artillery.

Time for consultation. In the summer of 1943, the latest information from the reconnaissance units is short-circuited with the commander of a unit of Marder III tank destroyers. In the background is a StuG III-G.

## Advance to the Dnieper: 17 July to 23 December 1943

The centre of gravity in the fighting now shifted to the south. According to Stalin, this was the key to final victory. The Soviets enjoyed a great advantage on the ground, the Voronezh and the Steppe Front having a local superiority of 3: 1 in men, 4: 1 in artillery and 3: 2 in aircraft, while the ratio in tanks and assault guns was 6: 1. A major reason for this superiority was that the Soviets had been able to recover and repair their tanks damaged at Kursk because they controlled the battlefield after the fighting ended. In addition, Soviet tank production now far exceeded German.

On 17 July, the Soviets attacked the First Panzer Army, followed a little later by an attack on the positions of the Sixth Army, the new name of the Army Abteilung Hollidt, near the River Mius. The Sixth Panzer Army was assisted in the local counter-offensive by the SS Panzer Korps, which soon had to expend all its energy on repelling a massive attack by the units of the Voronezh Front under Vatutin in the Belgorod region. Vatutin then ordered the First and Fifth Guards Tank Armies to advance in the area between the Fourth Panzer Army and the Army Abteilung Kempf, ignoring Kharkov and advancing towards Poltava. The aim of the Soviets seemed to be a deep attack to reach the Sea of Azov behind the German units of the 29th Corps. The gap between the First Panzer Army and the Army Abteilung Kempf grew to more than 50km. The 11th Corps in Kharkov was now threatened with isolation, but did not receive permission from Hitler to withdraw. Although the 11th Corps held its own in Kharkov, the corridor along which this Corps could withdraw became increasingly narrow. On 22 August, von Manstein felt that the resistance in Kharkov had lasted long enough and ordered the evacuation of the city. The 11th Corps was worth more to him than Kharkov. For Hitler this was a fait accompli; he simply had no choice but to accept it. Thus the fourth and final battle for the city came to an end. As the units withdrew from the city, the Sixth Army came under increasing pressure at the Mius. The target of the Soviet offensive there was the Donets basin and in particular the city of Zaporizhzhia, downstream on the Dnieper. If this city were taken, the Soviets could close off Crimea, isolating the Seventeenth Army on the Kuban Peninsula.

Von Manstein realized that he could not hold the front at the Mius. His Heeresgruppe had lost 133,000 men in recent months, of whom only 33,000 could be replaced. The front on the Mius became increasingly porous, and the Soviets finally managed to break through the German lines on the night of 27/28 August and advanced rapidly towards Mariupol on the Sea of Azov. They successfully encircled the 29th Corps, but the 13th Panzer Division was able to establish a corridor on 30 August through which 29th Corps could be evacuated and then repositioned behind the new defensive lines. In the weeks that followed, the Soviets steadily increased the pressure. Von Manstein and Von Kluge pleaded with Hitler to be allowed to fall back behind the Dnieper. He refused, although he allowed the Seventeenth Army to be evacuated from

A street scene in Kharkov, which changed hands several times and bore the marks of months of fighting.

the Kuban peninsula. At the front, the Soviets succeeded in breaking through in several places in the first weeks of September and constantly pushed the Germans onto the defensive. The situation changed immediately when the Voronezh Front managed to force a final breakthrough on 14 September and advanced rapidly towards the Dnieper. There was now an acute danger that the Soviets would cross the Dnieper and attack the German rear. Von Manstein realized that it was impossible to hold the area east of the Dnieper any longer and advised Hitler to withdraw all units on the west bank. Von Manstein was called back to headquarters in East Prussia, where he told Hitler that there simply was no alternative: holding on to the area east of the Dnieper was doomed to failure. Hitler was forced to give in again, and on 15 September Von Manstein ordered a retreat.

The Dnieper was of strategic importance in several respects. Not only was it the last major river in the Soviet Union, but west of this river lay the most important resources in raw materials of the Soviet Union. At that time, these were supplying more than 30 per cent of the German arms industry's needs. If the Soviets were able to cross the Dnieper, access to these raw materials would be lost and the Romanian and Polish borders acutely threatened. The oil from Romania, in turn, was the main source of energy for the German war machine.

Fortunately for the Germans, the Soviets did not have the type of divisional commanders who, as the Germans were used to doing, dared to advance deep

All tanks of the earlier series were equipped with *Schürzen* ('aprons'). These PzKpfw IV tanks have them around the turret and on the side to protect the tracks.

behind the front; otherwise the Soviets could have won the race to the Dnieper and its bridges in this first phase of the offensive. Now, on 19 September, the first German units reached the bridges at Kiev, Kanev, Cherkassy, Kremenchug and Dnipropetrovsk, and other units followed in rapid succession, protected by the German tank divisions at the rear. The Soviets did manage to establish a number of small bridgeheads on the west side of the Dnieper, but these were of little significance. They consisted of small units that had improvised river-crossings with boats and rafts and posed no threat to the Germans. The Germans had taken possession of all bridges and succeeded in evacuating most of their units to the west bank. The Soviets then decided to build a large bridgehead near Bukrin. To this end they deployed paratroopers for the first and last time in the war: three brigades of the 5th Parachute Guard with a total of 7,000 men were dropped at nightfall on 24 September. However, they ended up in the middle of the units of the 10th Panzer Grenadiere Division and were wiped out in the following hours; only 2,300 of them survived. The Soviets concealed this fiasco for years and would conduct no further airborne landings.

However, on 26 September some Soviet soldiers managed to cross the Dnieper near Lyutezh. Although the initial group consisted of no more than ten men, the Soviets, with their inimitable perseverance, succeeded in transferring more men and equipment over the following nights. On 30 September, two regiments supported by artillery were on the west bank, and Vatutin ordered rapid further exploitation of the opportunities offered by this bridgehead. But although they eventually succeeded in getting tanks into the bridgehead, the units were at first unable to break out. Vatutin convinced Stalin that this bridgehead had more potential than attempting to cross the river at Bukrin. To mislead the Germans, however, the Soviets pretended to make a second attempt to cross the river at Bukrin, meanwhile preparing for a breakthrough at Lyutezh. The offensive from this bridgehead was aimed at destroying the Fourth Panzer Army and occupying the important communication hubs west of the Dnieper such as Zhimoter, Berdichev and Vinnitsa, the site of Werewolf, Hitler's last headquarters in the Soviet Union. The capture of Kiev on 6 November, the day of the revolution, was seen as an important intermediate goal.

The offensive began on 3 November and the Soviets soon broke through the German lines and advanced west. On 5 November they reached Kiev, defended only by the 88th Infantry Division. It was unable to withstand the superior forces of the Soviets and by the end of the day its survivors had left the city without their vehicles or heavy equipment The Soviets quickly advanced west and captured Fastov, the communication hub through which all supplies for the northern flank of Heeresgruppe Süd passed. There was fierce fighting

> **The great crossing**
> The crossing of the Dnieper was a chaotic operation due to the lack of pontoons and bridges. The Red Army had to cross the river with 'self-found resources', sometimes in wrecked boats, sometimes on rafts and sacks of hay, only to be caught on the other side by the Germans. It is estimated that 20,000 men died in these attempts, and their bodies floated downriver in the weeks that followed, accompanied by crows feasting on the flesh. Victor Astafyev describes how sappers pushed the corpses away from the shore in the hope that civilians further down would fish them out and bury them. But 'near and under some corpses, rats had already managed to give birth and hide little naked rats under rotting soldier's clothes. Startled, they fiercely defended their nest and attacked people screaming. We beat them with shovels and stones, trampled them with boots.' (7: 127)

for the city, which changed hands several times. The Germans eventually had to settle for giving up the city and retreated to the higher ground outside it. Zhitomir, an important logistics centre containing considerable supplies, was also captured by the Soviets, but the Germans managed to regain control of this city. Despite Hitler's constant insistence, it was no longer possible to launch an offensive towards Kiev. The Germans did manage, however, gradually to slow the advance of the Soviets.

Meanwhile, the southern flank of Heeresgruppe Süd on the east bank of the Dnieper still extended to the strategically important city of Zaporizhzhia on the southern stretch of the Dnieper. This position protected the German units in Crimea. On 10 October the Soviets launched an attack on Zaporizhzhia, which the Germans had to abandon after blowing up the large hydroelectric dam on the night of October 14/15. In capturing this city, the Soviets held the key to the downstream parts of the Dnieper and Crimea. The Germans tried to stop the Soviets on their right flank, the Wotan line, at the Sea of Azov. Despite the provisional nature of this line, it held out for two weeks, especially in the area around Melitopol. This city finally fell on 23 October, when the Soviets succeeded in splitting the Sixth Army in two. Undeterred, both elements managed to fight their way back to the Dnieper. The southern part crossed this river at Kherson, and the northern, main part at Nikopol. The end result was that all German units were now on the west bank of the Dnieper and a complete German army, the Seventeenth, was left isolated in Crimea. In view of the actual situation, the Soviets renamed the different fronts: the Central Front became the Belorussian Front, and the Voronezh Front, Steppe Front, while South-West and South Front became the 1st, 2nd, 3rd and 4th Ukrainian Fronts respectively.

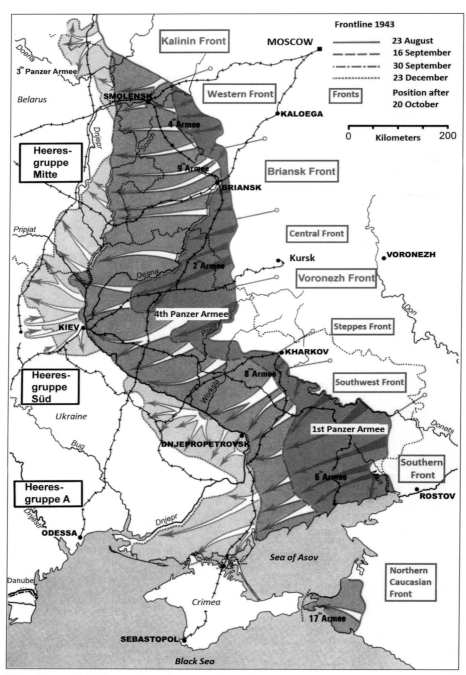

The advance of the Soviets from August to December.

The commander of a unit of T-34 tanks discusses new targets with his commanders.

From mid-1943 until the end of the war the initiative would lie with the Soviets. They had won some resounding victories in recent months, having dealt the Panzerwaffe a crushing blow at Kursk and pushed the Germans back across the Dnieper. Now the summer offensive came to an end, winter set in and the Soviets prepared for new offensives in the coming year, 1944. The new front line roughly followed the Carpathians and the pre-war Russo-Polish border and from the German point of view came dangerously close to central Europe.

After having sketched the main course of the battle, we will now describe the experiences of individual units. We will reflect on Raus's experience with the Soviets on the Don River in August 1943. These battles illustrate the almost inhuman tenacity of the Soviets. The details are taken from the book *Panzers on the Eastern Front: General Erhard Raus and His Panzer Divisions in Russia 1941–1945* by Peter Tsouras, which in turn is based on the post-battle reports of General Raus when he was a prisoner. They give an excellent insight into the fighting on the Eastern Front. Raus was a gifted writer who produced seven very interesting books about his wartime experiences.

We then describe the fate of the 25th Panzer Division, which travelled from France to the Eastern Front in December 1943 in much the same circumstances as the 6th Panzer Division under Raus a year earlier (see *The German Way of War on the Eastern Front 1941–1942*). However, things would turn out differently for this unit than for the 6th Panzer Division: ill-prepared and equipped with inferior materiel, it was deployed piecemeal upon arrival, only to perish almost completely in less than a month.

## 5.  At the front

### The swamp battalion (3 and 4 August)

We have already seen what the Soviets were capable of. The vicissitudes of the units commanded by General Erhard Raus give a good picture of the perseverance and creativity of the Red Army. The combat situation described takes place in the area of the Don, in August 1943. After Operation Zitadelle, the units involved, four infantry divisions, had retreated to their previous positions on the west bank of the Don on both sides of Belgorod. In the preceding month the divisions had endured heavy fighting and its combat strength had fallen to 40–50 per cent of its original numbers. The retreat to the west bank of the Don had gone smoothly, and the Soviets had followed the German troops cautiously, fearful that the retreat would turn to a sudden counter-attack. In early August the regiments of the 320th and 106th Divisions were about 30km south of Belgorod on the northern and southern flanks of a valley traversed by the large north-south Belgorod-Kharkov roadway. Preserving this valley and its roadway was of great strategic importance, as was the preservation of Belgorod. At the point where the valley met the Don, the terrain was swampy and covered with reed beds. The Germans were on the higher west bank and the Soviets on the lower east side. It was clear that the Soviets were at a disadvantage: the river was difficult to cross and the Germans were able to track their movements between their old trenches and fortifications on the other side of the Don. They were also able to shell all points of the Don valley from their well-camouflaged bunkers, and it would have been impossible for the Soviets to make preparations for a possible crossing during the day. In daytime, therefore, there was deathly silence on the other side of the river. At night, however, there was lively activity. Russian scouts looked for places to cross the river, and later, groups of soldiers appeared on the west bank, reconnoitring the German positions. In order to capture individual Germans, they crossed the river at night and crept up to the guard posts in the trenches, then waited, often for hours, for a good moment to overpower the occupants. The prisoners were then gagged and dragged back

As the Soviet Air Force grew in strength, the need for adequate anti-aircraft defences grew. Here the crew of a quadruple 20mm Flak scans the sky for possible danger.

to the Russian positions. Everything was conducted in complete silence. The only way for the Germans to guard against this was to increase the number of sentries, ensure that they remained in constant contact with each other, instal obstacles, possibly lay minefields and use trained guard dogs. This was another example of the creativity and perseverance of the Soviet soldiers. If they didn't succeed the first night, they kept going until they did. If they discovered that special measures had been taken, they did their best to circumvent them. In this way the Soviets were able to collect meaningful information about the German defensive positions which they would use with great skill in future actions. Here the Soviets quickly learned that the German lines were thinly manned, particularly the section north of the valley.

The Germans in these positions had, however, been warned, had mined the routes used by the scouts and aimed machine guns and mortars at key points along any possible attack route. They anxiously awaited the events of the following nights. As expected, enemy units appeared on the opposite bank before dawn, preparing to cross at three different points. But their surprise was complete when the leading men on the west bank ran into the mines and the others, still on the east bank, came under covering fire from machine guns and mortars. The units were dispersed and suffered heavy casualties.

However, the Soviets tried again the next night at the same point, but this time with more men and equipment. The Germans fired on them again, and again the Soviets suffered heavy casualties. However, a small group had managed to reach the west bank and were now out of reach of German fire at the foot of the steep bank. German patrols successfully drove these units into the swampy area during the day. There they remained, chest-deep in mud and barely protected by the reeds, putting up a tough resistance against the Germans until nightfall. To the surprise of the Germans, they were still there the next day; in fact, they were now accompanied by two further Soviet units! The Soviets had formed a 'swamp' bridgehead on the west bank, 300 metres from the German lines. The Germans assumed that these units would not last long in the swamp. From a nearby church steeple, they could see the helmets of the Soviets among the reeds. The Soviets had hung their weapons in the reeds, ready to fire, and seemed to be waiting for something. It soon became clear what for.

### An enemy battalion fighting in German uniform (4 August)

Meanwhile, other units north of the area described above had become acquainted with an equally unusual Soviet way of operating. Their sector was characterized by a very hilly and wooded terrain with dense vegetation. This meant that the field of view and fire was severely limited. The western bank was bordered by a steep but also thickly vegetated ridge. It would be difficult for the Soviets to settle in here. However, if they succeeded, experience had shown that such terrain could only be recaptured with the commitment of many men, perhaps in combination with flamethrowers or flamethrower tanks, or by setting fire to the forest. Given the available manpower and materiel,

Katyusha rocket launchers, also called 'Stalin's organs', were weapons feared by the Germans because of their notorious inaccuracy, mobility and destructive power.

this would be virtually impossible. The Soviets recognized the possibilities of the terrain and were soon busy transferring people and equipment to the other bank. During the day they managed to establish a bridgehead, which was attacked by ground support aircraft and fired upon by artillery. A Soviet battery was knocked out by accurate fire from a 210mm howitzer battery after noise soundings. The situation seemed to have stabilized somewhat, although 'Stalin's organs' (Katyusha rocket launchers) bombarded the German positions at irregular intervals. The problem with these mobile launchers was that immediately after firing their missiles they took off and were therefore difficult to target. After some time, however, it became clear that they were operating from three or four positions at different road intersections. To put an end to their activities, the coordinates of the four launch positions were entered, and as soon as missiles were launched from one of these positions, all were simultaneously fired on by the German artillery. After a number of devastating barrages, Stalin's organs stopped harassing the Germans.

In the night, however, the Soviets resumed their activities and attempted to cross the river despite artillery barrages and machine-gun fire. They succeeded in transferring considerable numbers of men and equipment, helped by the fact that the accompanying artillery fire had punched holes in the German lines. Despite offering stiff resistance, the German units were slowly but surely pushed back and some were even surrounded. All they could hope for was relief from nearby units or from the regiment's reserve, and soon they heard the familiar sound of German machine guns from the woods behind them and bullets began to fly. The trapped Germans breathed a sigh of relief as heavily armed patrols drove the Soviets off and pushed them back to a small section of the west bank. There they stubbornly held out, effectively supported by their artillery. It was clear that the Soviets did not want to give up and that the units on the west bank would be reinforced by water. Facing them were weakened German units, which no longer had reserves at their disposal. When all attention turned to the previously described situation in the southern sector of the front, the Soviets managed to cross the Don in the northern sector of the front and resume the attack. They drove back the Germans, who were forced to take up defensive positions in a deep canyon in the forest. During the day, the German units received help from a few assault guns and a hundred engineers. In addition, reinforcements arrived in the form of soldiers recalled from leave, wounded discharged from hospitals and men from the support units. Mines were laid in the gorge and positions fortified, and the men awaited further Soviet attacks.

In the southern sector, meanwhile, the German lines were about to collapse and there was a real chance that Soviet units could break through and carry out an encirclement. Suddenly, however, something completely unexpected happened: in the area between the two sectors, German soldiers appeared who reported in perfect German that reinforcements were on their way. Everyone breathed a sigh of relief and the news spread like wildfire. At that moment the Soviets attacked along the entire line, and the Germans had to fight with all their might against the danger of being overrun. While all attention was focused on the frontal attack, the newly arrived 'German' units suddenly opened fire on the Germans' rear and flanks near the gap. Absolute chaos broke out, with everyone appearing to be shooting at each other; no one understood what was happening. The newly arrived units turned out to be Soviets, who now threw themselves at the German units, shouting, 'Hooray! Hooray!'

The situation was completely out of control, until the battalion commander gave the order to retreat to the nearest village. He passed the order to the officers nearby, and they formed small units, fighting their way back through the woods to the village with the aid of their machine guns, hand grenades and daggers. All Russians in German uniform they encountered and recognized by their Slavic facial features were killed. In the village, the units that had managed to escape the fighting in the forest regrouped. The regimental staff, once alerted, ensured that reinforcements arrived quickly, including assault guns, which were brought in on trucks. In the course of the afternoon the Soviets tried several times in vain to attack the village from the forest. The Germans could look forward to the arrival of more and more of their comrades, who had found their way back from the combat zone via detours. By nightfall the battalion was more or less complete again and a counter-attack could be planned. When it started to get light the next day, 4 August, the Soviets attacked first. Under cover of artillery and mortar fire, wave after wave attacked the German positions. However, when the Soviet attack was well under way, they were surprised by German ground support aircraft and bombers. The Soviets were forced to retreat into the woods, but hot on their heels came the Germans, who still had a score to settle. The fighting spread throughout the forest, and two hours after the start of the counter-attack the Germans had recaptured the original defensive line. Almost all the Russians who had worn German uniforms were killed in this action. This ended a critical situation for the Germans in an important sector of the front.

**Tanks on other tanks (5 August)**
The Soviets clearly wanted to cross the Don with heavy equipment. To this end, they began building a bridge at night at the place where the bridge destroyed by the Germans had stood, and the night was filled with the sounds of hammering and sawing. The Germans had long since entered all position

data into their fire control system, and just before midnight the bridge came under brief but heavy fire. In the light of the ensuing fire, the skeleton of beams and sleepers making up the half-finished bridge could be seen. Wounded Soviets were evacuated by comrades who rushed to the rescue. Half an hour later, however, construction noises were heard again. A second heavy shelling later in the night interrupted the work but did not put an end to it. The Germans then decided to deploy a battery of 210mm mortars, which carried out a precision bombardment at irregular intervals. The degree of accuracy could be deduced from the behaviour of the Soviets: if a shell fell on the target, it took some time before work was resumed; if a shell only fell near the bridge, then they continued undisturbed. Despite the losses of men, the Soviets continued to work, and there was a real danger that the bridge would be ready by daybreak. To prevent this, the Germans deployed carefully camouflaged machine guns, which fired at the soldiers on the bridge from the flank. This was an exceptional measure, because the positions of these machine guns should have been kept hidden and they were not supposed to come into action until an actual crossing started. As a result, work on the bridge was halted. As dawn broke, the Germans were faced with a horrifying sight: between and under the remains of the bridge lay or hung the remains of many Soviet soldiers. The injured were sheltering in water-filled craters, and the surrounding area was littered with burnt-out and destroyed vehicles, dead horses and construction tools.

However, the Soviets did not give up, and the following night, the events were repeated. Based on their experience of the previous night, the Germans deployed machine guns against the engineers on the bridge and howitzers against the equipment and vehicles. Heavy casualties were inflicted on the Soviets, and by midnight work was halted. On the east bank there was now only the sound of tracked vehicles which, at least in the Germans' opinion, were dragging all the bridge-building material away to a safer place. However, the sound of tracked vehicles had not diminished by morning; on the contrary, it became louder and seemed to be getting closer. The tracked vehicles turned out to be tanks, which had already reached the west bank of the river and opened fire on the fortifications of the village closest to the river in the valley! This was the signal for an all-out attack. The Soviet artillery began to fire on the village and on the German fortifications in the hills surrounding the valley. The aforementioned units from the swamp also joined the battle with the aim of cutting off the Belgorod-Kharkov roadway together with the tanks. A German barrage and the minefields and other obstacles prevented the Soviets from succeeding immediately.

As it was getting light, the situation gradually became clear. Soviet tanks had already passed the outer fortifications of the village and were moving towards the centre of the village, followed by infantry. The 'swamp' battalion had joined the attackers and one by one the German fortifications were taken. Soon they had reached the northern end of the village, only to be stopped by anti-tank guns. As the Soviets' flanks grew longer and more vulnerable, German fire from the hills became more and more accurate. By noon the attack had been halted and the Soviets were trapped in a long but narrow area, unable to move forward or backward. Any attempt to reinforce the units from the east bank was repelled by the Germans. But it was clear that the units had to be prevented from being reinforced during the night. Hence, in the course of the morning, a unit of nine assault guns and a company of engineers had prepared themselves for a frontal assault on the Soviet positions. The units were well coordinated and had sufficient supporting weapons in the form of machine guns, anti-tank guns and anti-aircraft guns. A number of ground support aircraft could also be deployed.

Meanwhile, efforts had been made to discover how the Soviets had managed to get tanks across the river. The engineers in particular, were keen to find out how it had been possible to cross the river with so many tanks, a question on everyone's mind. The river was too deep to drive across, and in the preceding German offensive a 70-ton bridge had to be built to get tanks over. Tracks of tracked vehicles could be seen from one of the southern hilltops on the east bank, ending at the waterline. The only conclusion was that amphibious tanks must have been deployed. The corps commander was the only man who had encountered amphibious tanks, but that was just six of them in July 1941, and they had been much smaller than the T-34s on the west bank. The possibility of amphibious tanks was therefore ruled out, but this made the question of how the tanks had got across all the more pressing.

During the afternoon house after house was recaptured from the Soviets, and the T-34s were knocked out one by one in direct confrontations with the assault guns. As the assault guns approached the tanks, German infantry from the hills attacked the Soviet infantry on the flanks. After ground support aircraft were deployed, the Soviets gave up their stubborn resistance and by noon the attack was halted. The curious engineers now advanced to unravel the riddle of the crossing. Even up close, at first they could not work it out. It was only after they probed the water that they discovered that an underwater bridge had been built 50cm below the surface. This in itself was nothing special; the Soviets often did this to prevent detection from the air or otherwise. But this bridge was built incredibly quickly, and under heavy artillery fire. It was only after a closer inspection of the bridge's foundations that the mystery became clear: two rows of tanks had been driven into the water, then planks had been hastily mounted on them and tied with ropes to form a roadway. The fact that a few tanks had come off this and crashed into the river was a minor matter, since most had managed to reach the other bank. The tank bridge was blown up by German engineers the next day, but it was another example of the creativity and perseverance shown by the Soviets. (56: 176–92)

## Sacrificed: the misfortunes of the 25th Panzer Division

The 25th Panzer Division was one of the divisions that had to make up for the losses of the past year. It was established in Norway, manned by occupying troops and issued with captured equipment. The division was led by General von Schell, a colleague of Guderian in the Defence Department in the 1920s and 1930s. Von Schell had studied the effects of large-scale motorization in the United States and had returned to Germany with many innovative ideas. Shortly before the war, he was given an important position on the staff of the Wehrmacht and became the armed forces' most important adviser in the field of motorization. He managed to convince Hitler of the benefits of standardization and was consequently appointed Under-Secretary of State at the *Reichsministerium für Transport*, with special responsibility for the development of transport and logistics. The standardization and rationalization of the production of military vehicles now took place within the framework of the '*Von Schell Programm*'. Light passenger cars were replaced by two- and four-wheel-drive Volkswagens, and the various truck types were replaced by three types of 1.5, 3 and 4.5 tons respectively. The two-wheel-drive version could be used for commercial purposes, the four-wheel-drive version was for the military. Half-tracks were also reduced to eight types, including the *Kettenkraftrad* and two types of *Maultieren*.

Von Schell soon encountered resistance from captains of industry and leading figures within the party to his views on standardization and rationalization of production processes. The project came to an end after the war started too quickly for his ambitious standardization programme to be fully implemented. Only the VW Kübelwagen and the Mercedes Benz and Steyer type 1500 series for crew transport entered mass production. We have already described the consequences of the lack of standardization and mass production on the number of trucks available, and the ensuing problems of the production and logistics of spare parts.

Von Schell was transferred to Norway, a theatre of war where no startling developments were expected. Through hard work he had quickly turned the troops there into a highly deployable fighting force, and Guderian supported his desire to transform them into a tank division. This wish was granted, and later in 1943 the division – now the 25th Panzer Division – was transferred to France to take over the duties of divisions that had recently been moved to the Soviet Union after Operation Zitadelle. The division was given new equipment and was due to undertake thorough training in how to handle this and how to survive on the Eastern Front, since that was one of the possible areas of deployment.

At the beginning of October, however, this division was ordered by Hitler to transfer 600 of its new vehicles to the 14th Panzer Division, another newly created tank division which was destined for the Eastern Front. The reason for this was that both the OKW and the OKH at that time still assumed that the 25th Division would remain in France for a longer period of time and could make use of captured French equipment. When the order to travel to the Eastern Front came on 14 October, the division was short of equipment in a variety of fields, ranging from support and service trucks to artillery, armoured half-tracks and anti-aircraft guns. Guderian personally asked Hitler to delay departure until he had had an opportunity to inspect the division himself. After this inspection, Guderian concluded that the division needed at least another month to receive new equipment and undergo basic training. Separately, OKW (Supreme Military Command), OKH (High Command of the Army) and Hitler decided that the division should move to the Eastern Front on 29 October. The entire logistical transport plan corresponded neither to the wishes of the divisional staff nor to the tactical situation at the front. For example, the anti-tank battalion was spread over the various trains. Also, sPzAbt 509 with its new Tiger tanks, which Guderian had added to support the division, had not yet received all its equipment and ultimately did not travel to the Eastern Front at all.

The division was hurriedly transferred to the area of Heeresgruppe Süd, where it was decided that the wheeled vehicles should be unloaded at Berdichev-Kosatin and the tracked vehicles at Kirovograd; the two places were three days' march apart and communication between the two parts of the division was difficult because a large number of the telephone lines were out of action. It was decided that the units ready to move to the assembly areas should move out in separate marching columns as quickly as possible. However, the division was not given the opportunity to assemble as a whole in the agreed assembly area, since on 5 November the Soviets broke through the lines near Kiev. The 25th Panzer Division was now placed under the command of the Fourth Panzer Army and was ordered on 6 November to advance to Fastov and hold it at all costs. The wheeled vehicles had to leave for Fastov during the day and would have to look after their own protection, while the tracked vehicles would join them from Kirovograd as soon as possible. Von Schell became commander on site and, in addition to the 25th Panzer Division, he had two *Abteilungen Landesschützen* (national reserve) and a regiment of the SS Panzer Grenadiere Division Das Reich at his disposal. Because partisans had blown up all the bridges, the various units had to try to reach Fastov over country roads.

Early in the evening of 6 November, the units headed by von Schell took off. During the night they encountered retreating Luftwaffe units, which caused considerable delay. It then started to rain heavily, and the next day the roads turned into muddy tracks, forcing the wheeled vehicles to make long detours. The tracked vehicles had less trouble with the terrain. However, the various marching groups lost contact with each other, as any form of communication was prohibited. Around noon on 7 November, von Schell learned that Fastov had already been occupied by the Soviets. He went on a reconnaissance with his adjutant in two half-tracks and was confronted by a number of T-34s. These opened fire on a company of the division's Panzer Grenadiere Regiment, which promptly panicked. When von Schell rode back, the entire second battalion of this regiment was already retreating. He managed to get them back in line and ordered them to advance towards Fastov. He stayed with the units to intervene in case they panicked again and ordered them to dig in at nightfall.

During the night, however, Soviet tanks managed to reach the battalion's headquarters and partially destroy it. Von Schell now decided to break through the tanks in an attempt to reach Fastov. With a Kampfgruppe consisting of one company in front, one in the rear and the heavy weapons and vehicles in between, von Schell managed, after heavy fighting, to break through the lines. On 8 November he reached the headquarters of the XLVII Panzer Corps in Biala Zerkov. Part of the other marching groups led by Freiherr von Weichmar had meanwhile advanced further towards Fastov via other routes. On 9 November the units merged and advanced to Fastov, which was held by a strong Soviet force. On the same day a suburb was taken, and on 10 November the attack on Fastov itself was launched. However, the Soviets put up strong resistance, and von Schell and his units were unable to take the city itself.

But the drama was not over yet. From 24 to 30 December, this unfortunate division was deployed to hold a front of more than 40km against an overwhelmingly superior Soviet force. The division was ground down in battle and the remaining units were withdrawn from the front. The division would have to be rebuilt from the ground up. Hitler and the OKH wanted to dissolve the division entirely, given its history, but Guderian managed to prevent this, because in his opinion it could not be held responsible for the course of events. Von Schell fell ill and had to leave the front. He suffered greatly from the fate of his unfortunate division, which he had built up so energetically, and he was not given a command for the rest of the war. (20: 316–22)

## 6. Security behind the front in 1943

The security situation behind the front began to become an increasingly acute problem for the Germans in 1943. Partisan numbers grew in the area of Heeresgruppe Mitte from 57,000 in January to 103,600 in September, according to German estimates. In the entire hinterland, their numbers increased from 130,000 to 250,000, and the Wehrmacht began to lose control of large parts of the area behind the front. By August 1943 Heeresgruppe Mitte reported that it controlled only 23 per cent of the area, while 46 per cent was partisan-controlled and the rest was questionable. The Germans were increasingly forced to withdraw to larger towns and cities in order to protect the routes that were logistically and economically important. Thanks to a steady stream of supplies brought in by the Soviet Air Force and better training and leadership, the partisans continued to grow in strength.

**Explosive growth of partisans in early 1943**

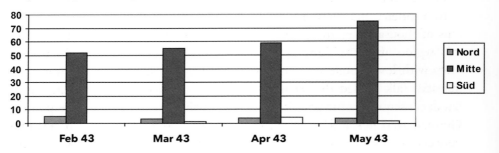

This table clearly shows the growth in almost all areas, but it is clear that the problems in the area of Heeresgruppe Mitte were significantly greater than in other places. While the numbers in the areas of Heeresgruppe Nord and Süd are more or less negligible (together fewer than 10,000 men), the Wehrmacht in the area of Heeresgruppe Mitte was faced by 75,000 partisans in mid-1943, a number that increased in the following year.

We now follow the vicissitudes of 221st Sicherungsdivision, as mentioned in *The German Way of War 1941–1943*. Despite its relative successes in 1942, the 221st Sicherungsdivision began to lose control of its area in the spring of 1943. The partisans were able to blow up economically important buildings and installations and carry out almost daily attacks on villages they suspected of being pro-German, looting houses and killing key individuals. While the number of clashes with partisans was 59 in February, this had risen to 131 in May. Between April and May the number of attacks on villages rose from 140 to 308 and sabotage actions from 87 to 233. In the same period, the division had to relinquish three of its battalions to be deployed elsewhere, and the level of training, as well as discipline and morale, declined. In addition, its units increasingly encountered partisans better armed than themselves. The *Ordungsdienst* (security service), which had provided the necessary support in the past, became increasingly unreliable and had to deal with deserters to the partisan ranks.

The 221st Division persisted in the belief that the civilian population should be spared as much as possible. In July, for example, when it learned that a Hungarian-led Operation Csobo, aimed at collecting food supplies, was getting out of hand in the area under its jurisdiction, the leadership immediately asked the Hungarian units involved to 'refrain … from deportations, destruction of villages or reprisals during the operation. The division would like to emphasize that as a rule burning down villages and taking measures against the population is strictly prohibited by order of the commander of Heeresgruppe Mitte.' The Hungarians paid no attention to this, slaughtered 900 civilians and complained to Heeresgruppe Mitte about the weak attitude of the 221st Division.

In February the division was confronted with the unexpected arrival of tens of thousands of troops from the Eighth Italian Army, who had fled to this region after the fighting around Stalingrad. These were undisciplined units with low morale who terrorized the local population. Moreover, their defeatist talk fuelled the feeling of the local population that retreat was at hand; consequently, the population was less willing than in 1942 to respond to German overtures, and in the course of 1943 this led to a worsening of relations between the two. In July, the 221st Division made one last attempt to turn the tide. With no fewer than 178,000 copies of newspapers and magazines, 60,500 brochures, 250,000 maps and 813,700 leaflets and picture books for children, the propaganda department of the division tried to convince the population of the good will of the Germans. It was in vain, however, and the voluntary turnout for the celebration of Operation Barbarossa, the 'day of liberation', was almost nil. In addition, the partisans were increasingly able inflict economic damage, and the Germans were increasingly unsuccessful in recruiting workers for German industry.

As a result of these developments, the idea grew among the division's leadership of keeping certain parts of their area firmly in their hands, while leaving other parts to the partisans and applying scorched-earth tactics to them. These would take the form of requisitioning grain and cattle from those villages suspected of acting as bases for partisans, then burning them to the ground and carrying off all able-bodied men for forced labour. The units carrying this out had to be restrained from using too much force, since it would be combined with propaganda efforts aimed at explaining and justifying the action. Economic staff officer Klinsky reported that 'Between July 1 and July 11, Moglin district was largely evacuated and burnt down. In a few weeks, the remaining crop is due to be harvested ... Similarly, in Slinka district, twelve villages have been burnt down during a military operation.' Such reports paint a horrifying picture of devastation and mass deportation by a division which had previously been characterized by a high degree of restraint and a positive attitude towards the civilian population. The aim was no longer to win over hearts and minds, but to crush the partisans in order to further the war effort and the economic exploitation of occupied territory.

The attitude of the 221st Division can be compared with that of the 201st. Even in 1942, the policy of the latter was to treat the partisans without mercy. If there was any restraint at all, it disappeared completely in early 1943, and the activities of this division began to spiral out of control in the spring that year. For example, in three actions in the first three months of 1943, 6,500 'partisans and involved parties' were killed, compared to 159 Germans, a ratio that is hard to believe. The presence of SS units in the region undoubtedly contributed to the large number of casualties. For example, 1,200 of the 6,500 prisoners transferred to these units by the Sicherungsdivision were shot by them. As a result, the Sicherungsdivision kept its hands clean, leaving the dirty work to the SS. In contrast, relatively few Einsatzgruppen (killing squads) were active in the 221st Division area and they limited their activities to screening suspects. This was immediately reflected in the figures. In summary, we can see that the views of the divisional leadership on relations with the local population, their way of dealing with the partisans or people suspected of sympathy with the Soviet regime, combined with the presence or absence of SS units in the area under their jurisdiction, strongly determined the way the Sicherungsdivisionen fulfilled their tasks. (53: 148)

It is interesting to examine a picture of the economic effects of the partisan struggle, as in the following table:

**Forestry production from August 1941 to April 1943**

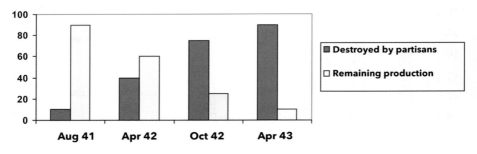

This clearly shows how strong the partisans were in wooded areas. In the end, forestry production was almost completely halted by partisan actions over a period of about two years. The partisans also focused their actions on the wood-processing industry: capacity fell by 42–58 per cent, eighteen sawmills were destroyed by fire and 232 workers and foresters were killed.

The Germans also collected data on economic damage in the field of the production of cereals, meat and oils. Below are the data for 1942 and 1943.

**Loss of grain production due to partisan actions 1942/1943**

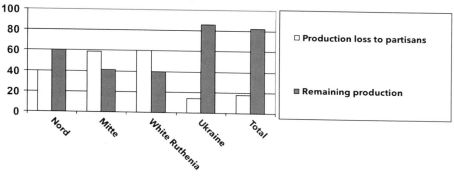

**Loss of meat production due to partisan actions 1942/1943**

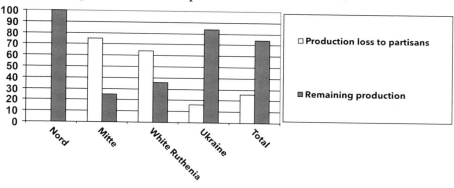

**Loss of animal fat production due to partisan actions 1942/1943**

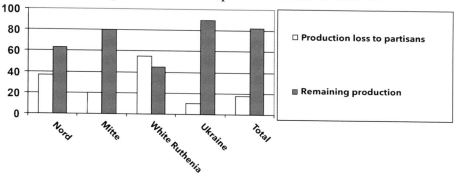

**Loss of mineral oil production due to partisan actions 1942/1943**

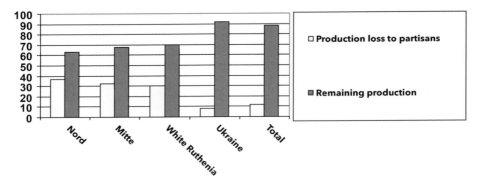

These figures clearly show that the partisans were least active in the Ukraine and that their effect varied in the other regions. The Ukraine was also the area that was by far the largest producer of grain, meat and oils. Hence, the actions of the partisans in the various regions had an effect on production of these regions, but much less on total production, since this was largely determined by that of the Ukraine. (21: 457)

The Soviet population, however, suffered under the German policy of forced requisitioning for the Wehrmacht and especially for Germany itself, and hunger in the occupied territory continued to become more acute. Lieutenant Emerich Pohl wrote home in a letter:

> Crooked, half-dead shadows creep here and there along the road …
> At night they dig seed potatoes from the ground. A boy was arrested
> yesterday who carried a large package under his arm, which contained an
> old fur. When asked what he intended to do with it, he explained that he
> wanted to take it home to eat by pulling out the hair and boiling the skin
> in water until it could be eaten.

Hellmut Prantl, a non-commissioned officer in a *Sonderkommando* (work unit of death camp prisoners), wrote: 'A human life is not important here. A woman will shoot her husband for a piece of bread, a child will report his parents to get something to eat.' (53: 151) The Soviet population could only try to survive and wait for better times.

## 7. The Reichsbahn (national railway) in 1943

In 1943, due to the threat of partisan actions, ever greater attention was paid to the protection of railway tracks. The Wehrmacht was responsible for this and focused its efforts mainly on the larger stations and important bridges. These were guarded against partisan attacks by units of the German *Landschütze* (local militia), units of German allies and so-called *Hiwis* (*Hilfswillige*, local volunteers). The latter were particularly unreliable. In August 1943, nearly 600 armed *Hiwis* defected to the partisans. The partisans also became increasingly brutal. Sometimes they raided track posts or smaller stations in broad daylight, locking up or simply shooting railway employees and then blowing up installations and the track. The German units were too thinly spread to counter such actions. Occasionally, drastic remedies were used. For example, the short but important stretch of track between Shlobin and Gomel, which had been blocked by constant partisan actions, was at one point guarded by a soldier stationed every five metres. However, even this did not prevent the partisans from carrying out several successful attacks.

To prevent attacks between services, trains travelled behind each other at a speed of 20kph in a column. During the day, individual trains ran at a maximum speed of 40kph, while at night the speed did not exceed 20kph. Trains did not run at all at night on stretches that were rarely used, but waited at a station. The next day, the route was first checked for mines by units of the Wehrmacht or trained railway personnel.

The Germans built wooden fortifications along the railway to guard the track and to have men on the spot in case of sabotage actions or attacks by partisans.

Once an attack had occurred, special construction trains turned out to make the track passable again. These were accompanied by a military unit of between fifteen and thirty men, often in bulletproof wagons, the so-called *Berta-Wagens*. Any derailed but undamaged wagons were hoisted back onto the rails, while damaged wagons were pushed off the track. As an emergency solution, on two-track routes, the rails of the second track were used to repair the damaged one in order to keep at least one track operational. If both tracks were blocked, trains were held at the nearest station, then sent forward again as soon as at least one track was passable. In areas where the partisans were especially active, troop and ammunition trains in particular were diverted over routes that were relatively safe, but losses of material such as rails, points, locomotives and wagons were considerable. For example, sabotage with a magnetic mine at a station between Minsk and Gomel destroyed a train carrying fuel, two trains carrying ammunition and a train carrying brand-new Tiger tanks. The damage to locomotives in particular had a major effect. In July 1943, 649 locomotives were hit in the GVD Osten, 357 of which were so badly damaged that they had to be towed to Germany for repairs. In the course of 1943, to protect the locomotives, two empty wagons were placed at the front of the train, so that in the event of an attack these wagons, and not the locomotive itself, would be blown up.

The pressure from the partisans increased, as can be seen from a diary entry of Hans Frank, head of the General Government, dated 25 May 1943 following a conversation with one of the managers from his area:

> The number of sabotage actions and raids on stations and railway installations has increased from February to May of this year continuously. At present, an average of 10 to 11 raids per day is seen as normal. Some routes can only be travelled under escort … Another route can sometimes only be used for one day after a lot of effort on our part, after which it is completely blocked again.

This forced the Germans to take more and more measures to defend themselves against the partisans. Outlying stations and sectional posts were surrounded by palisades. Fortifications were built, and even small water tank sites were turned into fortresses. In wooded areas, the *Eisenbahnpioniere* (pioneers) cut down trees and bushes 200–300m from each side of the track, and anyone who entered this area risked being shot. In addition, the *Forschungsabteilung* (research department) of the Reichsbahn developed a number of exotic installations that were supposed to detect sabotage actions at an early stage. The first was an automatic alarm system consisting of wires stretched along the rails, which when touched set off an alarm bell in the nearest station or block post. This was unsuccessful because the partisans regularly removed the entire installation. A second was the so-called *Güwa*, the *Gliesüberwachungsanlage*, an electrical installation that checked per block whether the rails were intact by sending pulses of current through them. If the rails were blown up or unscrewed, this would be immediately noticed. A third weapon that was thrown into the fray was an unmanned railcar that travelled ahead of the train with a wagon full of scrap in front of it. The idea was that this railcar and its wagon would detonate any mines laid by partisans in order to spare the train following behind. The partisans managed to circumvent this precaution by means of timed ignitions, after which the Germans in turn succeeded in generating an electromagnetic field via an antenna under the railcar that disrupted the ignition mechanism. This arms race between the two parties could have continued for some time, had it not been for the fact that by the end of 1944 the Wehrmacht occupied hardly any part of the Soviet Union. (42: 107–13)

Thanks to the above and other measures, the ultimate goal of the partisans, to paralyse railway traffic, was never achieved. However, they were able to completely shut down rail traffic on certain routes for days and sometimes weeks, thus inflicting great damage on the military and economic efforts of the Germans. Movement of troops and supplies was hindered, a feeling of insecurity grew behind the front, and train journeys sometimes became a perilous undertaking. The partisans managed to undermine the working of the railways, which were particularly important in a country with a limited road network.

A locomotive of the Baureihe 52 has just been derailed by a mine near Minsk.

## 8. Fate

### The life of an ordinary infantryman

That the Soviet army survived the first years of the war and rose again stronger than ever in 1943 was in no small part due to the steadfastness of the infantry. That is why it is necessary to take a closer look at the life of the ordinary infantryman. The memoirs and reminiscences of various writers, filmmakers and journalists offer a broad albeit fragmentary picture of the vicissitudes of civilians who went to war. In the run-up to the war, all men born in 1919–1922 had been called up for military service. In two waves of mobilization, in June and August 1941, young men born in 1923 and the older men born between 1890 and 1918 were called up. Mobilizations also took place in 1942 and 1943, so that in the end almost everyone below a certain age was under arms. Medical examination of conscripts was generally cursory. During the initial period of training, regular recruits were assigned to a 'reserve regiment' or a 'practice regiment'. In the literature everyone agrees that these regiments had an extremely bad, forbidding reputation: too little food, hard drill, ill-fitting, used uniforms and footwear, and inhuman accommodations (dirty, smelly, damp) were no exception. Many recruits fell sick with exhaustion, dysentery, bronchitis and anaemia. Those who felt most at home were the criminals released from prison, who terrorized their fellows and robbed them of their scarce possessions.

The period in these training regiments was so unbearable that men longed for the front. The stories of bullying by officers, political indoctrination, searches for food in rubbish bins, corporal punishment and 'educational' executions are legion. In addition, SMERSH (military counter-intelligence) officers recruited informants from among the recruits, but these informers had to be careful because, in the words of Vladimir Boet, 'at the front the informants are not forgiven and the bullets are not marked.' Guns were often unavailable and training was done with wooden rifles. In some cases, the recruits slept nine together in a pit in the ground with just two army coats as blankets. All in all, this poor training and the weakened condition in which the recruits were eventually deployed to the front led to heavy casualties. (7: 209–10)

When the 'training' was completed, men were allotted to a marching column, with decent equipment and uniform. Rifles were often only handed out at the front. It was no problem if they had not used the real thing before: 'Whoever is not beaten in the first fight will learn how to shoot. It's not that hard,' Dmitry Sergeyev was told by his officer. The soldiers were usually taken close to the front by train. The journey could take many days, in boxcars with bunks and a small heater in the middle. Stops were a chance to trade, with all kinds of military clothing changing hands. In this way mixed companies of Russians, Tartars, Kazakhs and other peoples of the Soviet Union travelled together. After the train journey, exhausting marches followed, usually at night, towards the front.

---

**On the way to the front**
Sergei Polyakov describes a trip in February 1943:

'The first days of the trip there was a blizzard. We walked in the short day, we walked in the twilight of night. During short breaks, the soldiers dropped into the snow, many fell asleep immediately. Officers ran along the column, waking the people, getting them to their feet. I had learned to sleep during a march, you walk with closed eyes and sleep. It is important that there is no bend in the road, because in a bend you get out of line and you fall down.'

In ten or twelve days he covered 300km to the front. Just before they got there they received warm food for the first time in ten days. Then came the last metres to the front. 'Our mortars are carried by horses that look like skeletons ... Two soldiers support the horse on the left and right, others push the sleigh from behind.' (7: 211–12)

---

Soldiers and non-commissioned officers were short-haired and soberly dressed. No one had watches – they were prized spoils of war. There were helmets, but these were not worn; the men wore a *pilotka*, a hat with a red star on it, and in winter a fur hat with earflaps. If you did wear a helmet, you ran the risk of being shot at by your own troops, because Germans wore helmets as standard. Helmets were used to hold water or light fires in. Incidentally, washing was done in the evening because an old soldiers' superstition stated that someone who washed in the morning would not make it to nightfall. Footwear consisted of shoes with puttees; boots were scarce at first. Not everyone had a tent tarpaulin, which also served to keep rain off the uniform and the puttees dry. All in all, a less than military image was presented. Golitsyn describes his pioneer company, which advanced to the west in 1944, as follows: 'With thirty carts including two kitchen trucks, carts with our belongings, our smithy, our liquor boiler [!], a motorcycle with sidecar for our captain, and our cows, sometimes as many as ten of them, our company was about half a kilometre long. It resulted in a less than military sight.' (7: 213)

Soviet soldiers generally slept in the open. In the summer this was not a problem; in winter a pit was dug in the snow with branches on the bottom, and men slept close together. Trenches provided some protection, but every

**New recruits**

After 1942, the advancing Soviet armies rapidly recruited all the men who had lived under German occupation. These hastily mobilized individuals were called 'booty' soldiers and were seen as unreliable and inferior. Moreover, some of them came from areas that had been loyal to the Whites (anti-communists) in the Civil War. These 'soldiers' were deployed without training, sometimes even without weapons, in their black auxiliary uniforms under the 'protection of the shielding detachments from the rear'. The members of these units called them 'blackcoats'. It was these soldiers who attacked the well-defended village of Grebennikov in the spring of 1943; hungry, poorly dressed, scarcely trained and without tanks or artillery, they attacked several times a day for almost a month. When one of the commanding officers asked why his units were treated this way he was told that they were 'from the south, the Don, the Kuban, the North Caucasus [and those] have always been a stronghold of the Whites. And even now it is a hostile nest, one even more a traitor than the other.' It is unclear whether deliberate revenge was being taken here or whether the manpower shortage was so great that there was no alternative but to deploy them in this way. (7: 125–6)

season had its problems. In the winter digging trenches was difficult because useful material was often lacking; in the spring the water table was so high and the trenches therefore so shallow that they were no deeper than the soldiers' waists; in the autumn there was glutinous mud. Trenches had their own smell, a mixture of damp, gunpowder fumes, sour sweat, rye bread, tobacco smoke and machine grease. The soldiers were seldom relieved or given leave, and tensions between men could therefore run high. It is not surprising that a large number of them suffered from battle-fatigue and became careless out of fatalism, considering the statistic that in periods of fighting an infantryman's average survival time was less than eight days. Relations between front-line soldiers were generally amicable, including with NCOs, who rarely insulted or humiliated the men. As in any army, men expected care, fairness and skill from their officers, but Red Army officers generally treated their subordinates poorly, and there was a wide gulf between officers and enlisted men. The officers were also ill prepared for their task, partly because of the purges of the higher echelons in the years before the war. They were often inexperienced, overconfident and indifferent to losing, a mentality they had adopted from their superiors. Officers received a modest extra ration in the form of chocolate, which they were supposed to share with their subordinates. Soldiers who had their own opinions were not popular with officers. 'Keep your mouth shut', 'obey orders' and 'don't philosophize' were favourite reprimands. In critical situations, officers were authorized to shoot their subordinates without trial.

**At the front**

On his way to the front, David Samolyov encountered the first signs of battle: 'And with concern we looked at the carts with the wounded. Farm horses slowly pulled narrow wagons in which two or three wounded lay, covered against the rain with tarpaulins so that you could only see part of a bandaged head, arm or leg. You feared the alarming imminence of death.' Kondrarjev described the first experiences of recruits at the front: 'In the night we arrived at the front and the next day we were immediately deployed … What I saw was very different from during exercises. A field full of corpses, and an ill-considered, ill-prepared attack. We were chased against machine guns, straight through a minefield.' After two months, having been used only three times, there was almost nothing left of his brigade.

Corporal punishment was no exception at the front. Unsurprisingly, soldiers were sometimes more afraid of their own officers than of the enemy. Officers who treated their men with respect, on the other hand, were adored.

With the above in mind, officers had a certain fear of their subordinates, because they would often leave wounded officers on the battlefield or even help them into the next world. If officers behind the front suddenly became friendly to their men, this was a sign that the march to the front was imminent, because 'where there is fighting, there must be no room for mutual resentment'.

The gulf between enlisted men and the staff officers was even wider. In the eyes of the men the staff lived in a completely different world, one in which washing, shaving and clean clothes were commonplace. They wrote

A T-34 crosses a shallow area of a river. Infantry riding on tanks were particularly vulnerable during combat.

notes, ate in canteens and were startled by the sound of a plane, as Dimitri Sergeyev observed.

An exception was some of the officers from the reserve. These were teachers, technicians, who paid more attention to the needs of the soldiers than the professional officers and also seemed to have more military-strategic insight. Despite it all, as we have seen, the ordinary Soviet soldier displayed unprecedented tenacity. Ergeni Nosov, then a soldier, later a man of letters, summarized it as follows:

[War is] above all, having patience, long marches, carrying heavy things, digging with a shovel that you picked up in an empty yard, feeling cold, your teeth chattering, stamping your feet at your post with frozen felt boots, enduring moisture, rain, thirst and heat patiently, sometimes waiting days for a lost field kitchen somewhere, gnawing at that poor, stale bread because you have nothing else, smoking dry grass or moss, with a flint of fire, sleeping with your boots on on damp ground or in a snow pit, enduring all kinds of bullets and brutal mortar shelling, not to mention the fighting itself, when you have to face a machine gun openly or fight with grenades against a tank.

Vlacheslav Kondrarjev said that 'his daily life, his days and nights, are bloody, hopeless, because only death or injury can free the soldier from the permanent, inhuman efforts, which were incredibly difficult to sustain.' The same fatalism was found in Vsevolod Osten, who spoke of 'patience bordering on and passing over to the willingness to die'. Genatoulin argued that two months in battle was already too much, because 'in that time you become so exhausted that you have only one thought: die or get hurt as soon as possible to stop tormenting yourself, there is a limit to what a man can endure.' (7: 215–16) Despite this, the front was often seen as a liberation because 'in the rear areas the food was scant and the treatment brutal'. Anyone who was wounded and ended up in a hospital wanted only to return to his own unit, to the friendship and comradeship of the soldiers at the front.

On the other side of the front, Soviet citizens also suffered through the war. In addition to starvation, from 1942 they were threatened with being taken for forced labour, either locally or in Germany itself.

## Labour force for the German Reich

In the past two years, the demand for labour in Germany had grown greatly. The German government therefore set up a programme to meet this need with foreign workers. On 21 March 1942, Hitler appointed Fritz Sauckel as

GBA, or *Generallbevöllmachtigte für den Arbeitzeinsatz* (general representative for work deployment). He was ordered to recruit as many workers as possible for the German Reich from the annexed and occupied territories of Europe. First on a voluntary basis, but from April 1942 also increasingly under duress, civilians in the occupied territories were recruited for work in Germany. In the Soviet Union, up to 30 June 1944, a total of 2,800,000 civilians were recruited in this way to work in Germany. Half of them came from areas under the military, the other half from areas under civilian rule. The bodies mainly responsible for recruitment were the so-called Sauckel Commission and the *Wirtschaftsstab Ost* (Eastern economic staff).

The OKH had mixed feelings about this system. It needed workers itself, but it feared that forced and sometimes violent recruitment would have a negative effect on the relationship with the civilian population.

### Overview of recruitment per area per year within the jurisdiction of the OKH
(21: 369)

|        | Süd     | Mitte   | Nord    | Total     |
|--------|---------|---------|---------|-----------|
| 1942   | 636,601 | 118,155 | 50,440  | 805,196   |
| 1943   | 116,118 | 91,475  | 4,557   | 212,150   |
| 1944   | 211,162 | 101,996 | 68,027  | 381,185   |
| *Total* | *963,881* | *311,626* | *123,024* | *1,398,531* |

In order to provide for its own labour needs, the Wehrmacht in the territories under its authority fell back on the decree of 5 August 1941 issued by Reichsminister Rosenberg which laid down that civilians in the occupied territories could be compelled to work. The Wehrmacht used this decree to recruit civilians in the areas under its authority for agriculture, industry and the construction of roads, railways and fortifications. As the war progressed, the labour shortage became more and more acute. To meet this increasing need, the OKH published an additional decree on 6 February 1943 which established a general obligation to work in the war zone. The *Ortskommandanturen* (local commanders) were responsible for introducing this labour obligation and did not shy away from harsh punishments in cases of refusal to work or sabotage. As a rule, the German employment service implemented the measures, supported by the local authorities. They mapped out the labour population, matched the number of workers to each requirement and divided them up among the various parts of the army. However, the employment service was only an administrative organization, so that units of the Wehrmacht and local auxiliary police were deployed for the actual implementation of recruitment. In this way, too, the Wehrmacht was forced to become ever more corrupt.

## German prisoners of war

The year 1943 was a turning point in the war in several ways. One was that for the first time large groups of German soldiers were taken prisoner. Becoming a prisoner of war was often the beginning of agony for men on both sides. According to German figures, during the war as a whole about 3,200,000 of their men were taken prisoner. The Soviets speak of 2,389,560 men, the largest number being made prisoner towards the end of the war. According to German figures, approximately 1,100,000 of the 3,200,000 did not survive captivity. The number of German prisoners of war steadily increased: at the end of 1941 only 9,417 German soldiers had been taken prisoner, but by March 1944 252,028 had been, of whom 105,285 were still alive. The last year of the war and the eventual armistice eventually yielded the largest number of PoWs, nearly 3,000,000.

The most dangerous period for captured Germans was the moment they surrendered and the days immediately after. In the years 1941 and 1942, a large proportion of the Germans who surrendered were killed during this time. Many also died during the marches to PoW camps, since those who could not march were killed. For example, of the 8,000 German prisoners of war in a camp near Prokopyevsk between 13 March and 1 May 1943, 6,189 perished, 1,526 on their way to the camp, the rest from starvation.

---

**Bitterness and retaliation**

Udo von Alvensleben's unit made a gruesome discovery on 17 August 1941: 'A few hundred metres from Girogowo station we find the corpses of about 150 men of the 6th company of the 79th Schützenregiment. The Russians have tortured them to death with everything that a devilish mind can think of in that field. At the same moment word comes from the east bank of the Ingul, where men of the division are found killed in the same circumstances. My own unit is always very good-natured towards PoWs, but now the call for revenge knows no bounds.' (5: 195)

---

Even if they survived this crucial period immediately after capture, and the marches deeper into the Soviet Union, the Germans struggled. For example, of the 91,000 German prisoners of war taken at Stalingrad, 85,000 perished in captivity. Some were not repatriated from the Soviet Union until 1955 after a visit by Chancellor Adenauer. The fortunes of the 6th Panzer Division defending the Don River, as described in this book, are also illustrative. On 14 April 1945, they surrendered to Patton's US Third Army near Brno in Czechoslovakia. Since they had been continuously deployed to the Eastern Front in the previous period, they were handed over to the Soviets in May. After many hardships, the last men did not return home until 1955.

All prisoners of war were put to work, clearing rubble, building houses and factories and constructing power stations. They were housed in camps, garages, monasteries and residential houses. Some did all right. For example, Viktor Sofronov once saw German prisoners of war working in a village where Russian women brought them bread, biscuits and potatoes. When one of the Germans was killed in a fall from the roof, all the women cried. Even during the march to the camps the Germans could sometimes count on the compassion of the population. For example, German prisoners of war were given drinks by Russian peasant women during short stops, while the Soviet guards pretended not to notice.

Some individual cases stand out. In the steppes near the Don, Sergei Golitsyn came across an Austrian soldier who had been left behind by his unit, Friedrich Stettiner, a car mechanic from Vienna. His knowledge came in handy when several of Golitsyn's engineering unit's trucks broke down on the side of the road. Stettiner got them going again and won a place in Golitsyn's unit. Despite his explicitly racist views about Slavs, he repaired gramophones, clocks, sewing machines, in short, anything mechanical, in the Russian villages along the way. He eventually married a Russian girl and was taken to a PoW camp only after the war. At the time that Stettiner joined the unit of Golitsyn they passed through an area that had never been in German hands. To Stettiner's surprise, half naked or naked corpses of Germans lay everywhere, and he realized that these were prisoners of war who had been shot while in transit. This was far from an isolated example of how the Soviets treated their PoWs. Around February 1943, Boris Slutskis was on a train that stopped at Mitjoerink station. On the other track there was a train carrying Italian, Romanian and Yugoslav prisoners of war. In the open boxcars dozens of yellowing corpses could be seen; the cause of their death was hunger. (7: 183)

PoWs who eventually managed to reach a camp were also subjected to 're-education' in the form of indoctrination, lectures, anti-fascist clubs and various courses. The effect of these measures was generally not great. Captivity did, however, lead to an explosion of plays, novels, operettas and paintings among the Germans. Before the PoWs could be repatriated after the war, the Soviet Ministry of the Interior first demanded 'a political account of their PoW life' because of its 'great significance for the refutation of defamatory and provocative statements abroad'. Repatriation depended on this, and those who did not change their attitude could count on facing trial. In the period up to 1950, 30,000 prisoners of war were sentenced by Soviet courts. For example, the last commander of Berlin, General Weidling, was given twenty-five years in prison for refusing to 'confirm Stalin's version of Hitler's flight from Berlin'.

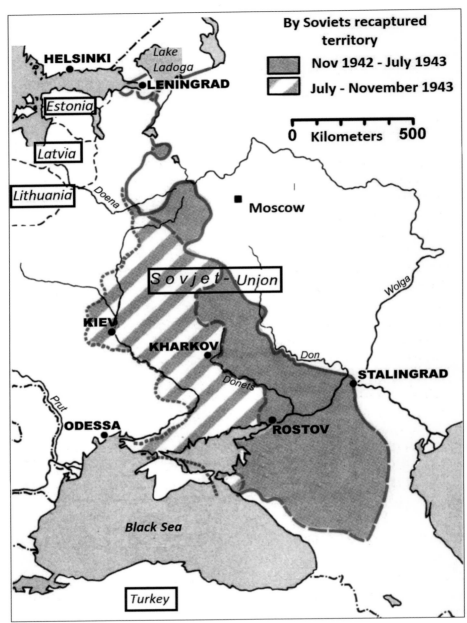

The course of the front in December 1943, showing the areas recaptured by the Soviets.

We end this chapter with the image of German prisoners of war. Their capture in numbers shows that 1943 can be seen as a watershed in the war on the Eastern Front. From now on the Soviets would hold the initiative, until they finally took Berlin in May 1945.

# Chapter 3

# 1944: A Year of Decisions

*The year 1944 saw the Germans being increasingly pushed back to the west. All they were capable of was conducting strategic defensive actions: they could hold up the Soviets, but they could no longer hold them back. While in the previous year after Kursk the battle had mainly taken place in the south, the Soviets now focused on the area of Heeresgruppe Mitte. Their summer offensive, Bagration, which started on 27 June, was an immediate success, and in the following weeks the Germans were pushed so far west that on 19 October the Soviets finally managed to occupy some German territory, albeit briefly. The situation was not very different in the south. In a series of offensives they managed not only to drive out the last German units there, but also to occupy Romania, Bulgaria, Yugoslavia and eventually most of Hungary. Although the course of events might suggest otherwise, German industry was in fact in full swing in 1944, and tanks and armoured vehicles, including new types, were leaving the factories in unprecedented numbers. On the other hand, the entire German training system was slowly but surely collapsing, because the war on the various fronts consumed ever more men. All this had a negative effect on German battlefield performance, which made the difference between slowly but surely giving way to being overrun by the Soviets. All in all, by the end of 1944, everyone was waiting for the final Soviet offensive that would bring a premature end to the Third Reich.*

In this chapter we will first discuss the adjustments that were made in the organizational structure of the German armed forces to deal with the pressing shortage of manpower. We then look in more detail at German arms production in 1944, the various new weapon systems and the shortage of industrial workers. Both the Soviets and the Germans changed their doctrine and tactics in 1944, the latter forced to do so by unfolding events. The security situation will also be reviewed, as will be the fate of various units and individuals in the larger context of events at the front.

## 1. Structure of the German Army

### The infantry division, early 1944

During 1943 the shortage of men had become increasingly acute. The Germans simply could not find enough suitable recruits to be deployed at the front. In addition, the troops needed more firepower. The solution to the first problem was found in the reorganization of infantry divisions. Their overall size was reduced by 28 per cent and the size of the infantry units themselves by 31 per cent. These divisions eventually totalled approximately 12,500 men each. New weapons such as the 120mm mortar had already been introduced during 1943, and the divisions' firepower increased by about 10 per cent compared to that of the standard division in 1939, somewhat compensating for the reduction in manpower. The slimmed-down nature of the division made it easier to provide replacements for units that had been reduced in size by combat. This prevented these divisions from having to keep fighting until they eventually had to deploy their highly trained and therefore valuable specialists (artillery, engineer and liaison units) in the front line as infantry. The first new divisions built along these lines were operational by the end of 1943. Existing divisions could easily be converted and followed quickly: one infantry battalion from each regiment was disbanded and each company lost 30 per cent of its combat strength due to the disbandment of one platoon.

### Volksgrenadier infantry divisions, late 1944

But in the end these measures were not enough. In the autumn of 1944, the Germans were forced to go one step further: on top of the previous cuts in the spring, there was a further 18 per cent reduction in manpower and a 16 per cent reduction in firepower. The divisions thus created were called 'Volksgrenadier Divisionen'. The fact that the combat power of these formations was even lower in practice is not apparent from the figures but is clear from the fact that these divisions were so hastily formed. Twelve were built from the ground up, the remaining thirteen were formed from divisions that had been so weakened in combat that they could not be rebuilt. The units of the Volksgrenadier Divisionen had an average training period of two months. Their fighting power ranged from 'as good as that of an old division' to that of a mere 'armed band'. The reason for this was a lack of training and team building, in addition to a shortage of weapons and equipment.

### The Panzer Division of 1944

This was a stripped down and standardized version of the armoured division of 1943. The Germans had resigned themselves to the fact that they were no longer able to bring the 'fully tank-equipped' division of 1941 into the field. Although one of these divisions' regiments was designated as 'motorized infantry', only one infantry battalion in the division was equipped with half-tracks – at least in theory, since in practice often only one company had these vehicles. This was compensated for by more and heavier weapons. The tank regiment had only two battalions, one with PzKpfw IVs and one with PzKpfw Vs (Panthers). One battalion of the artillery regiment had eighteen self-propelled guns. (11: 125)

## The motorized infantry division of 1944

This almost corresponded to the armoured division of 1944, but with the following differences: the tank regiment had been exchanged for an assault gun battalion and there was an extra infantry battalion per regiment, but an infantry battalion with armoured personnel carriers was missing. All other units corresponded to those of the armoured division. The motorized infantry division on the Eastern Front functioned in much the same way as the armoured divisions. Its firepower was more or less equivalent to that of an armoured division and its flexibility and mobility was as great, if not greater. The latter was the result of a lack of heavier tanks, the transport of which always caused logistical problems and therefore delays. (11: 124)

## New naming of units

The reality of the front necessitated an adjustment of the names of the various Heeresgruppen. At the beginning of 1944, Heeresgruppe Süd was renamed Heeresgruppe Nordukraine. This Heeresgruppe was commanded by Colonel General W. Model. Heeresgruppe Gruppe A was renamed Heeresgruppe Südukraine under Colonel General F. Schörner, a dedicated Nazi.

## The end of manpower planning

We have already seen that the Germans were at a considerable disadvantage in terms of numbers of men. Until the end of 1943, the superiority of the Soviets in this field could be offset by better training of the men and better leadership by the (non-commissioned) officer corps. In 1944 this would also change, for two reasons. In the first place, there was simply not enough manpower available to meet the needs on all fronts. Secondly, in 1944 the entire training and education system began slowly but surely to collapse. When the war started, the Germans had almost immediately faced a labour shortage. Of the total male working population of 25,900,000, 1,400,000 were under arms in May 1939. A year later, after the campaign in the west, the available male labour force had fallen to 20,400,000 men, since 5,600,000 men were now under arms and 100,000 had been killed in action or were no longer able to work. This labour force, supplemented by between 14,000,000 and 15,000,000 regular female workers, was regarded by the Germans as the minimum necessary to keep civilian production going. Its size, however, was wholly inadequate to meet the demands of a country fighting a war on several fronts. Hence, workers began to be recruited from the occupied territories, voluntarily at first, but soon under duress. In total, the Third Reich recruited approximately 7,500,000 foreign workers to fill the gaps caused by German men being called up and killed in increasing numbers.

By the end of 1944 a total of 13,000,000 Germans had been mobilized and 3,900,000 had died, were missing, had been taken prisoner or were no longer available for other reasons. As a result, the male working population had fallen to 13,500,000 men. That was far too few, even with the (forced) labourers, to keep combined civilian and war production going. The Germans could have solved this problem by bringing more women into the workforce, as all their opponents had done, but they chose not to do so on political grounds. This would ultimately have a major effect on the output of German industry. Despite that, however, production reached unprecedented heights in 1944, as we shall see.

**Number of foreign (forced) labourers as a percentage of the total working population in Germany** (33: 223)

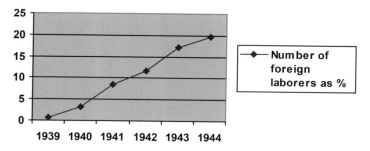

When it comes to the military, there were in total 9,100,000 men under arms in 1944. Of this number, 4,000,000, including 500,000 Waffen SS, were assigned to the Army.

**Absolute and relative strength of the Wehrmacht 1941–1944**

| | 1941 | | 1944 | |
|---|---|---|---|---|
| | | % | | % |
| Feld Heer | 3,800,000 | 52.7 | 4,000,000 | 44 |
| Ersatz Heer | 1,200,000 | 16.6 | 2,000,000 | 22 |
| Waffen SS | 150,000 | 2 | 550,000 | 6 |
| Luftwaffe | 1,680,000 | 23.3 | 1,800,000 | 20 |
| Kriegsmarine | 400,000 | 5.5 | 800,000 | 8 |
| *Total* | *7,200,000* | *100* | *9,100,000* | *100* |

What emerges from these figures in particular is the growth of the Ersatz Heer (replacement army). Since June 1941, the Ersatz Heer had trained 128,000 men per month. The basic training took four months, with an additional two to four months for specialists (maintenance, logistics, artillery, engineers). In addition to the basic training, there was a six-month course for non-commissioned officers, and an additional nine months officer-training after that for promising recruits. In other words, training a regular soldier took four months, a specialist six to eight months, a non-commissioned officer ten months and an officer nineteen months. After their training, the new units were gradually introduced to the front through the Ersatz battalions, which acclimatized recruits and taught them about the intricacies of their sector of the front.

This whole training and education programme was slowly but surely eroded. First of all, in 1942 the 'training division' was introduced. These divisions, twenty-six in total, consisted of training battalions with no further support or other units. They served to train recruits and to take the place of combat divisions in occupied countries. Due to the deployment of these training battalions, the combat divisions thus released formed a welcome addition to the front. The training and education of the training divisions was, incidentally, constantly disrupted by partisan actions when these formations were stationed in more hostile regions. On the other hand, such actions could be seen as good training exercises. As war drew fearfully close to home in 1944, the training divisions were hastily converted to or merged with normal divisions. This seriously disrupted the training and education programme, especially that of specialists, with the result that the entire programme had more or less ceased to exist by the end of 1944. Men and (commissioned) officers were prepared for service at the front as quickly as possible, and this thoroughly undermined the quality of the German Army, which had owed its edge over its opponents to its excellent officers and non-commissioned officer corps, and its high morale. With these elements falling away, the basis of its greater combat effectiveness was undercut, and the army began to show symptoms of disintegration. Even without this, however, given the balance of power between the Germans and the Soviets, the German Army would have slowly but surely been crushed.

## Materiel

Although the course of events might suggest otherwise, in 1944, thanks to Speer's efforts, the Germans were better equipped than ever before. In total, more than 19,000 armoured vehicles rolled off the production line that year, despite the Allied bombing raids on Germany and the other occupied countries of Europe.

**German production of main types of armoured vehicles 1943/44**

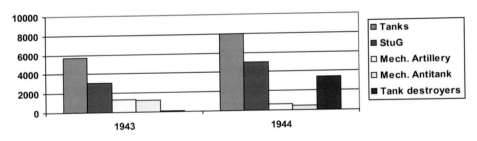

This covers 8,328 medium and heavy tanks, 5,751 assault guns, 1,617 mechanized anti-tank guns, 1,246 pieces of self-propelled artillery on various chassis, 3,400 tank destroyers and many other variants.

The Hummel was built on the chassis of a PzKpfw IV and equipped with a 150mm howitzer.

## Types of armoured vehicle in 1943 and 1944

| Species | Type | Numbers | |
|---|---|---|---|
| | | **1943** | **1944** |
| Tanks | PzKpfw IV | 3,013 | 3,126 |
| | Panter | 1,768 | 3,749 |
| | Tiger I | 647 | 623 |
| | Tiger II | - | 377 |
| Assault Guns | StuG III | 3,011 | 3,840 |
| | StuG IV | 31 | 1,006 |
| | StuG M 42 | 159 | 135 |
| | StuG M 43 | - | 18 |
| Mechanized Artillery | PzKpfw 38(t) with sIG33 | 215 | 154 |
| | PzKpfw II Wespe | 514 | 162 |
| | PzKpfw IV Hummel | 368 | 289 |
| | Mounted on various chassis | 256 | 52 |
| Mechanized anti-tank guns | PzKpfw II 75 mm Marder II | 204 | - |
| | PzKpfw 38(t) 75 mm Marder III | 618 | 323 |
| | PzKpfw III/IV 88 mm Nashorn | 345 | 133 |
| Tank Destroyers | Ferdinand | 90 | - |
| | Hetzer | - | 1,457 |
| | Jagdpanzer IV | - | 769 |
| | Pz IV/70 | - | 767 |
| | JagdPanter | - | 226 |
| | Jagdtiger | - | 61 |

Another new model was the Jagdpanzer IV with the chassis of the PzKpfw IV and the proven 75mm gun. (*Model D. Lister*)

In 1944 the arms industry reached its peak, as the graph below shows.

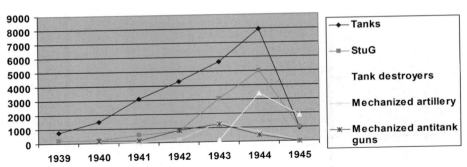

## Production of armoured and mechanized vehicles

The second generation of tank destroyers (Jagdpanzer) made its appearance at the end of 1943 in the form of the Hetzer, the Jagdpanter and the Jagdtiger.

The Hetzer, based on the chassis of the outdated PzKpfw 38(t), was distributed among the anti-tank battalions of infantry divisions. The superstructure had angled corners and 60mm armour; the Hetzer had a 75mm L/48 gun on the right side of the fighting compartment. Mounted on top was a remote-controlled machine gun that could rotate through 360° and was controlled from the fighting compartment. The Hetzer was admired for its design, but space for the four crew members was limited. The commander sat to the right of the gun, the driver, gunner and loader to the left. The Hetzer could carry forty-one shells, and despite its limitations, served well at the front.

The Jagdpanter was in many ways the opposite of the Hetzer. With its 45 tons and 88mm-L/71 gun, it could easily take on any tank the Western

The Hetzer was characterized by its low profile and was therefore ideally suited for its role as a tank destroyer. (*Model C. Schwach*)

The Jagdpanter combined the excellent characteristics of the Panther tank with the effectiveness of the 88mm gun. (*Model C. Hain*)

Allies or the Soviets could throw into battle, and it is often seen as the best tank destroyer of the war. It was built on the chassis of a Panther and featured an angled armoured superstructure, with 80mm frontal armour providing the same protection as its 160mm vertical equivalent. The Jagdpanter had a speed of 45kph, could carry eighty grenades, and the five-man crew could defend themselves against attacks from close range with a machine gun in the sloping front section. Its 700hp Maybach engine gave it a speed of 50kph, and the engine and drive train were very reliable. The main limitations of the tank were the limited manoeuvring space for the gun and its relatively great height of 2.72m. A total of 228 tanks of this type were produced in 1944.

The Jagdtiger is generally seen as the supreme tank destroyer. Built on the Tiger chassis, the Jagdtiger, with its 128mm L/55 gun, was the most heavily armed tank destroyer of the war. Its shells were split into two parts for greater manoeuvrability, resulting in a slower rate of fire than other tank destroyers. The Jagdtiger's armour was 250mm at the front, 80mm at the sides and 40mm on top. Despite weighing 72 tons, it could reach a very acceptable speed of 37kph. The limitations of the Jagdtiger lay in the technical complexity (and sensitivity) of its mechanical part and the fact that the weight of the tank made towing difficult. A total of forty-eight tanks of this type were produced in 1944.

These types of tank were mainly used on the Western Front. On the Eastern Front they were only available in limited numbers and, like the sPzAbten, were used as 'fire brigades' in crisis areas.

The Jagdtiger was the supreme tank destroyer. (*Model J. Teleszynski*)

Despite all the efforts of Speer and the German arms industry, the attrition and loss of weapons and vehicles was so great that Germany was slowly but surely losing the battle in this field as well. (41: 188)

## 2. Tactics and doctrine

### Changes in German tactics and doctrine

From mid-1943, the Panzerwaffe, the offensive weapon par excellence, had to adapt to the changed circumstances, and the Germans were forced to rapidly adopt all kinds of new defensive tactics. The active defence of 'sword and shield' changed to a 'hammer and anvil' tactic. Enemy attacks were halted by a strong front of anti-tank guns, after which tanks attacked the flanks and rear of the enemy. In a variant of this, Tiger tanks (the anvil) caught the Soviet tanks, and Panthers (the hammer) took out the stalled tanks from the flanks. In addition, the deep thrust into the enemy hinterland, successfully demonstrated by Von Manstein in February 1943, proved to be a workable concept, as did a variety of other techniques such as delaying and blocking tactics, defensive outflanking manoeuvres and flank attacks with the aim of creating an encirclement. In terms of tactics, this traumatic period shows what well-led and coordinated units, when deployed within the concept of mobile defence, were capable of. In the course of 1944, however, the Germans began to lose control of events and were rarely able to take the initiative, so the tactics outlined above became less and less effective.

### Changes in Soviet tactics and doctrine

The Soviets had also learned a lot in the past years. They found that despite the fact that the Germans operated more skilfully and were tactically superior, the Red Army was more and more able to bring its offensives to a successful conclusion, even though the Soviets accepted that they had to pay a high price for this. They were increasingly able to maintain control and coordination over their large armoured and mechanized units, but their success was based on the rigid and unimaginative execution of detailed plans and their deep penetration of the hinterland, and it lacked the finesse and perseverance of the German units. The introduction of command centres in the front lines, however, enabled them to control every phase of their breakthroughs and further penetration. In addition, their C3I capability as well as their logistics had improved significantly. This was due in no small part to Allied supplies in the form of more than 10,000 sets of radio equipment, 1,500,000km of telephone cable, 1,500 locomotives, 9,800 wagons, 540,000 tons of rails, nearly 400,000 trucks and 50,000 jeeps. The trucks, in particular, were crucial to the long-range operations envisioned by the Soviets. It is true that the Soviet soldier was able to survive without many supplies for long periods of time, but tanks and other motor vehicles simply came to a halt if they were not refuelled in time.

All this led to the Soviets being able to launch frontal offensives combined with attacks on one or both of the German flanks. While in 1943 these offensives were between 25km and 30km deep with the aim of encircling between six and twelve divisions, in 1944 they were much more ambitious, at a depth of between 150km and 200km with the aim of encircling up to eighteen divisions. The Red Army had also taken a step forward in materiel. In 1943 it had 150–180 pieces of artillery and 30–40 tanks, tank destroyers and self-propelled artillery per kilometre of front: by mid-1944 this had risen to 200–250 artillery pieces and 70–85 tanks, tank destroyers and self-propelled guns. This gave them a 3.5:1 superiority in men and a 6.8:1 superiority in tanks and artillery, as well as a 3.5:1 superiority in aircraft.

All this was the result of a huge increase in production by the Soviets. In 1944, no fewer than 29,000 tanks, assault guns and tank destroyers were manufactured, including 11,000 T-34s equipped with an 85mm gun in an enlarged turret. In addition, 2,000 Josef Stalin-2 (JS-2) tanks left the factory, the first of which made their appearance at the front in the spring of 1944. The JS-2 was a formidable tank with a 122mm L/45 gun and 160mm of frontal armour, slightly more than the 150mm of the Tiger 2. They were an unwelcome surprise to the Germans and a threat to the Tiger tanks. These could only take them out at a range of less than 2,000 yards, at which point they themselves were within range of the Soviet tank's 122mm guns. The era in which the Tiger could control the battlefield at a safe distance was over, and they were now vulnerable to these Soviet tanks.

The JS-2 was a formidable tank which was not only reliable, but also produced in large numbers. This tank and its successor, the JS-3, made the Western Allies realize in 1945 how outdated their tank designs were.

The Soviet offensive in the coming period was to be characterized by successive waves aimed at weakening German resistance and creating gaps in their defensive line. Mobile Soviet units would then advance deep into the German hinterland through these gaps. The size of these attacking units could

The JSU-152 was the Soviet answer to the Tiger. With its 152mm howitzer it was an impressive weapon in many ways.

vary. At the front they involved one or two tank armies or one or two tank corps combined with one or two mechanized cavalry units; at the level of an army they were made up of one or two tank or mechanized corps supported by additional artillery and anti-aircraft units.

Once the German defensive positions had been breached, the tank armies advanced behind the front along parallel lines in predetermined columns. These were ready to repel counter-attacks by the Germans at any time if necessary. Many troop movements took place at night, and these units were expected to advance between ten and fifteen kilometres in a 24-hour period. All kinds of other units operated ahead of these columns; their task was to occupy strategically important positions such as bridges, railway junctions and roads and to prevent the Germans from taking up new defensive positions. An even more telling innovation was the way the Soviets dealt with encircled German units. While previous encirclements were effected by two cordons – one to pin down the defenders and a second to repel any relief attempts – now only one cordon was deployed; the Soviets assumed that the Germans no longer had the strength to mount a relief effort. From now on, the Soviets would launch offensives in rapid succession at various points along the front, and the Germans would never again be able to check the relentless advance of the Red Army.

## 3. The security situation

Partisan activities peaked in 1944. In the summer, in the rear areas of Heeresgruppe Mitte, the section that had the greatest problems with partisans, more than 300,000 of them, a total of 199 brigades, were active, and they could rely for logistics and communications on the support of an even larger group of sympathizers. They were directed by the Central Committee of the Communist Party of Belarus and were in close contact with the military staffs

German units plough their way through the woods during Operation Frühlingsfest. The first two vehicles, an SdKfz 7 with a 37mm gun and a StuG, are brand new and still have the factory sand colour. Two PzKpfw-35(t) tanks can be seen in the background.

of the various fronts. The partisans controlled large parts of the hinterland and were dropped weapons, ammunition and radio equipment by C-47 Dakotas supplied by the Americans. They were led by regular officers, and key personnel had been trained by the Red Army. This all had a positive effect on the training level and discipline of the units; nevertheless, the partisans were unable to hold down substantial numbers of frontline soldiers.

Heeresgruppe Mitte undertook three major operations against the partisans in the spring. The first two, Regenschauer and Frühlingsfest, were aimed at the fighters of the Usachi Partisan Republic, who had entrenched themselves behind minefields and fortified positions in the area west of Vitebsk and Orsha. Despite the occasionally ferocious actions mounted by the partisans, their resistance was broken by mid-May. Subsequently, the last anti-partisan operation, Kormoran, took place in the Minsk area. This followed the same pattern as previous operations: the partisans offered uncoordinated resistance and were soon forced back into an increasingly smaller area. Operation Kormoran was eventually brought to an end prematurely because on 27 June the Soviet summer offensive, Bagration, aimed at Heeresgruppe Mitte, began.

---

**The other side**

Pro-Soviet partisans were not the only irregulars. There were also many nationalist groups who initially fought against the Soviets and later turned on the Germans, after it became clear that there was no chance of gaining independence. They remained active even after the front line moved further and further to the west. General Vatutin of the 1st Ukrainian Front was one of their victims: they attacked his escort in March 1944 when he was on his way to visit one of his units and shot him dead. Marshal Rokossovsky mentions in his memoirs that he had to travel in an armoured train to visit his southern units 'because the woods are still teeming with groups of Bandera and other fascist followers'. Bandera was leader of the Ukrainian Liberation Movement. Unwilling to tempt fate, Rokossovsky flew back to his headquarters. After the war, this independence movement was brutally wiped out by the Soviets. (1: 79)

---

In the days leading up to Bagration, the partisans carried out more than 10,000 attacks, particularly on the railway connections in the hinterland of Heeresgruppe Mitte. The effect of this on the movement of German units is unclear, all the more so since mobile repair teams were generally able to restore connections quickly. Of greater importance was the tactical coordination between the partisans and the Red Army in the days and weeks that followed. The partisans disrupted the work of the German support units in the hinterland, provided the advancing Soviet units with information, helped regular units to capture bridges and road junctions, repaired roads and guided Soviet units through difficult terrain.

These were the last actions of the partisans; after the successful completion of Operation Bagration, the entire Soviet Union had been liberated. To their dismay, the partisans, after a short break, were conscripted into the Red Army and served the rest of the war with regular units.

## 4. The course of events

### The struggle for Ukraine

Liberating Ukraine was the goal of the next Soviet offensive. Now that the Red Army had crossed the Dnieper, it was only a matter of building up enough fighting power in the bridgeheads on the west bank of the river. The Soviets' ambition was to encircle substantial amounts of German units. The 1st Ukrainian Front under Vatutin would advance south-east towards Pervomayisk on the Bug River, while the 2nd Ukrainian Front under Konev would advance more or less west towards the same place. In this way the German First and

On the run from the Soviets, these German soldiers try to cross the frozen Dnieper to safety near Kiev.

Eighth Armies would be surrounded and the road to Romania would be open, the Germans having left an inviting corridor between Kanev and Cherkassy.

The Soviet offensive started on 5 January, and by 7 January the 2nd Ukrainian Front had surrounded the German units in the town of Kirovograd, an important industrial centre. This was one of the cities that Hitler wanted to hold onto at all costs. In Kirovograd the 3rd and 14th Panzer Division, the 10th Panzer Grenadiere and the 367th Infantry Division were trapped. However, the designation of these units as divisions is misleading; in reality, the Germans had only 65 tanks and 109 assault guns at their disposal, compared to an estimated 620 tanks on the Soviet side. The units were also spread thinly across the front. For example, the 10th Panzer Grenadiere Division with only 3,700 men had to maintain a defensive line 17km long. The commander of the 3rd Panzer Division was Bayerlein, one of Rommel's old commanders, who had no intention of being boxed in and planned a breakout. Since contact with the outside world had been lost, he could claim not to have had the opportunity to discuss his plan with the higher echelons. On the night of 7/8 January, his units broke through the Soviet lines. This left the 3rd Panzer Division as the only unit able to confront two Soviet tank corps, which had broken through the German division north of the city in the morning. Bayerlein succeeded in stopping the Soviet units, and on 10 January the Germans were able to withdraw from the city, thanks in part to the deployment of units of the Panzergrenadiere Division Gross Deutschland, which in turn was threatened with encirclement. The fighting in the region was settled by the deployment of the newly arrived SS Division Totenkopf, which launched an attack as soon as it arrived, surprising the Soviets as they gathered behind the front. Once again, the Luftwaffe's intervention was crucial: the German anti-tank ace Rudel with his Stuka Geschwader sowed death and destruction among the Soviet tanks.

The Soviets had deployed no fewer than thirty-one divisions for this first offensive of the new year, but these had been so weakened by the fighting that some regiments numbered no more than 300–400 men, and the number of operational tanks had dropped to 120. Despite this, the position of the Germans had not really improved: on Hitler's orders, they were not allowed to shorten the front line and remained chronically short of reserves.

## The encirclement of XI Corps and XLII Corps at Cherkassy

As an advance deep into the German lines appeared impossible, the Soviets adjusted their objectives. On 25 January, the 2nd Ukrainian Front launched a westward attack followed by the 1st Ukrainian Front with a south-westerly attack on the area north of Kirovograd. The aim was to encircle the German units in the bulge around Cherkassy created by the offensives in the north and south. In this bulge were the XI Corps under Lieutenant General Stemmermann and the XLII Corps under Lieutenant General Leib. The offensive went smoothly, and on 28 January the spearheads of both Fronts met: the German units were surrounded and formed a 'hedgehog'. Hitler reacted sensibly this time and ordered a two-axis offensive to relieve the units and restore the front. The III and XLII Corps could be deployed for this offensive. III Corps would attack from the south-west and be supported by XLII Corps attacking the Soviets' southern flanks. However, the latter corps had suffered greatly from the fighting at Kirovograd and its capabilities were further undermined by constant Soviet counter-attacks: by 3 February it had only twenty-seven tanks and thirty-four assault guns left at its disposal. In addition, the mud prevented rapid movement and neither corps was unable to advance more than 10km. To break the deadlock, Hitler ordered III Corps to launch an attack along the most direct route to Cherkassy. This attack began on the night of 11/12 February and finally stalled on 15 February at Hill 239, no more than 4km from the perimeter of Cherkassy. The units in the hedgehog position reported that they seemed unable to bridge the gap themselves and looked for other breakout options. A final attempt to take the hill was made on 16 February, but after some initial success, the units had to abandon the captured positions.

The men in Cherkassy had already lost contact with the Third Army and, in accordance with the plan, began their own attempt to escape during the night of 16/17 February. In a dramatic breakout, and leaving behind all their equipment, about 35,000 of the original 50,000 men were eventually able to reach German lines. The Germans had paid a heavy price: more than six divisions had been knocked out as fighting forces. Later, we will consider these events in more detail and discuss the heroic role played by the Tiger and Panther tanks of the Schwere Panzer Regiment under Lieutenant General Dr Bäke in the battles around Cherkassy.

### The retreat of the First Panzer Army

After this battle, the Soviets were already planning another offensive. Gehlen, the commander of Fremde Heeres Ost, warned Von Manstein to look out for a pincer movement aimed at encircling Heeresgruppe Süd. He believed that the 1st Ukrainian Front would attack towards Poland, then turn south and move along the Dniester to cut off the German rearguard and support units from their fighting troops. At the same time, the 2nd Ukrainian Front would try to break through the Eighth Army and, in cooperation with the 1st Ukrainian Front, encircle the First and Fourth Panzer Armies. Hitler rejected this scenario because, in his view, the mud would halt any Soviet initiative. But as we have seen, mud played no part in the Soviets' considerations.

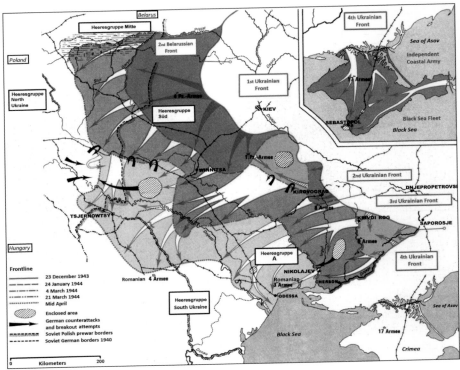

Overview of the offensive in the south of the Soviet Union in early 1944.

The offensive did indeed proceed more or less along the lines outlined above. On 4 March, the 1st Ukrainian Front attacked Von Manstein's northern flank and cut the Fourth Panzer Army in two. At the head of this Front was Zhukov himself, because Vatutin had been mortally wounded by pro-German partisans a few days earlier. Zhukov sent his Eighteenth Army through the gap thus created in the front. A day later, Konev launched his offensive by the 2nd Ukrainian Front, which broke through the lines of the Eighth Army in several places. His units raced through Uman to the Bug River, crossed it and sped towards the Dniester. On 16 March, the important Lvov-Odessa railway line fell into his hands, depriving the south-western flank of Heeresgruppe Süd of its supply route. By 17 March Konev had reached the Dniester, and his units turned north to encircle First Panzer Army with its twenty-two divisions.

Zhukov's units had advanced more slowly, but managed to cross the Dniester on 29 March and were now able to advance on a broad front behind Heeresgruppe Süd; the First Panzer Army was thus surrounded. Von Manstein wanted to evacuate them as soon as possible, but Hitler opposed this and argued that the line should be held at the River Bug. In the end, the First Panzer Army was allowed by Hitler to fight its way to the German

In a hurry, Soviet soldiers cross an emergency bridge over the Bug River.

lines, on condition that it also had to hold the line at the Bug: a contradictory command, rather like his orders at Stalingrad. Von Manstein now gave Hitler an ultimatum: he would order the First Panzer Army to withdraw unless he received reinforcements immediately. Hitler gave in, and the next day, Von Manstein ordered Hube, the commander-in-chief of the First Panzer Army, to retreat. There were two alternative routes for this retreat, one to the west and one to the south-west, and a discussion ensued between Hitler and Von Manstein as to which was preferable. Here, too, Von Manstein's view ultimately prevailed, and so Hube and his First Panzer Army began the retreat to their own lines via the western route on 28 March. On 6 April, his first units, the SS Panzer Division Frunsberg, managed to break through the last Soviet lines and re-establish contact with the German front. We will describe this breakout in more detail later.

For Von Manstein, the master of defensive strategy, this was his last victory over Hitler. On 30 March, he and Von Kleist were picked up by Hitler's special Focke Wulf Condor to be transported to headquarters in Obersalzberg. There they received swords to their Iron Crosses from Hitler, were thanked warmly for their efforts and sent home. With their departure, Germany's best armoured commanders were all dead, prisoners of war or had been dismissed. Hitler could now nominate his own favourites, commanders who might have been able to hold their own at the tactical-operational level, but who by no means always grasped the strategic-tactical dimensions of the war on the Eastern Front. To show that a wind of change was blowing, Heeresgruppe Süd was renamed Heeresgruppe Nordukrain under Colonel General Walther Model, formerly commander of Heeresgruppe Nord. Model would also become responsible for Heeresgruppe Mitte on 28 June and then take over command of the entire western front on 17 August. Heeresgruppe A, part of which was landlocked in Crimea, was renamed Heeresgruppe Südukrain under the ambitious Colonel General Friedrich Schörner.

The mud, meanwhile, had halted the Soviet offensive on the southern sector of the front. Although the Soviets had hitherto paid a terribly high price in blood for liberating the motherland, their army was constantly growing in strength, despite the losses in men and materiel. The Germans knew that when the mud dried up, the Soviets would resume the offensive with renewed vigour. But despite the events of the recent past, the morale of the German soldiers remained unbroken.

### Crimea

Meanwhile, the Seventeenth Army, part of Heeresgruppe A, with Jaenecke as its commander, was still in the Crimean peninsula, having become isolated there in the autumn of 1943. They now prepared to break out towards the southern flank of Heeresgruppe Süd. Not entirely unexpectedly, Hitler refused to approve this, and the Seventeenth Army remained where it was, waiting for Soviet initiatives to recapture Crimea, although a few inconclusive attempts in the autumn achieved almost nothing. The Germans, meanwhile, were supplied by German and Romanian ships, which maintained a shuttle service to Sevastopol from Romania. The Soviet Navy hesitated to engage in a confrontation for fear of falling victim to the Stukas. In the spring, the Germans did draw up emergency plans for a withdrawal and possible evacuation via Sevastopol – not without reason, because on 7 March an offensive was launched by the 4th Ukrainian Front under Tolbukhin aimed at liberating Crimea. On 9 April, the German units were ordered to retreat to the Gneisenau Line, a circle around Sevastopol that contained all the major roads. Despite the fact that the retreat was announced prematurely by Romanian units, who set fire to their buildings and blew up their stores of surplus ammunition, the operation was a success and the evacuation by sea was able to begin on 12 April, after which 7,000 men were transferred every day. However, again Hitler demanded that Sevastopol be held and that only support units be evacuated. Schörner, the commander of Heeresgruppe A, immediately urged Hitler to reconsider his decision. Since the evacuation of the support units was to be completed by 19 April, a decision had to be made quickly. Schörner tried to press Hitler in the same way that Von Manstein had, saying that retreat could only be avoided if reinforcements were brought in. Hitler agreed to this, and reinforcements began to arrive in dribs and drabs. By 20 April the city had come within range of the Soviets' artillery, and by 27 April the situation had become extremely precarious. Jaenecke now demanded the two divisions he had been promised and was promptly dismissed. All the elements for a drama in Crimea were now in place.

## Leningrad

During this period, an important event took place in the area of Heeresgruppe Nord: the lifting of the siege of Leningrad. By early 1943 the Soviets

---

**War at the top**

On 20 July, a bomb attack on Hitler, organized by the resistance group around Lieutenant Colonel Von Stauffenberg, failed. The bomb placed in the meeting room of the command centre Wolfsschanze in Poland inflicted only minor injuries on the Führer, and a coup d'état in Berlin and other European capitals failed to get off the ground. This bombing changed Hitler's relationship with the Wehrmacht forever. He would never trust his generals again, and to show his contempt for them he banned the military salute on 23 July. Suspicion and fear would characterize the relationship between Hitler and the officer corps in the future. General Ludwig Beck, former chief of staff of the Wehrmacht, was compromised by the bombing, as was General Erich Höpner. Beck, who was positioned to become head of state after Hitler's death, was given the opportunity to commit suicide, while Höpner was put in front of a firing squad. There is no doubt that many generals had been aware of the assassination plan. They faced a dilemma: to side with the plotters would betray the army's neutral role and be high treason; on the other hand, they did not want to betray their fellow officers. Another victim was Zeitler, chief of staff since 1942. His initially good relationship with Hitler had deteriorated in the period leading up to the bombing and he had asked the Führer several times to remove him from his post, having tried to induce him to come to terms with reality. Hitler sacked him the day after the attack and forbade him to wear a military uniform any longer. In his place, Hitler surprisingly appointed Guderian, one of the few generals he still trusted. Hitler considered himself lucky to have placed the Panzerwaffe under its own Inspector General: no Panzerwaffe unit had had any connection with the conspirators. The armoured units, moreover, were too spread across the different fronts to be able to play an active role in the coup. However, Hitler immediately made it clear to Guderian that only he could make decisions and that Guderian was to act as his lieutenant: absolute control of Germany's armies was now in Hitler's hands. In the months that followed, generals who had served Germany faithfully in recent years would be fired at a rapid pace.

had succeeded in establishing a narrow corridor between their lines and Leningrad, and in January 1944 they planned to achieve full contact. All in all, Heeresgruppe Nord only served to keep Finland in the war; the Germans had in fact long since given up their ambitions to conquer Leningrad. A logical consequence of this would have been the withdrawal of German units to the Baltic countries. This would have shortened the front line by many hundreds of kilometres and would have freed up units for the much-needed strategic reserve. But retreat was out of the question, and on 14 January the Soviets launched an offensive against Heeresgruppe Nord with the aim of pushing the Germans back to the borders of Estonia and Lithuania. The offensive of the Forty-Second, Fifty-fourth, Fifty-ninth and Sixty-seventh Armies was successful, and in the period up to 30 January the Germans were forced to retreat more than 75km. The siege was now finally lifted, and the city was out of reach of the German artillery. A second phase of the offensive pushed the Germans back even further, until they actually controlled only the Baltic countries, White Russia and the part of Poland that the Soviets had occupied in 1939.

## 5.  At the front

**Tactical-strategic pirouettes: the offensives of XLVIII Panzer Corps**
The events described below took place in November 1943 and give a good picture of the cycle of offensive/defensive actions that would characterize the activities of the Germans in 1943 and 1944. The action in the Zhitomir region can be divided into three phases:

- Phase 1: the capture of Zhitomir and the stabilizing of the front west of Kiev: 15–24 November
- Phase 2: the neutralizing of the Soviet units north-east of captured Zhitomir: 6–10 December
- Phase 3: the encirclement of Soviet forces and the retreat to defensive lines: 15–25 December

*Phase 1*
In November 1943 General Hermann Balck received orders from Colonel General Raus, in his new function of commander of the Fourth Panzer Army, to recapture Zhitomir in the north and to stabilize the front west of Kiev. Balck had the XLVIII Panzer Corps at his disposal, which formed the iron fist of the Fourth Panzer Army. At that time, this XLVIII Panzer Corps consisted of the 1st, 7th, 19th and 25th Panzer Divisions, the 1st SS Panzer

Division Leibstandarte SS Adolf Hitler, a Kampfgruppe of the 2nd SS Panzer Division Das Reich and the 68th Infantry Division. It was the most formidable armoured force available at the front at the time. Balck envisaged an action along three spearheads: The 1st Panzer Division and the Panzer Division SS Leibstandarte Adolf Hitler would advance in the centre; the left flank was to be covered by the 7th Panzer Division and the 68th Infantry Division; and the right flank by the 25th Panzer Division and Das Reich's Kampfgruppe.

The German offensive began on 15 November, and the attackers broke through the Soviet lines almost immediately. On the night of 17/18 November, Zhitomir was taken without any problems. The Third Guards Tank Army launched two counter-attacks in the following days, neither of which was successful, and this prompted Balck to attempt to encircle the Soviet units. On 20 November, the Panzer Division SS Leibstandarte Adolf Hitler attacked the Soviets from the west, while the 1st Panzer Division did so to the north, with the 7th Panzer Division on its left flank making an outflanking manoeuvre. From the south-west, the 19th Panzer Division advanced with the aim of making contact with the 1st Panzer Division to complete the encirclement. The plan succeeded and the Soviets were thus trapped by the Panzer Division SS Leibstandarte Adolf Hitler to the west and the other divisions to the north, south and east. By 24 November the area was completely in the hands of the Germans. The booty was considerable, consisting of 153 tanks, 70 artillery guns and 250 anti-tank guns. A total of

Another winter. German soldiers have found protection against the cold in a Soviet village towards the end of 1943.

3,000 Soviets were killed, but a significant number, including the officers and staff, managed to escape.

*Phase 2*
Following these initial successes, Balck was ordered at the end of November to attack the Soviet units north-east of Zhitomir, since they posed a threat to the flanks of a possible German attack towards Kiev. He decided to have the 1st Panzer Division and the Panzer Division SS Leibstandarte Adolf Hitler jointly break through the Soviet front, while to the north the 7th Panzer Division would launch an attack deep into the Soviet rear. This last operation was the most daring, and the day before the attack, armoured reconnaissance vehicles moved engineering units deep behind the front to secure and repair bridges and roads to ensure a rapid advance for the 7th Panzer Division. The utmost secrecy was also observed to prevent the Soviets from learning of the Germans' intentions. For example, no written orders were issued and the units only went to their assembly points at the last moment.

Thanks to the support of the Luftwaffe and to excellent planning and preparation, the offensive launched on 6 December was a great success. The area between the Rivers Teterev and Irsha was completely cleared of Soviet units within a few days. In an encirclement near Radomyshl, more than three divisions were surrounded and neutralized, while 36 tanks and 204 anti-tank guns were destroyed. Large stocks of ammunition were also found, a sign that the Soviets had themselves been preparing for an offensive in this area.

*Phase 3*
While units of the XIII Corps occupied the newly conquered territory, the XLVIII Panzer Corps was redeployed to the north-west with a new assignment. Soviet units in that area were said to be about to launch an offensive aimed at the XVII Corps south of Korosten. On 15 December, the 7th Panzer Division crossed the Irsha and managed to establish a bridgehead around Malin. The 1st Panzer Division and Panzer Division SS Leibstandarte Adolf Hitler first moved west and then turned north and crossed the river. Balck now gripped the enemy from three sides, but he had no idea of their strength. In the following days he tried to encircle the Soviets, but they were not intimidated and fought back hard. Only on 21 December, when papers were found on a captured Soviet officer, did it become clear how large the fighting force was that opposed the Germans: no less than three Tank Corps and four Infantry Corps of the 1st Ukrainian Front under Vatutin had been assembled to recapture the area around Zhitomir. Balck wisely refrained from further attempts to encircle the enemy and took up defensive positions. However, the Soviets went on the

StuGs rush forward. Although the Germans were still tactically capable of winning victories in late 1943/early 1944, they were unable to turn the tide.

offensive almost immediately and quickly recaptured all the territory they had lost in the previous month.

These events are illustrative of this phase of the war on the Eastern Front. Despite the fact that the Fourth Panzer Army had destroyed two Soviet armies in the previous period, inflicted heavy casualties on a third and destroyed 700 tanks and 668 artillery pieces, the Soviets were able to launch a counter-offensive without any problem and recapture all the lost territory. Neither Balck's tactical-operational ingenuity nor the skills and experience of his men could compete with the superior force of the enemy. The cyclical character of offensive/defensive operations on the German side would continue to dominate the picture in the coming year: however successful it was, any German offensive would be followed by a Soviet counter-offensive that pushed the Germans ever more onto the defensive and further to the west. (41: 170–4)

## Tigers and Panthers in action: sPzAbt 503 and the battle for Hill 239

In 1943 and 1944 the achievements of the two new tanks, the Panther and especially the Tiger, had taken on almost mythical proportions. To get an idea of how they functioned in the harsh reality of the front, we will follow the sPzAbt 503 in the period January/February 1944. The sPzAbt 503 received a total of forty-five new Tigers on 3 January 1944. On 11 January, sPzAbt

503 with its new Tigers was merged with the 2nd Abteilung of the 23rd Panzer Regiment with its forty-seven Panthers. Together with a battalion of self-propelled artillery and a battalion of engineers specializing in bridge construction, they formed the Schwere Panzer Regiment Bäke, named after Supreme Commander Oberstleutnant Franz Bäke. The Schweres Panzer Regiment Bäke would play an important role in the following weeks in the relief of German units in the hedgehog position at Cherkassy. The units in Cherkassy consisted of XI Corps under Lieutenant General Stemmermann and XLII Corps under Lieutenant General Leib. There were ten divisions in total, including the 5th SS Panzer Division Wiking and the Wallonia brigade of Belgian volunteers. The whole was known as the Gruppe Stemmermann and consisted of approximately 50,000 men. The battle for Cherkassy can be divided into three phases.

In the first phase, the Schweres Panzer Regiment Bäke was to prevent Soviet units from five tank corps from completing the encirclement of Gruppe Stemmermann. To this end, the Regiment launched an attack at 0600 hrs on 26 January in the Vinnitsa region and destroyed no fewer than 267 Soviet tanks and 156 artillery pieces (!) in the following five days. They themselves lost three Tiger tanks and four Panthers, one of the Tigers being knocked out by a Panther. Despite these successes, however, they were unable to stop the Soviets, who were eager to complete the encirclement and destroy the German units within the hedgehog position. By 6 February the encirclement was complete and the Soviets began to increase pressure on the units within the hedgehog; the circumference of the position shrank by 8km to just 13km in the following weeks.

After its teething troubles were cured, the Panther became one of the most effective tanks of the Second World War.

It is interesting to take a look behind the scenes of sPzAbt 503. During this period, the unit had problems with both the supply and maintenance of its tanks. Supply was problematic due to a shortage of available half-tracks and because itinerant Soviet units and partisans made the supply routes unsafe. The half-tracks were critical because there were no roads in the area and the mud made transport very difficult. During the battle, more and more vehicles broke down, and at one point only 68 of the 111 available half-tracks were operational. This meant that only 119 of the 234 tons of fuel and ammunition needed daily could be transported to the front line. The partisans also wreaked havoc among the units: the maintenance crew of the 1st Company were all killed by partisans. How unclear the course of the front line could be is shown by the fact that when the Schweres Panzer Regiment Bäke was repositioned for the relief of Cherkassy, the station yard that was to serve as a loading area turned out to be occupied by the Soviets. After a short and fierce battle, forty-six Soviet tanks were knocked out and the whole Kampfgruppe was able to be loaded onto the train – just in time, since a superior Soviet force was preparing to recapture the station.

In the second phase of the fighting around Cherkassy, the Schweres Panzer Regiment Bäke was deployed to open a corridor to the positions of Gruppe Stemmermann. Schweres Panzer Regiment Bäke was at that time part of the III Panzer Corps, which consisted of the 16th and 17th Panzer Divisions, supplemented by the 1st Panzer Division and the Panzer Division SS Leibstandarte Adolf Hitler. The presence of these last two divisions,

---

**The technique of the Tiger**

The Tiger tank was one of the most formidable weapons of the Second World War, capable of changing the course of a battle. However, it had its limitations. For example, fuel consumption was very high: when full with 540 litres, the tank could cover 195km by road or 110km over land. In comparison, a T 34/76 with its 480 litres of diesel could, in theory at least, cover 455km. Guidelines for refuelling the Tiger were given in the manual *Tiger Fibel*: ideally, the tanks would be refuelled within friendly lines after they had moved from the emplacement area to the front. In order to spare the Tiger's drive train as much as possible, it was recommended that the tank be given ample space so that it had to change gear as little as possible. It was also pointed out that moving these tanks in general led to traffic congestion. It was recommended that they be moved as little as possible, and forced journeys were discouraged because of the great wear and tear that these could cause. It was emphasized that the average speed was 10kph during the day and 7kph at night. After heavy fighting, it was recommended that the units not be deployed for two to three weeks, in order to get them technically up to standard. If this was not done, the number of mechanical failures could increase rapidly. (57: 31–36)

which we have already seen in action above, shows how these 'elite' units were constantly rotated along the front and deployed where the fighting was fiercest. The attack began at 0600 hrs on 4 February and was preceded by a heavy artillery bombardment. The spearhead was formed by the Schweres Panzer Regiment Bäke with sPzAbt 503 in the leading position, followed by the 16th Panzer Division on the left and the 17th Panzer Division on the right flank. The first day, the units advanced 30km thanks to a lack resistance by the enemy. This changed the next day when the Soviets threw 130 tanks from the 5th Mechanized Corps and 5th Guards Tank Corps into battle. As a result, the two tank divisions lost contact with each other. Schweres Panzer Regiment Bäke was ordered to restore the line and engaged Soviet units positioned between both German tank divisions on 6 February. Bäke used a tactic that would also prove successful in the coming period. The Tiger tanks of sPzAbt 503 pinned down the Soviet force with their fire at long distance, while the Panthers carried out a large outflanking movement. These Panthers, suddenly appearing behind them at 0830 hrs, surprised the Soviets. At that point, Bäke ordered the Tigers to advance, and the Soviets were caught between the Tiger and Panther tanks, a prime example of the dreaded 'hammer and anvil' tactic. This action broke the Soviet resistance and allowed Schweres Panzer Regiment Bäke to advance further towards Cherkassy. However, they failed to break through the Soviet lines and make contact with the encircled units, because of a combination of supply and maintenance problems and the mud, which made rapid movement impossible. In the *Erfahrungsberichte*, Bäke later reported:

> The progress, especially of tracked vehicles, was hampered by the roads being completely reduced to mud. The Grenadiere may serve as an example of the type of struggle against the mud. The Grenadiere took off their boots and walked barefoot through the swamp and mud. This was easier than taking one step at a time and then having to dig the boots out of the mud.

The Soviets clearly had less trouble with the conditions underfoot: they were able to move the 5th Guards Tank Corps and the remnants of the 3rd and 16th Tank Corps to the battlefield. How the Germans struggled with the terrain is shown by the fact that on the day that sPzAbt 503 successfully managed to break through, a large number of the Tiger tanks were used to tow half-tracks through the mud, while the others guarded the convoys and the front. Horst Krönke, the tank commander we met in 1943, described the situation as follows:

For days no supplies, neither ammunition nor food reached us, because the eternal rain had turned the roads into mudslides. Each time, attacks by Soviet tanks and infantry were beaten back. Our base stock was eventually reduced to a few grenades. A fourth tank eventually brought us fifteen shells for our three Tigers.

Because a crucial bridge over the River Gniloy Tikich proved unable to support the heavy Tiger tanks, Schweres Panzer Regiment Bäke aborted an attempt to relieve the units at Cherkassy via this line of attack. In the meantime, Gruppe Stemmermann had managed to move the border of the hedgehog position further west by shortening their lines. By 9 February sPzAbt 503 had returned to its starting position, ready to make another attempt to contact the encircled units. But the fighting of the past few days had left its mark: only twenty Tiger tanks were operational, the rest were under maintenance; of the unit's seventeen officers only three were fit for action.

The Germans prepared yet another attempt to relieve the units in Cherkassy via a different route, an example of the Germans' determination never to leave surrounded units behind. Schweres Panzer Regiment Bäke with sPzAbt 503

Tiger tanks were constantly deployed where the need was greatest. Here a Tiger Tank Company is on its way to relieve cornered units.

would again play an important role in this plan and was reinforced by sPzAbt 506 with twenty-seven Tiger tanks, of which about half were operational. The third phase of fighting around Cherkassy began on 11 February and lasted until the 16th. This attack was also successful at first. The tanks made steady progress towards Cherkassy and on the first day managed to capture a bridge on the River Gniloy Tikich, over which at least the Panther tanks could reach the north side of the river, while the Tigers remained behind on the south bank.

Reconnaissance showed that there was a ford downstream, and not much later the Tigers were able to join the Panthers near Frankovka. The Soviets deployed a blocking force consisting of the 5th Guards Tank Corps and the 20th Tank Corps, with eighty tanks and fifty anti-tank guns. Using the coordinated deployment of Stuka bombers and the same 'hammer and anvil' tactics of a week earlier, Bäke broke the Soviet resistance on 12 February, losing just four Tigers and four Panthers, and destroying seventy Soviet tanks and forty anti-tank guns. Over the next few days the unit fought its way via the Medwin-Lisyanka road towards the encircled units, successfully repelling continuous Soviet attacks. However, the number of operational tanks of sPzAbt 503 was steadily declining: on 13 February twelve Tigers were still operational, but by 14 February this had fallen to nine. The villages along the road were secured by German units that followed the vanguard so that the tanks could continue to operate up front. The fog now rolled in, and Horst Krönke described the situation as follows:

> We remained in our positions … and had to repulse at least four attacks by groups of five to seven tanks, probably weakened Soviet tank companies. At least twenty tanks were destroyed by us during these battles. The Soviet infantry was also getting closer, but luckily more and more German infantry was coming forward too, so that we were better protected against their tank destruction teams. Snow squalls and fog muffled the sound of the fighting; the poor visibility meant that enemy tanks could suddenly appear nearby.

In this ghostly atmosphere sPzAbt 503 launched an attack on the morning of 15 February to bridge the last kilometres to the encircled troops. The attack was repulsed by the Soviets, whose numbers were constantly increasing. The same day, it became clear that Hill 239 was a key position in the escape route for the German units, which would try to break out the following evening. To cover this breakout, sPzAbt 503 was ordered to capture a town in the vicinity of this hill, which they succeeded in doing by nightfall. At that time sPzAbt 503 had only seven operational Tigers left and were short of almost all supplies.

However, Ju-52s of the Luftwaffe brought relief: during the morning of 16 February the unit was supplied from the air, and parachutes fell carrying petrol barrels and ammunition. After the tanks had been refuelled and the ammunition loaded, sPzAbt 503 carried out a successful attack with its remaining tanks on the hill 2km away. The importance of the hill was not lost on the Soviets, and they concentrated the 20th Tank Corps and elements of the 3rd Tank Corps in the route between sPzAbt 503 and the units in Cherkassy. Later that day, these were reinforced by two infantry divisions and an anti-tank brigade. Although the Soviet units were well below their nominal strength, they could dispose of eight or ten tanks, as well as thirty to thirty-six pieces of artillery and mortars per kilometre of front. Thanks to the efforts of their maintenance units, the Germans were eventually able to deploy eight Tigers, nine Panthers and twelve half-tracks. The Tiger tanks charged, destroying twenty Soviet tanks and reaching the hilltop intersection. After a short time, however, they were forced by heavy Soviet artillery fire to leave the hill and retreat a few hundred metres to the south-west. The units of Gruppe Stemmermann were unaware that this central hill was not in German hands and began their breakout at 2300 hrs the same day. The first German units infiltrated past the Soviets and managed to make contact with the Tiger tanks of sPzAbt 503 at 0430 hrs the following morning. The evacuation would take on a dramatic character in the course of the day. Stemmermann and Liebe had had to make the most difficult decision of their lives: their wounded would be left in the care of a few doctors due to a lack of transport capacity, while the nurses would, for obvious reasons, be evacuated. Everyone knew that the Soviets showed no mercy and that these men's death warrants had effectively been signed.

The outbreak from Cherkassy itself had started at 2300 hrs on 16 February. Through the night, columns of men, horse-drawn artillery and farm carts, trucks and tanks moved slowly through the gently sloping wooded landscape. Around 0700 hrs, the vanguard units were spotted by the Soviets, who immediately opened artillery fire, which increased in intensity at dawn. Because only a small number of tanks managed to drive through the icy mud and up the hills, a large part of the heavy equipment, artillery and vehicles had to be left behind. In a desperate attempt, Liebe and the remaining tanks managed to break through the Soviet lines between them and Hill 239.

How heavy the fighting was is shown by the account of Leon Degrelle, the commander of the Wallonia brigade:

We had hardly begun to climb the hill when we saw cavalry rushing down a hill from the south-west. At first we thought they were German Uhlans. Looking through my binoculars, I could clearly see their uniforms.

> **Dark days**
> Grossjohann's unit had to withdraw under pressure by Zhukov's 2nd Ukrainian Front in early March. They crossed part of the Umaka River on horseback and hid on the other side, while Soviet units occupied the east bank. However, wounded infantrymen were still left on the other side. 'I will never forget the heartbreaking scenes that played out before our eyes as we waited. Each time, at short intervals, we heard the loud cries for help from our wounded comrades on the other bank. Unfortunately we couldn't help them. If we had tried, the Soviets would have shot us to pieces, it was a true shooting paradise. After some time we saw Soviet tanks with men on them driving in the direction where the cries for help came from. For me, forced to watch this happen without being able to help, this was one of the most horrible experiences of my life.' (19: 110)

They were Cossacks. I recognized their little nervous brown horses. They came after us, fanning out in all directions. We were stunned: the Soviet infantry machine-gunned us, Soviet tanks chased us, and now the Cossacks rushed after us to finish the job.

Only one obstacle now separated the Germans from the safety of friendly lines, the River Gniloy Tikich, which was between 7.5m and 12.5m wide and 2.5m deep. To bridge this, the last tanks were driven into the river at 1300hrs to form a roadway for the remaining units.

Meanwhile, sPzAbt 503 had been ordered at 1100 hrs to support the cornered units with the aim of shortening the route for the troops to be evacuated. It managed to take the hill in a quick action by Tiger and Panther tanks and repelled several attacks by Soviet tanks. While the first evacuees reached the rear German lines at around 1600 hrs, sPzAbt 503 had to withdraw due to shortages of petrol and ammunition. By this time it had only eight Tigers and six Panthers tanks at its disposal. The evacuation was a relative success: of the 50,000 trapped men, between 30,000 and 35,000 managed to escape. However, they had left all their equipment behind and had to be fully re-equipped; the Wallonia brigade was effectively lost.

Although sPzAbt 503 had failed to force a breakthrough towards the units withdrawing from Cherkassy it had made an important contribution to the escape of the majority of the trapped Germans and was always to be found where the fighting was toughest. Although it is unclear exactly how many Soviet tanks sPzAbt 503 knocked out during this period, a conservative estimate gives a total of 329. sPzAbt 503 itself had lost twenty-two Tigers, six of which were destroyed by their own crews because they could no longer be towed away from the battlefield. (57: 78–86 and 41: 176–8)

German soldiers hitch a ride to safety on accompanying tanks. In 1944, despite an unprecedentedly high rate of production, the shortage of vehicles grew dramatically.

sPzAbt 503 was withdrawn from the Soviet Union after this fighting to be refitted with the new Tiger II tanks. Its place at the front was taken by sPzAbt 509.

**Moving hedgehog defence positions: the First Panzer Army's fight to freedom**
The year 1944 was characterized by, among other things, the phenomenon of the moving hedgehog defence position. In this period of the war described as the era of *Kesselschlachten* (cauldron battles, the tactic became necessary as the result of a combination of rapid advances by the Soviets and Hitler's refusal to sanction retreats. Since the Germans had been the masters of encirclement at the beginning of the war they were particularly aware that at the beginning of an encirclement it was essentially a matter of perception as who was exactly surrounding whom. The sooner an escape was attempted, the more likely it was to succeed. This is how the concept of the 'moving hedgehog' was born, in which encircled units fought their way back to their own lines through the mass of their opponents. It should be clear that the success that the Germans enjoyed with this tactic was due to the experience built up in the previous years and their knowledge and skills in this field.

A good example of the 'moving hedgehog' is the experience of the First Panzer Army in the Kamenets-Podolsk region in March 1944. The First Panzer Army at that time consisted of nine tank divisions, a Panzergrenadiere division, ten infantry divisions and a number of smaller formations such as the aforementioned Panzer Regiment Bäke. Although it was an impressive fighting force on paper, all units were well below strength. The First Panzer Army was commanded by General Hube, who had built up extensive experience in the Soviet Union and in Sicily. By March it had become clear to Hube that his Army was in danger of being surrounded by the 1st and 2nd Ukrainian Fronts from the north, east and south. To give himself extra flexibility, therefore, he had already had all administrative and support personnel transferred to safer areas before preparing for a retreat across enemy territory. By 25 March the encirclement was complete and Hube and von Manstein drew up plans to break out. There were two possible routes:

- A retreat south via a bridgehead over the Dniester at Hotin
- A retreat west to new positions already occupied there by German units

The first alternative was a relatively easy route and would lead the Army to Romania. Its disadvantage was that the Army would no longer be part of the German front line, and a long march would be necessary to unite it with other German units in the near future. In addition, it was the more obvious route, and the Soviets were undoubtedly already taking measures to frustrate a retreat along it. Moreover, there was a real danger that the Army would eventually become isolated and be surrounded again by the Soviets. This would therefore mean only a stay of execution.

The second alternative required a trip over difficult terrain, crossing three rivers. But it was the shortest route to the German lines and possible to reach out from there to the retreating units. Von Manstein ordered Hube to prepare for a retreat to the west and flew to Hitler to convince him that giving up the position of the First Panzer Army was absolutely necessary, and that sufficient units from the reserve had to be deployed to support the retreat. After fierce debates, Hitler finally relented and promised the deployment of the newly formed 2nd SS Panzer Corps. This formation consisted of sister divisions the 9th SS Panzer Division Hohenstaufen and the 10th SS Panzer Division Frunsberg. Both had been active as Panzergrenadiere Divisions until October 1943. This 2nd SS Panzer Corps, together with the 101st (light) Division and the 367th Infantry Division, formed a fighting force that could be used for relief.

Hube, meanwhile, prepared carefully for the breakout to the west. He split his tanks into three attacking forces: Kampfgruppe Nord, Kampfgruppe Süd and Rückzug. He set up an elaborate deception plan involving radio traffic and vehicle movements to give the impression that a southward sortie was being planned. To limit fuel consumption, all unnecessary vehicles were destroyed and transport was switched to horse-drawn Russian farm wagons. His staff meticulously prepared the route and the timing of all troop movements, and all troops were extensively briefed. The morale of the units in the encircled area was high because they had previous experience of such situations and were confident that everything would turn out well. Meanwhile, in the Tarnopol region 200km to the west, the 3rd SS Panzer Corps prepared to support the breakout, and the Luftwaffe prepared to fly in supplies of petrol and ammunition if the hedgehog position moved west.

The breakout took place on the night of 27/28 March under cover of a storm that obscured the scale of the troop movements from the Soviets. The two Kampfgruppen, battalions with Panther tanks in the lead, broke through the Soviet lines without difficulty. They seized crossings over the first river, the Sbruce, the next day and advanced rapidly to the second river, the Siret, which they reached on 29 March. The Soviets, at first thinking that a breakout to the south had been initiated, now did not hesitate for a moment; Konev ordered his Fourth Tank Army to cross the Dniester and attack the German flank between the Sbruce and the Siret. However, Kampfgruppe Süd saw off the Soviet assault, and the evacuation of the First Panzer Army across the Siret continued undisturbed. The Soviets now began sending units from the north

Two worlds side by side. A technically advanced Tiger tank passes a horse-drawn wagon, the transport of choice for the Germans in the last year of the war.

and south into First Army's path in an attempt to intercept the Germans, while simultaneously attacking their rear. In this rearguard were concentrated the Tiger tanks, which had no trouble repelling the Soviet attacks.

However, the progress of the First Army was gradually threatened by heavy storms, which ravaged the area from 1 April. For three days the speed of the hedgehog dropped to just a few kilometres per day; the storms producing the type of mud that the Soviets managed better than the Germans. On the other hand, the Luftwaffe did an excellent job: it was able not only to bring in sufficient supplies at all times, but also to evacuate all the wounded, which was of great importance for morale, since no German soldier wished to fall into the hands of the Soviets. In addition, the 2nd SS Panzer Corps steadily fought its way east and finally managed to make radio contact with the First Panzer Army. The gap between the two units gradually narrowed, and on 15 April both Kampfgruppen of the First Panzer Army reached the third river, the Strypa, and were able to establish a bridgehead on the other side. The next day, the forward units of the 2nd SS Panzer Corps and the First Panzer Army met at Buchach. The evacuation of the First Panzer Army was successfully completed when the rearguard units finally crossed the Strypa with their Tiger tanks. During the fighting of the past weeks, Hube's units had destroyed no fewer than 357 tanks and 42 self-propelled guns in their remarkable push towards friendly lines.

The achievements of General Hube and his men are an example of the Germans' tactical-operational skill in extremely difficult circumstances. Hube himself was immediately promoted to colonel general and awarded diamonds to his Iron Cross on 20 April, making him one of twenty-eight diamond-decorated Iron Cross bearers during the Second World War. He was killed in a plane crash the next day. (41: 179–82)

This breakout was a success, but as the year progressed the Germans were less and less able to break through encirclements or relieve surrounded units: the Soviets were too strong, and the distance between the encircled units and friendly lines was often simply too great due to the rapid advance of the enemy. Then there was nothing left for men who had been surrounded but to find their way to their own lines alone or in small groups.

## 6. Operation Bagration: the collapse of Heeresgruppe Mitte

After the fighting for the Ukraine ended at the end of March, Heeresgruppe Nord and Mitte were relatively unaffected. Although Heeresgruppe Nord had lost ground, its combat power was not structurally impaired. The question now was where the Soviets would strike next. Several options were open to them. The first was to continue their advance towards Romania and the Balkans in the south. This option was politically attractive and would endanger the Germans' energy supply, but would result in leaving strong German units on the Soviets' northern flanks. A second option was to launch an offensive from the north of Ukraine via Poland towards the Baltic states. This option was also rejected, because it was beyond the strength of the Red Army and would also leave strong German units on the flanks. A third option was an attack in the north, but here the many natural obstacles would make a rapid advance impossible. In the end, a fourth option was chosen: a focus on Heeresgruppe Mitte, which was in the way of the fastest route to Warsaw and Berlin and whose planes could still reach Moscow. Stavka had analysed the winter offensive against Heeresgruppe Mitte and had come to the conclusion that it was not so much the strength of the Germans that prevented the Soviets from achieving the intended result, but the quality of the organization and command structure on the Soviet side. The chosen offensive would also lead to the liberation of Belarus, which was of great moral significance, as it was the last part of the Soviet Union occupied by the Germans. In addition, the way would be cleared for an advance to the Vistula from the Lvov area.

The Germans initially assumed that the next offensive would take place in the south and that Heeresgruppe Nordukraine would have to absorb the

Soviet anti-tank units and T-34 tanks with infantry on board cross a river near Lvov.

heaviest blows. The Soviets also did everything they could in the way of *maskirovka* to convince the Germans of this. Thus, the Soviet units opposite Heeresgruppe Mitte began to build defensive positions and intensified their activities in the north and especially in the south, launching an offensive by the Twenty-seventh Army and Second Tank Army across the River Prut towards Romania. This convinced the Germans that a future offensive would take place in the south. In line with this, LVI Corps of Heeresgruppe Mitte was transferred to the area of Heeresgruppe Nordukraine. This corps would play a role in the preventive offensive that the OKH had in mind there. However, moving this unit had drastic consequences for the fighting power of Heeresgruppe Mitte: it lost 15 per cent of its divisions, as many as 88 per cent of its tanks, 50 per cent of its anti-tank guns, 23 per cent of its self-propelled artillery and 33 per cent of its heavy artillery. Needless to say, all this played into the hands of the Soviets. (1: 65)

As the month of May progressed, it became clear that a large fighting force was gathering opposite Heeresgruppe Mitte, and the OKH began to view it as the target of a future Soviet offensive. The counter-offensive by Heeresgruppe Nordukraine was called off, but the units of the LVI Corps did not return to their positions within Heeresgruppe Mitte. Hitler would not have been Hitler if he did not have very particular views on the upcoming offensive: he assumed that its main axis would lie between the Pripyet Marshes and the Carpathian Mountains, on the southern flank of Heeresgruppe Mitte. This would take the Soviets towards Warsaw and the Vistula and also into the rear of Heeresgruppe Mitte. In itself, this was the most logical scenario, although the Soviets had already shown that they did not necessarily follow the obvious line. Hitler positioned his main reserves, including four tank divisions in Galicia, on the expected route of attack. He was convinced that he had seen through the Soviets and that they would not be able to penetrate the German defence line. In fact, Hitler and the leadership of the Wehrmacht were so confident that they disregarded all reports that the Soviets were targeting not the southern flank of Heeresgruppe Mitte but Heeresgruppe Mitte itself. The intelligence service of Heeresgruppe Mitte had a good idea of the sectors on which a possible Soviet offensive would focus, but it had no idea of the size of the troop build-up on the Soviet side, nor did it suspect that the strategic targets for the coming offensive would lie at Minsk and further west. Busch, commander-in-chief of Heeresgruppe Mitte, realized that his units were outnumbered and that the only way to hold back the Soviets was mobile defence. As we shall see, Hitler thought otherwise.

The Soviets did not need the kind of sophisticated plan that Hitler envisioned; the past few months had shown that the Germans simply could not stop a massive frontal attack providing it was conducted by enough men across a broad front. The Soviets realized all too well that the Germans could easily defeat almost any Soviet unit if they were not vastly outnumbered. But the Germans simply could not be everywhere, and where they were absent or were vastly outnumbered, Soviet force majeure could simply overwhelm the enemy and force a breakthrough.

The Soviets had also considered the terrain. The southern part of the front was dominated by the Pripyet marshes, which gave way to wooded and swampy ground with only a few areas where tanks could advance quickly. Further to the north-west the terrain was more open, and the area between Orsha and Vitebsk had been the site of major confrontations, both in the Napoleonic Wars and during Operation Barbarossa. During their winter offensive of 1943/44 the Soviets had tried to break through here. Cities in the area were important hubs. Vitebsk, Orsha, Mogilev and Bobruisk were on the easternmost side of the front, while Borisov was an important crossing point over the Berezina River. Behind it lay two important corridors for railways and highways towards Minsk. The rivers in the area ran from north to south and could be major obstacles to a rapid advance.

The main thrust of the Soviet plan was as follows. The 1st Baltic Front and the 1st, 2nd and 3rd Belorussian Fronts would launch the offensive with the aim of encircling and destroying the German units in and around the cities of Vitebsk, Orsha, Mogilev and Bobruisk, then take Minsk and advance west as quickly as possible. The Soviets had the numbers of men to give substance to their concept of force majeure: against the 400,000 men of Heeresgruppe Mitte under Busch, consisting of the Second, Third, Fourth and Ninth Panzer Armies, were no fewer than 2,500,000 men of the 1st Baltic Front and the 1st, 2nd and 3rd Belorussian Fronts. The superiority of equipment on the Soviet side was also significant: 4,000 to 900 in tanks, 28,500 to 10,000 in guns and 5,300 to 1,300 in aircraft. The Soviets were able to bring together this amount of men and equipment by reinforcing the Fronts involved with units from various other areas, such as Crimea, liberated in May. These added a total of more than 400,000 men, 3,000 tanks and 10,000 guns. The movement of these units took place at night in order to retain the element of surprise. Infantry divisions travelled on foot, some covering 150 miles in twelve nights, to spare the congested railway network as much as possible, while railway personnel struggled to get supplies and ammunition to the front in time. Despite all their efforts, the level of supplies remained critical, and there were problems not only in getting enough ammunition from the rail to the front in time, but also in re-supplying the units once the offensive had started.

**Americans at the front**
American Lend-Lease trucks were a crucial element in Soviet transport. Sergeant M. Fukson, technician in an artillery brigade of the 1st Baltic Front, described the importance of the American Studebakers: 'For the transport of ammunition we received sixteen American Lend-Lease Studebakers. The Studebakers were cars with powerful engines that could traverse marshy ground and all sorts of other difficult terrain. Soviet roads simply could not be compared with European roads. There were also swamps and the like, but the front line simply does not stick to the main roads. That's why the Studebakers helped us tremendously.' (1: 54)

With a sense of history, Stalin set the start of the offensive, codenamed Bagration, as 22 June, the date of the German invasion of the Soviet Union. Partisans were deployed prior to the offensive, just as at Kursk. In the hinterland of Heeresgruppe Mitte, as we have seen, the partisan movement was particularly strong. There was no anti-Soviet separatist movement active here as in the Ukraine and the Caucasus, and as a result the area had always been a hotbed of partisans. They were so active that certain parts were no longer under German control, and in other areas the Germans could only move in convoy. The partisans began their

American deliveries meant that the Soviets always had more than enough vehicles at their disposal, such as this M3A1 armoured reconnaissance car.

actions on the night of 19/20 June and blew up bridges and rail links in more than ten thousand places from the Dnieper to the west of Minsk, cutting off all supply lines for several days. In addition, all telephone lines along the railway lines were cut.

The first attack was launched on the northern part of the front, where the Third Panzer Army was confronted on both sides of Vitebsk by the 1st Baltic Front and elements of the Belorussian Front. Then, on 23 June, the 2nd Belorussian Front attacked the Fourth Panzer Army along the Dnieper in the area between Orsha and Mogilev. To complete the assault, on 4 June the 1st Belorussian Front struck at the Ninth Panzer Army in the direction of Bobruisk on the Berezina.

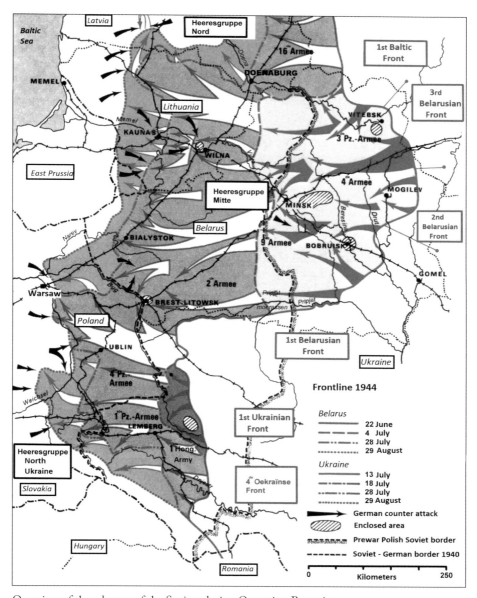

Overview of the advance of the Soviets during Operation Bagration.

Hitler initially assumed these were just diversions for the main attack, but he eventually realized that it was the main attack itself. During the previous year, the Soviets had tried to break through the German lines with similarly superior numbers, but without success; the Germans' use of mobile defence had meant the positions were held. But Hitler had failed to see how Von Manstein had been able to limit the damage by quickly moving units from place to place. Busch, as commander of Heeresgruppe Mitte, had proposed withdrawing his support units behind the Berezina to prevent them from being crushed in a possible Soviet offensive. In addition, he wanted to position the bulk of his combat units some 20km behind the front, out of range of the Soviet artillery, in order to counter any Soviet breakthrough through the relatively sparsely manned front line with a mobile defence. His aim was to frustrate the Soviets' careful planning by creating chaos in the area behind the front and launching rapid counter-thrusts from positions in the rear. This was the scenario Zhukov feared. But he need not have, because on 8 March, in the run-up to new Soviet offensives, Hitler had introduced a new defence concept, namely that of the fortified cities (*Festen Plätze*). These places would 'have the function of fortresses from historical times. They will ensure that the enemy cannot occupy areas of critical strategic importance. They will allow themselves to be surrounded, capturing large numbers of opponents' forces while also being able to launch counter-attacks.' In line with this, he had important communication and supply centres reinforced, with the idea that the units in these fortifications would hold the Soviets up.

For example, the towns of Bobruisk, Mogilev and Ohrsa in the front line of defence were occupied by just one division, while a town like Vitebsk was defended by three. In the hinterland, Minsk, Slutsk, Baranovichi and Vilnius were designated as *Festen Plätze*. Why Hitler arrived at the idea of fortified cities is unclear, since the past year had shown that the Soviets unhesitatingly ignored such places. The fact that they were unable to advance with their tank divisions deep into the enemy's hinterland had not prevented them from advancing quickly towards Kiev during their attack on Heeresgruppe Süd in the spring, bypassing all unimportant German units. Hitler failed to realize that a German force encircled by Soviet units was just as much knocked out as a unit ground down during a frontal attack. And the Soviets had enough units to keep these fortified cities isolated, especially if they were occupied by only one division. Moreover, these were precisely the divisions that the Germans so desperately needed as a mobile reserve to close the gaps in the front. Protests at the idea *Festen Plätze* came from various quarters within the Heeresgruppe Mitte, as stated by General Jordan, commander-in-chief of the Ninth Army:

> The Ninth Army is on the verge of a great battle, the size and duration of which cannot yet be predicted … And the Army believes that even under the present circumstances, it would be possible to stop the enemy, but not under the current directives, which require an absolutely rigid defence … The Army considers in particular the orders to create *Festen Plätze* as dangerous. The Army looks at the coming battle with bitterness,

Soviet units are warmly greeted by the residents of Vitebsk.

knowing that it is bound by orders that make tactical manoeuvring impossible and that in our previous successful campaigns led to the defeat of the opponent.

Busch did not comment, but referred to OKH directives.

The offensive started very well for the Soviets. Soon many of the fortified cities, including Vitebsk, were surrounded. The Soviets subsequently devoted little time or energy to these positions: they were small and would be dealt with later. The gaps in the front were so large, and the Soviets were advancing so fast and so deep, that help from German units or attempts at a breakout were out of the question. By 28 June, the front of Heeresgruppe Mitte had been breached in several places and Soviet units were advancing along the Minsk-Smolensk highway to Borisov and south to Slutsk. A large part of the Ninth Panzer Army was surrounded on 29 June at Bobruisk, east of the Berezina. The front was so destabilized that the Soviets reached this city after only four days, instead of the planned eight. The German units tried to break out, and 30,000 of the 100,000 encircled German troops eventually managed to reach their own lines, or what passed for them.

The Third Panzer Army was not much better off. It was already seriously weakened because it had had to give up part of its units as reserves to face the expected Soviet offensive in the south. In addition, one third of the remaining

Tired by their long marches, this German infantry unit seeks relief in the shade. On the right, a captured Soviet tractor pulls a trailer with some of their gear.

units, LIII Corps, had to defend the fortified city of Vitebsk where it was then surrounded. Hitler made another of his half-hearted decisions: LIII Corps was allowed to attempt a breakout, but had to leave one of its divisions behind in the city. The 206th Infantry Division was given the honour of remaining, but the units were in the end so weakened that they never attempted a breakout. On 27 June the curtain fell on the Germans in Vitebsk. The situation in the air had also changed considerably. After D-Day, an important section of the Luftwaffe on the Eastern Front had been transferred to the west to tackle the superior Allied air forces. It was no longer Henschels, Stukas and Ju-52s that influenced the battle on the ground, but Soviet ground support aircraft that knocked out artillery positions and made supply routes unsafe. They were particularly effective in the area of the Fourth Panzer Army. Gaining air supremacy would be one of the keys to the Soviets' success in the near future.

On 27 June, Zhukov sent forward the Fifth Guards Tank Army, and in the following days it moved through the area between the Dnepr and the Dvina, towards Borisov. It reached this place just ahead of the 5th Panzer Division, which advanced from Kovel but was stopped in its tracks by the Soviets. This was why Hitler fired Busch and replaced him with Model. As a result of this appointment, Model combined the command of Heeresgruppe Mitte and Heeresgruppe Nordukraine.

It was still unclear what could be expected of Model's appointment. In the south, the only major operation in which he had been involved was the final phase of the retreat of the First Panzer Army. The mud had then brought the front to a halt. Model realized that holding on to stationary positions

The supreme tank. The Tiger II (later called *Königstiger*) is often seen as the most impressive tank of the Second World War. However, only a limited number were produced, and technically these tanks were vulnerable.

would only lead to the sacrifice of more and more men, so he opted for mobile defence. But it was too late for that now, and on 3 July the Soviets took Minsk. While Model managed to gain traction with his new units and create a mobile defensive screen, Zhukov had his eye on Baranovichi, a railway hub. If this place could be taken, the entire southern part of Model's fighting force would be undermined. The Soviet offensive initially stalled in front of Baranovichi, but after personal intervention by Zhukov, the city fell on 8 July. In Chalin, the 39th Panzer Corps was encircled and, despite vigorous efforts to relieve it, was forced to surrender on 9 July.

As the arms of the pincers closed, Minsk fell, and German units began to withdraw without a clear line of defence to fall back on. The Soviets reached Vilna on 9 July and the city fell four days later. By mid-July, all of White Russia had been cleared of Germans and the Soviets had reached north-eastern Poland. As the Soviet units advanced towards the Baltic coast, the entire Heeresgruppe Nord was now threatened with isolation. The Germans, meanwhile, had completely lost control of events: on 24 July, the forward units of Rokossovsky's left wing reached Lublin, 150km east of Warsaw and 45km from the Vistula, and two days later, his units reached the river itself. On 31 July, Bagramyan's armoured units reached the Baltic at the Gulf of Riga and Heeresgruppe Nord was in practice cut off from the rest of the Wehrmacht. A southern flanking movement, meanwhile, had forced the Germans to retreat towards Warsaw. On 2 August, Konev crossed the Vistula at Baranov, 180km south of Warsaw. In the north, the Soviets captured Kaunas, the capital of

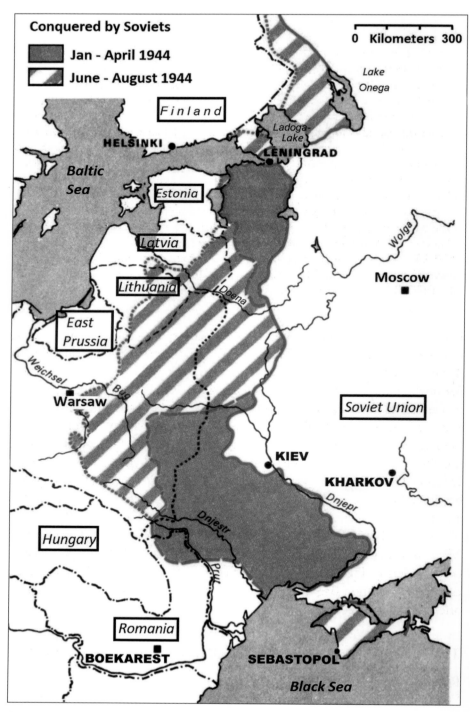

**Conquered by Soviets**

■ Jan - April 1944
▨ June - August 1944

0   Kilometers   300

Lake
Onega

*Finland*

HELSINKI

Ladoga-
Lake

LENINGRAD

*Baltic
Sea*

*Estonia*

*Latvia*

Wolga

*Lithuania*

*Doena*

**Moscow**

*East
Prussia*

*Weichsel*

*Bug*

**Warsaw**

*Soviet Union*

**KIEV**

**KHARKOV**

*Dnjepr*

*Dnjestr*

*Hungary*

*Prut*

*Romania*

**BOEKAREST**

**SEBASTOPOL**

*Black Sea*

Overview of the front line at the end of April and the end of August 1944.

**Out of control**

The Germans often lost control of events during Operation Bagration. This was due not only to the superiority of the Soviet forces, but also to fundamental mistakes made by the German commanders. For example, on 14 July, during a counter-offensive in the area between the Strypa and the Siret, the commander of the 8th Panzer Division, part of the XLVIII Panzer Corps under Balck, chose to use the main road instead of forest paths, something that Balck had explicitly forbidden. As a result, the division's columns were repeatedly hit by fighter-bombers. It took three days to reposition the division for the relief of XIII Corps in the north, and Balck sent his chief of staff, von Mellenthin, to assume temporary command. However, during the preparation phase, the commander of the tank regiment positioned his units only 30 minutes before the start of the attack and in full view of the Soviets. Von Mellenthin relieved him of command on the spot and called off the attack. These were mistakes that the Germans could no longer afford and they indicate that the officer corps was no longer up to standard. Despite the failure of the 8th Panzer Division on the 20th, the XIII Corps managed to fight its way to freedom, leaving its artillery and heavy weapons behind. (41: 193)

Lithuania, and advanced into East Prussia. The rapid advance had, meanwhile, provoked an uprising by the people of Warsaw, which would be bloodily put down by the Germans in the coming months.

Meanwhile, the Soviet offensive had slowly but surely fizzled out. Bagration had left a gap of 400km from north to south in the German lines and, after an advance of 720km to the west, came slowly but surely to a halt after five weeks. German reinforcements in the form of the 4th and 19th Panzer Divisions, the SS Panzer Divisions Totenkopf and Wiking and the Luftwaffe Panzer Division Hermann Göring managed to stabilize the front and prevented a breakout from the bridgeheads on the west bank of the Vistula. Counter-attacks in the north forced the Soviets to retreat there. But Bagration's effects had been devastating: the Soviets had pulverized Heeresgruppe Mitte, destroying twenty-five divisions. Of the forty-seven corps or division commanders of Heeresgruppe Mitte, thirty-one had been killed in action or captured. Operation Bagration can rightly be seen as one of the most decisive offensives of the Second World War.

## The disintegration of the front in the Balkans

### Romania

While this drama was unfolding for the Germans in the north and centre of the front, Antonescu, the Romanian head of government, had proposed that the German and Romanian units in the south withdraw to more defensible positions along the Carpathians. Hitler agreed, but wanted first to see clear signs of a Soviet offensive in the south. Until then, the units should remain in their existing defensive positions. While discussion was still going on, the Soviet offensive against Heeresgruppe Südukraine was launched on 20 August, focusing on the two sections of the front held by the Romanians. Hitler allowed an immediate withdrawal, but the Germans had to hold off the Soviets long enough to secure the bridges over the Danube which the Romanian and German units could use to withdraw. The main attack was carried out by the 2nd Ukrainian Front under Malinovsky and the 3rd Ukrainian Front under Tolbukhin. The 2nd Ukrainian Front attacked from the south and advanced along

Victorious Soviet soldiers enter Bucharest on American Lend-Lease GMC trucks.

both banks of the Siret River from Jassy to Galatz, and the 3rd Ukrainian Front advanced westward along the Dniester. The Romanians capitulated on 23 August and then immediately changed sides. They occupied the bridges over the Danube, isolating sixteen German divisions on the east bank, all of which could be considered lost. The Soviets did not hesitate and took Galatz on 27 August, the Ploesti oil fields on 30 August, and Bucharest on 31 August.

## Bulgaria

The Soviets now turned their sights onto Bulgaria. This country was one of the partners of the Axis and had declared war on Great Britain and the United States, but had given little more than moral support to the war in the Soviet Union. It had been involved militarily only in the invasion of Yugoslavia and Greece in 1941 and in fighting partisans in these countries thereafter. But Bulgaria had no wish to be crushed under the Soviet steamroller and declared that it would allow the Red Army free passage. To reinforce its intentions, it declared war on Germany on 8 September. This threatened to isolate the units of Heeresgruppe E and F in Yugoslavia and Greece respectively, and the Germans hastened to withdraw these units to Hungary. The Soviets then

The advance of the Soviets seemed unstoppable. Here, Soviet soldiers cross the Danube on a partially destroyed bridge.

entered Bulgaria with the aim of invading Hungary on the widest possible front via the Balkans.

## Yugoslavia

While this was playing out in Bulgaria, the Soviets were planning an offensive against the German forces in Yugoslavia. However, after the first Soviet

By the autumn of 1944 fewer and fewer German units were motorized. Here, on the retreat, two 105mm guns are pulled by eight horses each. Good camouflage was vital because of Soviet command of the air.

units entered Yugoslavia, Tito convinced them to take Belgrade, which they promptly did on 19 October. The Germans, who had not yet been able to establish a defensive line, retreated from logistical hub to logistical hub step by step towards Hungary, followed by the Soviets. This southerly route led the Soviets to advance through Yugoslavia to the north, eventually appearing on the Hungarian steppes earlier than the units that had advanced into Hungary via the direct route past Cluj. By the end of October Yugoslavia was completely in Russian hands and the Soviets could now focus on Hungary.

Further north, the 4th Ukrainian Front under Petrov had launched an offensive across the Carpathians that had taken them into Ruthenia and then west into Slovakia.

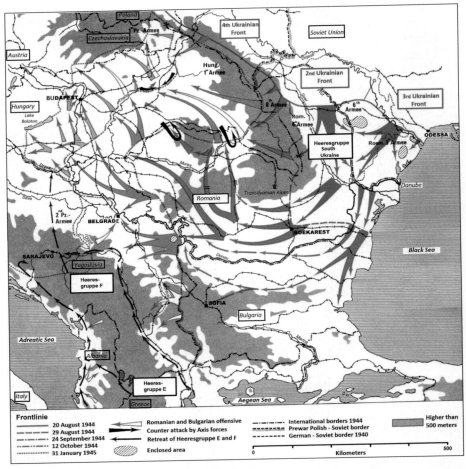

Overview of the advance of the Soviets in the Balkans.

## Hungary

The 2ⁿᵈ Ukrainian Front under Malinovsky continued its advance and launched an attack towards Budapest on 30 October with sixty-four divisions. The Germans and Hungarians were pushed back, and by early November the fighting had moved to the outskirts of Budapest. Bad weather frustrated an attempt to take the city by storm and gave the Germans time to prepare for a lengthy siege. To the north and east, the terrain and German resistance prevented further advance through Hungary towards Slovakia. One of the last major tank battles of the war took place in this region. On the Hungarian plains near Debrecen, an ideal theatre for tank operations, Colonel General Freissner's Heeresgruppe Süd, the renamed Heeresgruppe Südukraine, managed to encircle three Soviet Corps with the 1ˢᵗ, 23ʳᵈ and 24ᵗʰ Panzer Divisions. This

Fleeing the violence of war, these horses gallop through a heavily damaged city in Hungary.

successful action slowed down the Soviets' advance, but failed to stop it. In the weeks that followed the Soviets increased pressure south of Budapest, crossed the Danube near its junction with the Drava and reached Lake Balaton on 4 December. By Christmas Budapest was completely encircled.

### Finland and the Baltic States

The Finns, meanwhile, had made peace with the Soviet Union on 2 September, thus ending the conflict that had begun in 1939. On 10 October, the Soviet offensive in the north erupted again. The 1st Baltic Front reached the coast at Memel, while the 2nd and 3rd Baltic Fronts closed in on Riga and the Leningrad Front advanced through Estonia. The remnants of Heeresgruppe Nord under Schörner, some thirty-three divisions, were pushed back on the Courland peninsula and around Memel. They could no longer play a significant role. In the end, all units except the 12th and 14th Divisions were evacuated by sea in the last months of 1944 and the first of 1945.

The Soviets reached the Baltic coast at Memel in September 1944.

The Soviets gave the Germans no respite. On 16 October, they launched an offensive across a 140km-wide front in East Prussia. On 19 October, they occupied German territory for the first time by taking the districts of Goldap and Gumbinnen. A fierce German counter-offensive succeeded in pushing the Soviets back again on 5 November. However, the short Soviet occupation had left its mark: Wehrmacht and Volkssturm (Home Guard) soldiers discovered almost no survivors in the area.

### Revenge: the fate of Nemmersdorf

The testimonies of the Wehrmacht and Volkssturm soldiers before a military court in Neu Ulm in July 1946 paint a horrifying picture of what had happened in Nemmersdorf and other villages during the short period of Soviet occupation. Dr Heinrich Amberger, commander of a Fallschirmjäger company stated: 'On the road through Nemmersdorf, near the bridge over the River Angerapp, I saw a whole procession of refugees who had been run over by tanks. Not only the horses and carts, but also a large number of civilians, mostly women and children, had been crushed by the tanks. Along the side of the road and near the farm lay the corpses of civilians who had not all died in military action, but had been murdered more systematically.' Some of the women had been crucified, nailed naked to barn doors. Karl Pork, a Volkssturm soldier, testified: '[Behind the inn *Roter Krug*] in a barn we found a total of seventy-two women, children and an old man, all dead. They had been brutally murdered, except for a few who had been shot in the neck ... Sitting on a chair below was an old woman of eighty-four ... Half her head had been cut off with a shovel or pickaxe.' Also among the dead were sixty French prisoners of war. The Wehrmacht arranged for the international press to visit Nemmersdorf within a few days. An international medical commission determined that all the women had been raped before they were killed. The massacre at Nemmersdorf sent a shock wave through Germany, and a mass flight of civilians from the east began. (59: 60–4)

After almost six months of continuous fighting, many of the German units were close to exhaustion. The Soviets would give them no rest until Berlin was captured.

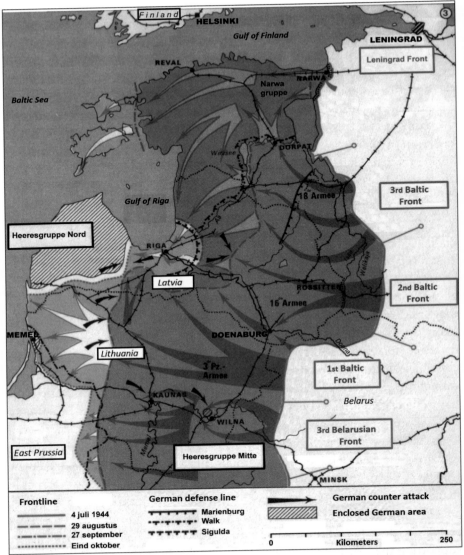

Overview of the Soviet advance on the Northern Front from July to the end of September 1944.

All now prepared for the final round. The Germans had lost more than 1,000,000 men on the Eastern Front in 1944, losses they could not replace. To compensate for this, very young and old men were called up for service and placed in the Volksgrenadier Divisions described earlier. Thirteen new tank brigades were also formed, numbered 100 to 113 and composed of vehicles that had just rolled out of the factory and men who had just completed basic training. The tank regiments were made up of one mixed battalion consisting of tanks and assault guns, one or two battalions of Panzergrenadiere and as many artillery and support units as could be scraped together.

In Germany itself, people were mainly concerned about whether the Allies or the Soviets would be the first to occupy the country. After the events in the east there were no illusions about what a Soviet invasion would entail. Meanwhile, the army leadership had built up a large central tank reserve in the form of two fully equipped Panzer Armies to stabilize the front in the east. Ironically, this force would end up being used by Hitler against the Allies during the Ardennes offensive, thus sealing Germany's fate. With the wasting of these last resources, the way for the Soviets into Berlin and the heart of Germany was open.

## At the front

### The way back

During Bagration, a good many Germans had managed to escape the encirclement of the Fourth Army and evade captivity. In the following weeks they tried to find their way back to their own lines in groups. They had no maps, little ammunition and few rations. A small number of them eventually managed to reach friendly lines, mainly the younger and fitter men; their elders had little chance of surviving the gruelling journey. The men moved through enemy territory at night and in foggy weather, sleeping during the day in fields and forests. They stayed away from villages, towns, thoroughfares and railways, because there was always the danger of encountering Soviet units. The Soviets, in turn, had set up sentries and sent out patrols to intercept retreating German soldiers. Larger groups split into smaller ones to reduce the chance of discovery and increase the possibility of finding food. Surprisingly, many Russian peasants gave these men food and drink. Some probably couldn't believe that the Germans were retreating and even asked them for receipts. Others feared the Soviets would come back again and hoped that by supporting the Germans they would prevent this happening

> **A merciful death**
> Heinz Fiedler was one of the soldiers who attempted to escape from Bobruisk. 'We tried to escape but we were shot at and panic broke out. There was a soldier, still a boy, sitting under a tree with his entrails bulging out of his belly. He yelled, "Shoot me!" but everyone just walked past him. I had to stop but I couldn't shoot him. Then a young second lieutenant of the engineers came and gave him the coup de grâce with a shot. At that moment I cried bitterly. I thought his mother should know how he met his end.' Heinz Fiedler was one of the few who managed to reach friendly lines. (44: 219)

German soldiers who fell into the hands of partisans had no chance of survival. The luckiest were immediately shot, but many were tortured to death. The retreating units encountered many mutilated corpses of their comrades. One report speaks of a hundred wounded Germans who remained behind after the fighting and were killed with a shot in the neck. In another incident, a group of PoWs were forced to strip naked, then beaten until their pulped remains were barely recognizable. It is unclear how many more of these incidents occurred, because only a small proportion of those who fell into the hands of the partisans survived to tell their story.

The most dangerous part of the journey was the last few kilometres through the Soviet front line to reach the German lines without being shot by one's own units. The Soviets tightly controlled the front line to prevent any exfiltration attempts. In one escape, a captain and a non-commissioned officer had come across a Soviet artillery position and hid under a pile of dried sunflower stalks. Soviet soldiers then arrived and began to move the pile, but the Germans coolly picked up some stalks and simply followed the Soviets through the minefields. When a Soviet soldier put a question to the non-commissioned officer, he cursed him in Russian. The two crossed the Soviet trenches and ended up in no-man's-land, from where they managed to reach the German lines.

Another group spent three days between the two front lines. By the third night they were determined to make a move. Tracer ammunition was flying through the air and gunfire was everywhere as they crept past the sentries. A flare was fired and shots came from both sides. They dived headlong into a shell hole, at which point one of them stepped on a German mine, which went off with a blinding explosion. One of the men went to get help from the German lines and eventually returned with a number of medics. They had succeeded in escaping. It is estimated that between 10,000 and 15,000 escaped the encirclements, but no more than 900 eventually managed to reach friendly lines. The most senior in rank was a major, bearer of the Iron Cross, who had managed to find his way back barefoot and alone. (1: 160–3)

## Panthers in action: force majeure at operational level

We have seen that on a strategic-tactical level the Germans had to surrender the initiative to the Soviets in the course of 1944. At the tactical-operational level, too, they failed more and more often, due to the inexperience of newly recruited officers and men. This did not alter the fact that they were still formidable opponents at the level of the individual unit.

An example is the following incident, which took place in August 1944 when the 35th Panzer Regiment was involved in an attempt to re-establish contact with Heeresgruppe Nord. After capturing a strategically important

Tanks and Panzergrenadiere on their way in their SdKfz 251.

Panther tanks and Panzer Grenadiere of SS Panzer Grenadiere Division Wiking in action in the summer of 1944 in the south of the Soviet Union. Perhaps one of the last actions in which the Panzerwaffe's operational methods were clearly visible. Here, preparations are being made.

Panzergrenadiere advance through the field along with Panther tanks.

After a battle, information is exchanged and the men assemble for the next action.

hill, NCO Christ's Panther tank began to malfunction. The driver reported an oil leak and steering problems, which quickly got worse. There was nothing to do but let the other Panther tank move on and await the arrival of the Werkstatt Kompagnie's towing vehicles. After a while, the crew heard the rattle of tracks and the sound of tank engines to their right. Panzergrenadiere reported seeing a T-34 at the edge of the forest opposite. Further investigation revealed that it was two T-34s, and that they were a special version known as the T-43, equipped with a 110mm gun. The Panther was laboriously manoeuvred into a good position to be able to aim at the tanks. The crew managed to take out the first tank with one shot and its crew fled, while the second tank burst into flames after the second shot. Almost immediately, Christ and his crew saw the muzzle fire of two other tanks, which were apparently firing at random without seeing the Panther. These tanks were also set on fire with a single shot each. Christ then decided not to take any chances and positioned his tank on the other side of a hill so that the turret could no longer be seen. His hunch had been correct: two other T-34s appeared and aimed their barrels at where they suspected the Panther was. While Christ directed his gunner from his turret, the Panther moved slowly up the hill to open fire on the tanks, with its barrel just above the top. One of the two newcomers was hit and blown up by an internal explosion. Surprisingly, the first T-34 now made itself heard again; apparently the driver had climbed back on board and was trying to get away.

This tank was hit again with a single shot, and black smoke began to spew out of it. The Panther had run out of ammunition during the battle, and the appearance of two new T-34s on the battlefield made the situation precarious. The driver and radio operator jumped out of the tank, at lightning speed retrieved fresh shells from one of the supply trucks that had shown up, and with the help of the Panzergrenadiere got them on board as quickly as possible. Any shell passed through the manhole was fired immediately – and successfully: the sixth and seventh victims of the day came to a burning stop a little later. The Soviet counter-attack had been halted. Christ and his men ended the day behind one of the Werkstatt Kompagnie's towing vehicles on its way to the regiment's mobile workshop. (41: 196–7)

## Deception

The Soviets successfully used a combination of *maskirovka* techniques in 1944 to mask the real objective of their summer offensive. Soviet actions in winter 1943/1944 had concentrated on the southern part of the front, and the Soviets wanted the Germans to believe that any future offensives would also target this area. To this end, the 3rd Ukrainian Front had to simulate the build-up along the front of eight or nine infantry divisions with additional tanks and artillery. The units opposite Heeresgruppe Mitte, on the other hand, had to create the impression that no offensive actions could be expected from them by constructing extensive defensive fortifications. Shtemenko stated that 'the troops were put to work perfecting their defensive positions. The news bulletins of the armies and divisions all along the front only published stories about defensive affairs. All the troops talked about was holding on to the current positions.' The units that had to reinforce the offensive were brought in by train. These trains were completely cut off from any contact with the outside world, and the men were only allowed to leave the train in a limited number of places and under supervision. Railway staff were told the numbers of the trains, but not their final destination. The assembly areas where the units had to position themselves were well camouflaged and controlled from the air. Only very limited reconnaissance was allowed, and the officers had to wear soldiers' uniforms. Tank crews had to exchange their clearly recognizable dark uniforms for normal soldier's attire. In other places, heavy road traffic was simulated and trains ran empty during the day to places behind the front, only to return full at night.

In the south, and to a lesser extent in the north, the Soviets engaged in all sorts of activities to suggest that an offensive in these areas was only a matter of time. In the south they launched a large-scale attack across the River Prut close to the Romanian border with the Twenty-seventh Army and the Second Tank Army. One of the most critical elements of the preparations was to move two tank armies from the south to the centre of the front. This action went off without a hitch, although the 2nd Ukrainian Front tried in vain to 'account for' some tank regiments and regiments of self-propelled guns in order to be able to use the equipment later for their own offensive. This combination of measures was extremely successful, and we have seen that Hitler and the German army leadership were completely surprised when on 22 June the Soviet offensive broke onto the front of Heeresgruppe Mitte. (1: 56–61)

The Soviets also used deception at a more operational level to confuse the Germans. For example, during the retreat of the Fourth Army over the Berezina, a lieutenant suddenly appeared and ordered the bridge, over which all kinds of units were still retreating, to be blown up. He was, however, exposed as a Soviet infiltrator and shot dead on the spot. This was not the only incident of this kind. In another case, the wounded commander of an artillery battery encountered two staff officers 2km from the Berezina. They gave as the direction for the retreating units a route that led into a swamp, claiming that the bridge ahead had been blown up. Since the commander had not heard any sounds of fighting, he determined to drive on, despite the officers doing everything they could to stop him. A member of the 267th Infantry Division reported that his unit was also intercepted near the Berezina by a major on horseback, who ordered all the vehicles to be blown up. The men were then to swim across the river with the remaining horses because the temporary bridge was not yet ready and the Soviets were already on the west bank of the river. The commanding officer investigated, concluded that the bridge was still intact and immediately had the bogus major shot. Not all units were so lucky; in another incident, an officer on a motorcycle convinced a commanding officer that his message came from divisional headquarters and that the unit in question should follow a different route to team up with tanks there. On arriving at the location mentioned, they found themselves under fire from artillery, mortars and finally Soviet infantry. (1: 55)

## Refugees

With the withdrawal of the Germans, a large flow of refugees to the west also began. This consisted of *Volksdeutsche* (ethnic Germans), collaborators and anyone else who had something to fear from the Soviets. In addition, large numbers of Soviet citizens were forcibly taken west for use in German war industry. This was in accordance with the Germans' scorched-earth policy, which, as the Soviets had done in 1941, aimed to render unusable as many of the means of production as possible. This strategy was only partially successful, often because the Red Army was advancing so rapidly.

Wirtschaftsstab Ost was responsible for planning the transport of refugees and destruction of industrial and other facilities. The actual implementation was left to the Wehrmacht, since Wirtschaftsstab Ost did not have the manpower, weapons or logistics for this work. The Ortskommandanten (local commanders) themselves had to determine when and how many troops could be deployed. The flow of refugees and deportees is shown in the table below.

### Numbers of refugees per Heeresgruppe (21: 388)

|  | Heeresgruppe Nord | Heeresgruppe Mitte | Heeresgruppe Süd |
|---|---|---|---|
| 15/11/42 – 2/7/43 | 22,545 | 190,000 | 150,000 |
| 2/7/43 – 31/12/43 | 260,240 | 885,000 | 520,500 |
| 31/12/43 – 28/3/44 | 237,436 | Unknown | 372,147 |
| *Total* | *516,221* | *1,075,000* | *1,042,147* |

The Germans tried to take as many cattle as possible with them on their retreat.

These journeys took place exclusively on foot and put an enormous strain on the affected civilians. Many of the elderly, children and the sick among the refugees did not survive these marches of often more than hundreds of kilometres. In addition, they had to leave hearth and home behind and face an uncertain future, while those deported for forced labour had to leave their loved ones behind as well.

Refugee flows were also occurring on the other side of the front. In 1943, Stalin had authorized the deportation of entire ethnic groups that he believed had collaborated with the Germans. It seemed pointless to him to find out which individuals had collaborated and which had not, so whole groups were deported. Among his first victims were the Kalmyks, who inhabited the steppes through which the Germans had passed in 1942 on their way south to Baku and the Caucasus. In October, Stalin confirmed the decision of the State Defence Committee to deport them and cleared the way for the 're-allocation' of the Kalmyks to areas far in the east such as Omsk and Novosibirsk. In December 1943, the NKVD was used by Beria to carry out these deportations. One of the officers involved, Lieutenant Nikonor, a dedicated communist, said, 'Looking at them from another point of view, I thought to myself: how could these people have helped the enemy? They looked so sad and pitiful.' (44: 195) On 28 December, the NKVD began driving the Kalmyks out of their homes, giving families two hours to pack. They were then transported to the nearest station and carried into the depths of Siberia by train, during which many died of cold, malnutrition and dysentery. It will never be known how many Kalmyks did not survive the journey. The only available figures relate to a transport to the Altai Krai region: of the 478 people deported, 290 died, a mortality rate of 60 per cent. Once they arrived in Siberia, the living and climatic conditions also took their toll, and many more died of malnutrition and disease. The Kalmyks who had fought loyally as conscripts alongside the Soviets fared no better: they were removed from the army and deported to labour camps in the Urals. In total, 93,000 Kalmyks were deported. However, they were not the only people to pay a heavy price in the aftermath of Soviet liberation. Others included the Karachai from the North Caucasus (68,000 deportees), the Chechens (500,000 deportees), the Balkars from the Caucasus (340,000) and the Tatars from Crimea (180,000). The total number of deportees will always remain unclear, but was certainly more than a million. (44: 192–5)

These great displacements of people were a dark prelude to what would happen in 1945 when the Soviets entered Central Europe and Germany itself.

# Chapter 4

# 1945: Towards the End

*By the beginning of 1945, as the Red Army advanced unstoppably from the Balkans and eastern Poland towards Germany, it was clear that the end of the Third Reich was only a matter of time. Before them the Soviets drove at first thousands but soon hundreds of thousands of refugees, all trying to escape Russian vengeance. The first months of 1945 still saw some major German offensives, but the Soviets were able to halt any German advance and break their enemy's resistance. In mid–April everyone prepared for the final conflict: the battle for Berlin. While Hitler still believed that his by now imaginary divisions could halt the Soviet advance, the reality was that the Red Army had fought its way through the hastily scraped together German units to reach the symbol of Nazi power, the Reichstag. On 1 May, the German units in Berlin surrendered. Thus ended the battle of the two giants. The price had been high: on the German side there were 3,800,000 dead or missing and 4,200,000 wounded; 2,200,000 civilians had also lost their lives. The losses on the Soviet side were even more horrific: 10,000,000 dead and 18,000,000 wounded, with probably an equal numbers of civilian casualties.*

## 1. On the run

### Flight

The year 1945 would be characterized by the large flows of refugees to the west that started when the Soviets approached German territory. The events in Nemmersdorf described in the previous chapter cast an enormous shadow, and many decided to err on the side of caution and flee. This was the beginning of the great displacement of many millions of Germans during and after the Second World War. It started in the second half of 1944 and can be divided into four phases:

- the flight of ethnic Germans from those areas annexed by the Germans after 1940
- the forced evacuation of Germans by the retreating German army. This was often announced at short notice, but was generally well organized

- the disorganized flight of hundreds of thousands of Germans who had not been evacuated in time
- the forced migration of Germans from the east in the period March 1945 to 1948 (59: 60)

The first phase started immediately after it became apparent what had happened in Nemmersdorf. Large groups of Germans, consisting mainly of women, children and the elderly, set off with horse and cart; their journeys were called 'treks' after the caravans of the South African Boers. In the first weeks the roads were not congested, but that changed as more and more people decided to pack up and flee from the Red Army. Explicit orders from Gauleiter Koch to stay and defend the homeland were ignored. The treks were often led by Allied prisoners of war who had worked on the farms and in the factories and who preferred evacuation with the Germans to an uncertain future under the Soviets. The refugees had to find their way west over icy roads and in

snowstorms. Horses slipped on the roads and carts often broke down. Food and drink were scarce, and as the flow of refugees increased it became increasingly difficult to find places to stay in the villages along the way. Soviet fighter and bomber pilots showed no mercy, and the treks were often machine-gunned or bombed from the air.

Because the overland route was long and dangerous, and the Soviets had cut more and more roads to the west, large numbers of refugees made for the coast in the hope of being evacuated by sea. The fate of refugees from the Königsberg region in the east and more southern regions was particularly harrowing. At the end of 1944, large numbers arrived on the coast with the aim of crossing over the water of the bay, the Frische Haff, to the Pilau

Children on a fully loaded wagon on their way to an uncertain future. During the fighting and the flight to the west in the spring of 1945, a total of 1,000,000 civilians died.

peninsula. The bay is about 20km wide, but the water was frozen over and no ships could be deployed. The refugees tried to cross the Haff on what was in many places very thin ice. The crossing often took more than eight hours, and many children and elderly people died of exhaustion and cold.

During the crossings the refugees were machine-gunned and bombed by the Soviet air force, and many disappeared into the waters of the Haff with their horses and carts. In February, when the temperature rose and the ice became even thinner, the crossing became even more dangerous: it was unclear where the weak spots were, and the journey began to resemble Russian roulette. It is estimated, however, that ultimately no fewer than 500,000 Germans from the East Prussian region successfully made the crossing over the Haff to Pilau. From there they could be evacuated by sea, albeit under constant bombardment by the Soviets.

### Evacuations by sea

The evacuations by sea were commanded by Admiral K. Engelhardt, who chartered every available ship for the rescue operation in the Eastern Baltic. He had a total of 790 vessels at his disposal, from the Kriegsmarine as well as from shipping companies and private individuals. Some ships made as many as twelve trips. The operation's duration, size and distance made it the largest ever evacuation by sea, but this was the fastest and safest way to get to the west. In total, between 2,000,000 and 3,000,000 civilians and soldiers, the latter mostly wounded, were transported up to May 1945. About 1 per cent of this group, between 20,000 and 25,000 men, did not survive the journey because their ships were torpedoed by submarines or bombed from the air. Probably the greatest maritime disaster ever was the sinking of the *Goya* on 16 April 1945 by the Soviet submarine *L-3*. This freighter was carrying between 6,000 and 7,000 civilians, of whom only 183 survived the torpedo attack.

The passengers on the *Wilhelm Gustloff* did not fare much better. The ship, with thousands of evacuees on board, was leading a convoy en route from Pilau to Mecklenburg when she was torpedoed by the submarine *S-13* on 30 January. Several hours out, she was hit by three torpedoes and began to list to port. The sea was rough, the deck was covered in ice and the lifeboats were frozen in. Protected by the rest of the convoy, the ship slowly sank, but due to the weather conditions only 838 people could be saved.

Another drama was the sinking of the *Steuben* on 10 February. This was a so-called *Verwundetentransporter*, with 3.500 wounded soldiers on board. All perished. This type of vessel could have been considered a *Lazarettschiff* (hospital ship), but she did not enjoy the protection of the Hague and Geneva Conventions since she had not been registered as such. All *Lazarettschiffe* and almost all *Verwundetentransporter* were recognizable as such by their white paint and red crosses. In practice, however, this made no difference because the Soviet Union simply disregarded the Conventions. A total of thirteen *Lazarettschiffe* and twenty-one *Verwundetentransporter* took part in the evacuation, and four *Lazarettschiffe* and eight *Verwundetentransporter* (25 and 38 per cent respectively) were sunk. Since these figures were higher than the total percentage of vessels sunk, it proves that the Soviets explicitly targeted these ships with their defenceless cargo.

Nevertheless, the Germans successfully managed to evacuate large numbers of refugees by sea until the very last moment. On 6 May, for example, 43,000 refugees were evacuated from the Hela peninsula, and on 8 May, the day on which the unconditional German surrender took effect, 25,000 soldiers from Hela reached Schleswig-Holstein. Many ships were still underway at midnight on 8 May, the time at which all hostilities were to cease; all ships that were still sailing at that time had to head to the nearest port. Ships carrying refugees generally tried to sail to ports held by the British and Americans. The *Julius Rütgers*, an old tanker with 300 people on board, was discovered by the Soviets sailing west in the early morning of 9 May, and torpedo planes promptly attacked her, but miraculously only one passenger was injured.

The Soviets showed no mercy to civilians. Here, a woman searches for her belongings among the remains of a trek hit by Soviet planes.

Another tanker, the *Liselotte Friedrich*, was less fortunate. On 9 May she was on her way to the nearest Danish port as agreed, but was torpedoed and sank off the island of Bornholm. Even weeks after the armistice, ships carrying refugees managed to reach the west safely, the last one docking after a long journey with a broken compass.

In addition to evacuation by road and by sea, a substantial number of people were also transported by train.

The way the Soviets treated civilians did not go unnoticed. George Kennan, then attached to the US embassy in Moscow and the initiator of the Truman Doctrine after the war, was deeply shocked. In his memoirs he wrote:

> The horrors that unfolded in these regions have no parallel in modern European history. There were large areas where, by all existing evidence, hardly a native man, woman, or child had survived the passing of the Soviet units; and no one believes that they had all succeeded in fleeing to the west. (59: 60)

His observations and analysis had a decisive influence on post-war American policy. Field Marshal Montgomery expressed himself even more directly:

> It quickly became clear from their attitude that the Russians, albeit good fighters, were in fact barbaric Asians, who had never known the same civilization as the rest of Europe. Their approach to every problem was completely different from ours and their behaviour, especially towards women, was absolutely reprehensible in our eyes. In certain parts of the Russian zone, there were no Germans left. They had all fled before the advance of the barbarians. (59: 72)

Once refugees arrived in the west they shared the fate of many inhabitants of large and medium-sized German cities, which suffered from the devastating British and Americans strategy of area bombing. When Dresden was bombed on the night of 13/14 February, there were approximately 600,000 refugees from Silesia in and around the city, most of whom had fled there by train. The city had never been bombed in previous years, because there were no military targets there to justify an attack. This did not stop the Allies from attempting to level the city in three consecutive air raids by more than 1,500 planes. The resulting firestorms destroyed 90 per cent of the ancient city and killed between 60,000 and 100,000 people.

**Strategic bombing**

We have seen that German industrial output rose to unprecedented levels in 1944, despite massive Allied bombing in the same period. It turned out that the bombers often had the greatest difficulty hitting their targets, even if these were whole cities, let alone individual military targets. That is why 'dehousing' (bombing the houses of workers) is often mentioned as the second strategic goal of bombing. In practice, this amounted to bombing whole cities, although the bombers did not always manage to hit the right places, as shown by the bombing of Nijmegen and Enschede in the Netherlands, both mistaken for German cities. The figures show the negligible effect that bombing had on industrial output. By the end of 1944, after a year of the heaviest bombing ever, only 6.5 per cent of Germany's industrial plant had been damaged. Six months later, not only had this been replaced, but German industrial capacity had even grown considerably. The same had happened in Great Britain in 1940: despite German bombing, only 1.7 per cent of British industry had been damaged. It is questionable whether the Allies' investment in bombers, the training of specialist air force personnel and all the necessary infrastructure justified the final result achieved in destruction of plant and production capacity in Germany. In contrast, the damage caused by Allied bombing to private property, infrastructure and public facilities throughout Europe was enormous. (33: 332–5)

## 2. The course of events

The Soviet offensive had come to a halt on the banks of the Vistula in July 1944. The Red Army had witnessed the Warsaw uprising and its bloody suppression, and had not intervened. The question was, what they were waiting for. The answer was simple: they had advanced at a rapid pace over the past year but had suffered heavy losses. They were now on the borders of the Greater German Reich and assumed that the Germans would resist as stubbornly as they had in recent years.

During December 1944, Gehlen, Chief of Intelligence, was able to report to Guderian, Chief of the General Staff, that he had identified 225 infantry divisions and 22 tank corps between the Baltic Sea and the Carpathians. Hitler assumed that Gehlen's analysis was based on unreliable information and deception by the Soviets. In his opinion, the enemy were not capable of fielding such a large force, and he refused to consider calling off the planned offensive in the Ardennes and deploying some of the divisions thus released to the Eastern Front.

On that front, Heeresgruppe Nord's twenty-six divisions had become isolated during the Soviet offensive, and Guderian wanted to evacuate these units to the German defence line. Hitler, of course, wanted nothing to do with this. In addition, he refused to permit a second defence line to be built 20km behind the first on the Vistula. The idea behind this was that if the Soviets attacked, German units could immediately fall back on this second line and allow the familiar Soviet artillery offensive to hit the abandoned first one. The Germans would also have more room to manoeuvre in order to deal with the Soviet attack. Hitler refused to accept so much territory being given up without a fight and ordered the construction of a second line only 3km behind the first. As history would show, the Soviet artillery offensive was able to hit both lines, so the construction of the latter proved futile. Hitler, of course, did not hesitate to blame the generals for positioning the two lines too close together. Only when the minutes of the various meetings were put on the table did he accept that he was the one who had ordered the distance between the lines to be reduced to 3km. The ordinary German soldier could not, of course, influence these pointless discussions, but it was he and his comrades who paid the price for Hitler's faulty orders.

Intelligence services advised Guderian to expect a Soviet offensive in the north around 12 January. There, the Soviets had an 11: 1 preponderance in infantry, 7: 1 in tanks and 20: 1 in artillery. The German positions would be further weakened by the transfer of the IV SS Panzer Corps from the front in Poland to Hungary in an unsuccessful attempt to relieve Budapest. Guderian's observation was that the entire front in Poland was no more than a house of cards: if the Soviets broke through, it would collapse completely.

The Germans faced five Soviet Fronts, from north to south:

• the 3rd Belorussian Front under Chernyakhovsky in Lithuania, aimed at East Prussia
• the 2nd Belorussian Front under Rokossovsky, aimed at the Baltic coast around Danzig
• the 1st Belorussian Front under Zhukov east of Warsaw, ready to advance west
• the 1st Ukrainian Front under Konev, aimed at Silesia
• the 4th Ukrainian Front under Petrov, aimed at Poland and Slovakia

The Red Army's main target was Silesia, Germany's second industrial region after the Ruhr, at least on paper. In addition, Stalin never lost sight of Berlin, and it was the task of Zhukov, the prominent commander of the 1st Belorussian Front, to advance in the direction of the German capital. The Soviets were also more mobile now that almost all of their infantry was motorized, thanks to the Lend-Lease programme. This would allow them to advance at a rapid pace without the previous need for frequent halts.

As predicted, the Soviet offensive was launched on 12 January. It began with an attack by the 1st Ukrainian Front, which broke out of the bridgehead

An SJU-152 tank ploughs its way through a forest in Poland.

at Baranov. This Front consisted of seventy divisions, which advanced 30km west within three days and then swung north, threatening the rear of the units opposite the 1st Belorussian Front. By 14 January the latter Front had moved to emerge behind Warsaw in a broad northward movement, while the other wing took Radom on 16 January. North of the 1st Belorussian Front, the 2nd Belorussian Front had launched its own offensive on 14 January and had already broken through the German southern defence lines in East Prussia. To complete the nightmare for the Germans, on 15 January the 4th Ukrainian Front began its attack, targeting Jaslo, south of Krakow.

Warsaw fell on 17 January and Krakow on the 19th. The Soviet offensive continued at a rapid pace, and after a week they had advanced 150km across a 600km-wide front. In the first week they took 25,000 German prisoners of war, in the second week, 86,000. The Germans were simply not mobile enough to escape the advancing Soviets, the loss of Romanian oil and the lack of industrial capacity to produce vehicles forcing them to continue the war on foot.

Meanwhile, the Soviet offensive seemed unstoppable. On 20 January, units of the 1st Ukrainian Front reached Silesia and the battle continued on German territory. The events of October 1944 in Nemmersdorf made it clear that the Soviets would show little mercy towards civilians and non-combatants. In the north, the commander of Heeresgruppe Nord, Reinhardt, was concerned that his Heeresgruppe would be isolated and requested permission to withdraw from the Narve region. This request was rejected by Hitler. Hossbach, the commander of the Forth Army, launched an offensive against the orders of

SU-76 self-propelled guns in combat near the Oder.

Hitler to the west on 22 January to reconnect with the German lines. Hossbach did not inform Reinhardt until a day later, and Hitler did not learn of this initiative until the Lötzen Fortress was taken by the Soviets without a fight. Reinhardt and Hossbach were promptly both sacked. On the same day, units of the 1st Ukrainian Front reached the Oder, near the main industrial areas of Silesia, over a 60km-wide front. By 26 January the front had already grown to 90km in the area south of Breslau.

By 20 January the 2nd Belorussian Front, advancing rapidly into East Prussia, had reached Tannenberg. The Germans had managed to move Hindenburg's sarcophagus in time and had blown up the monument commemorating his victory in 1914. The 2nd Belorussian Front continued its advance towards the Baltic coast and reached Allenstein on 21 January, cutting the main east-west rail link on the same day. On 26 January, the Soviet vanguard reached the

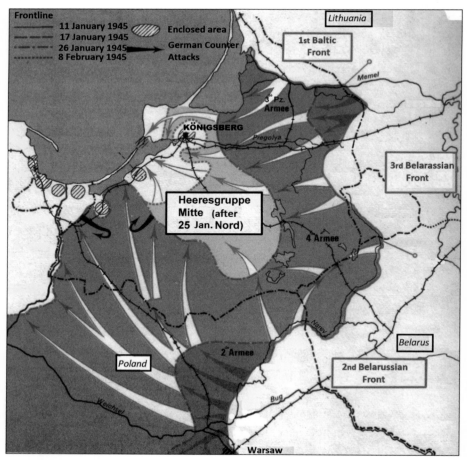

The advance of the Soviets to the Baltic coast in January 1945.

Gulf of Danzig. This isolated the German units, forty divisions in all, in East Prussia. Some of them retreated to Königsberg, others took refuge in three hedgehog positions, surrounded by the enemy.

In the centre, Zhukov advanced quickly over the Polish plain and on 23 January surrounded Posen, which was heavily defended, then entered Bromberg. Zhukov simply bypassed Posen, leaving it to be taken in the future, and reached Brandenburg and Pomerania in the last week of January, no more than 150km from Berlin. While Posen was under siege, Guderian was restructuring his forces. Heeresgruppe A was renamed Heeresgruppe Mitte, and Heeresgruppe Mitte was renamed Heeresgruppe Nord. In addition, a new Heeresgruppe was formed, which had to operate between the two, and Hitler believed that Heinrich Himmler would be ideally suited to lead it. Himmler, a loyal servant of the Führer, would never dream of retreating, even in the face of superior enemy numbers. Himmler's only experience of command was with Heeresgruppe Oberrhein, whose offensive had been halted by the Western Allies without much difficulty. And so the new Heeresgruppe Weichsel (Vistula) acquired a new commander with no combat experience but who had to prevent the entire front in East Prussia from disintegrating and the Soviets from reaching Berlin before the end of February. In addition, the only substantial reinforcements that could be found after the Ardennes offensive had come to a halt, the Sixth Panzer Army, had been sent by Hitler not to the east, but to Hungary to relieve Budapest.

The Soviets, meanwhile, were not standing still, and by the end of January most of Silesia was in their hands. Speer concluded that the war was lost now that industrial production from this region had been lost; the war could only be fought with what was available.

The Soviets did not delay. On 28 January, Zhukov crossed the Oder at Lüben and Steinau, 60km north-west of Breslau. On 31 January he was at Küstrin on the Oder, 60km from Berlin. In the first week of February he crossed the Oder at Küstrin and Frankfurt and managed to establish bridgeheads there. However, the offensive stalled due to the onset of a thaw. The Soviets became bogged down, and the melting of the ice on the Oder turned it into a real barrier again. Zhukov had to be satisfied with these two bridgeheads and meanwhile tried to re-order his long logistical lines.

However, the units of the 1st Ukrainian Front under Konev still had combat power left and on 9 February they broke out of their bridgehead at Breslau in the south and advanced north-west along the west bank of the Oder. On 13 February they reached Sommerfeld and on 15 February the River Neisse at its junction with the Oder. Konev and Zhukov could now combine their forces, and the German lines were now so shortened that even with their

Tiger II tanks (*Königtigers*) shelter in the protection of a forest. The dominance of the Soviet Air Force greatly limited the mobility of tanks and other units.

limited forces they were able to halt the Soviets for the time being. In addition, German units still remained encircled in various places, which the Soviets had to take into account. For example, in Courland there were twenty infantry and two armoured divisions, which were left alone because the Soviets did not yet

---

**Low morale**

Attempts had already been made to reduce the pressure on the German units in and around Budapest. In early January there had been three offensives, Konrad I, II and III, in which Schwere Panzer Abteilung 503 was involved, but not every soldier showed the same commitment. When this unit had to seize a Soviet trench on 9 January, the commander had to personally motivate the infantry to join the advance:

> Our own infantry remained behind our tanks and made no attempt to leave cover. Then I saw Hauptmann von Diest-Körber climb out of his tank and point his right arm forward, trying to get the infantry to advance. A scene from an old painting of a battle! We held our breath. We tried to pin the Soviets down with our fire and cover him. However, the infantry did not follow him. He stood alone at the edge of the trench and hastily hid behind our tanks. In the end we managed to get some infantrymen to join the advance.

Von Diest-Körber said: 'With the help of three corporals and a machine gun, we managed to take the trench and take 300 Soviets prisoner.' (57: 166)

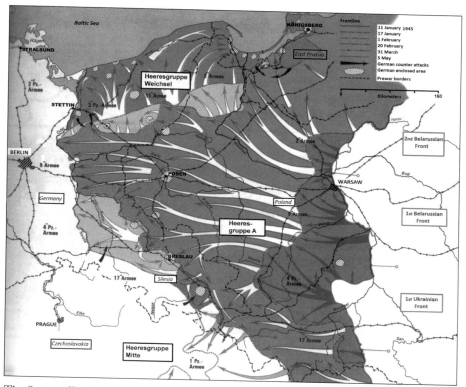

The Soviet offensive towards the Oder and Neisse in January/February 1945.

consider it necessary to reduce the size of the pocket and clear it of Germans. Around the city of Königsberg were the remnants of Heeresgruppe Nord, consisting of nineteen infantry and five armoured divisions. Here the Soviets were more active because the Germans occupied important road and rail connections. Guderian wanted to evacuate these units as quickly as possible so that they could somehow be used in the battle for Berlin. Finally, Hitler allowed the withdrawal of four infantry divisions and an armoured division from Courland. Although the other divisions tied up Soviet units, they would no longer play any significant role.

In addition to the action in Poland, there was a lot happening in the south. Budapest was completely surrounded in January, but both Germans and Soviets were determined to control the city. Some assaults had already been beaten off by the Germans, but the Soviets were preparing for a final attack.

On 18 January, the Germans launched an offensive between Lake Balaton and the forests of Bakony in an attempt to relieve the city. Although they reached the banks of the Danube, the Soviets managed on the same day to take the southernmost parts of Budapest. By 20 January the German offensive had

**The last ride of the Tigers**

In January 1945 in Hungary, Schwere Panzer Abteilung 509 was the only battalion fully equipped with heavy tanks, the Tiger II or Königstiger. Most Schwere Panzer Abteilungen at that time consisted of a core of Tiger I or II tanks surrounded by PzKpfw IVs and Panthers. On 18 January, the unit was deployed in the independent role originally assigned to it: to force a breakthrough in the enemy front followed by a deep penetration behind enemy lines. At 0800 hrs the forty-five Königstigers advanced in a V formation with the 1st and 3rd Companies in the lead and the 2nd Company as a second wave behind them. These forty-five tanks must have been an impressive sight. Throughout the morning, they fought their way through multiple Soviet defence lines, reaching their primary objective by noon. However, they suffered losses, especially among key personnel: all tank commanders of the 3rd Company were wounded, as well as the commander of the Abteilung itself. The commander of the 2nd Company, who had emerged from the battle relatively unscathed, was given command of the Abteilung, and a non-commissioned officer took over the 3rd Company. The remaining eighteen Königstigers launched an attack at 1400 hrs and drove the Soviets back to the Sarviz Canal. With 50 metres to go, the Soviets blew up the bridge over the canal, and since there was no other bridge that could carry the Königstigers, the attack continued without them. Further analysis shows that the Abteilung lost seven Tigers to enemy fire and four were damaged, while and no fewer than sixteen were halted by mechanical problems. They had, however, destroyed more than twenty Soviet tanks and many anti-tank guns. (57: 169–70)

lost momentum, although sporadic fighting was still taking place. The Soviets launched a counter-offensive targeting German units south of Lake Balaton on 30 January, followed by a second offensive between Lake Balaton and the Danube on 31 January. Clearly, their ambition was to cross the Danube and advance north.

Hitler had not been fooled by these developments: he wanted to retake the Danube in order to gain access to the Hungarian oil fields and was repositioning his SS divisions for this purpose. This brought him into conflict with Guderian, who wanted to use the SS divisions in Silesia and Pomerania for a pincer movement aimed at Zhukov's forward units. The Third Panzer Army was to attack in the north via the Pyritz-Arnswalde line and the SS Panzer divisions of the Sixth Panzer Army in the south via the Glogau-Guben line. Hitler wanted nothing to do with this, and the Sixth Panzer Army, led by the famous Sepp Dietrich, continued its journey to Hungary. The Allies got wind of the movement of this Army and bombed the more than 200 trains carrying the troops. Since Hitler also had no intention of evacuating his forces from Courland, Guderian had to make do with the units he had.

And that meant that Himmler had to take the lead with his Heeresgruppe Weichsel. Guderian pinned his hopes on Wenck, an able officer whom he had thrust upon Himmler as his chief of staff. Since Himmler, realizing that he had little to contribute, spent most of his time in his train carriage, Wenck had become the de facto commander of Heeresgruppe Weichsel. Guderian knew, however, that he could do no more than delay the Soviets for some time in the hope that Hitler would realize that it was only a matter of time before Berlin was attacked. The German offensive was due to start on 26 February, and Guderian could only wait and see.

## The German offensive

The offensive got off to a reasonably good start, thanks in part to Wenck's skill as a commander, and on 16 and 17 February the German units advanced steadily. However, on 17 February Wenck was injured in a car accident. He had been in Berlin that afternoon to discuss the state of affairs with Hitler, but on the way back his driver had become sleepy and Wenck himself had got behind the wheel. However, he too nodded off and crashed into a bridge. He was seriously injured and would not be able to play a significant role for the foreseeable future; the German offensive slowly but surely came to a halt. Wenck was replaced by Krebs, who although a skilled staff officer had little experience of operational command. On 18 February Himmler also began to take an active part in the battle, and when the German units hit minefields and strong anti-tank positions, the offensive came to a halt; it was effectively over when Himmler ordered the Eleventh Panzer Army to regroup. All the Germans could do now was wait for the Soviet attack on Berlin, which had already been expected in February.

The position of the Soviets did not follow their normal pattern. Although they had reached the Oder, they occupied a narrow front and their northern and southern flanks were vulnerable. Previously they had made sure to create a broad front after advancing deep into enemy territory. This gave them more options for follow-up offensives and avoided rendering them vulnerable to attacks from the flank. The German offensive had alerted them to the dangers to their flanks, and they now began to clear the east bank of the Oder of German units.

This lull in the fighting was welcomed by the Germans. They had lost 600,000 men in recent months, only half of whom could be replaced. In addition, war production had begun to be seriously disrupted. Instead of the 1,500,000 artillery and tank shells needed per month on the Eastern Front, only 367,000 were produced in January. Fuel was also growing scarce, and the Luftwaffe could only be deployed at critical moments or when no other resources were available.

With the aim of clearing the flanks, the 2nd Belorussian Front under Rokossovsky was the first to act. His objective was the Baltic coast, and on 24 February his units resumed their offensive. Within two days they were halfway to the coast, cutting the Third and Fourth Panzer Armies in half. Due to a lack of fuel and ammunition, the Germans could do little more than stand and watch. On 1 March Rokossovsky reached the coast. On the same day Zhukov began his northward attack, and his units in turn cut through the Third Panzer Army. On 4 March, he too reached the Baltic coast, and his right wing made contact with Rokossovsky's left. En route he had surrounded Kolberg, where the Germans would offer fierce resistance until 18 March. Zhukov's units would spend the next two weeks pushing the remnants of Third Panzer Army back to the coast. Rokossovsky targeted Danzig and Gdynia, but it would take him until the end of March to break all German resistance in this region.

In the south, the 1st Ukrainian Front under Konev focused from mid-March on clearing northern Silesia. The Germans suspected that this was the beginning of a large outflanking movement with the aim of advancing to Prague and then attacking Berlin from the south-west behind the back of Heeresgruppe Mitte. However, the Soviets did not entertain this grand ambition; they just aimed to push the Germans slowly back to the west. They knew that the enemy were not strong enough to stop them and they wanted to husband their strength. Konev's front moved on 15 March, and on 17 March he succeeded in encircling the German LVI Corps south-west of Oppeln in a pincer movement. With this resistance removed, Konev was able to advance to the Neisse. The Germans still assumed that this was the prelude to a much larger offensive, but they were mistaken; on 31 March, Konev's units came to a final standstill. The Soviets were now free to roll up the last pockets of resistance east of the Oder-Neisse line.

### The last German offensive

The Germans would launch their final offensive in Hungary in the following days. There, the units of the Sixth Panzer Army, which had just arrived by train from the Ardennes, would win the Panzerwaffe's last victory. The I SS Panzer Corps, consisting of the Leibstandarte SS Adolf Hitler and the Hitlerjugend Panzer Division, launched an offensive aimed at a bridgehead of the 7th Guards Corps. The position was manned only by infantry, while the closest tank units further behind the front were being re-supplied. On 17 February the Germans attacked the Soviets, who after months of success had not expected any serious German resistance, with 150 tanks and assault guns. Surprise was complete, and the Soviets were rapidly driven back; on

The Soviets push ever deeper into Germany. Here, Soviet tanks drive through a newly captured German provincial town near Berlin.

24 February substantial casualties forced them to abandon the bridgehead, leaving all their heavy equipment behind.

In line with this success, Hitler planned an offensive along two routes in Hungary. The intention was to cut the 3rd Ukrainian Front under Tolbukhin in half in two phases. The first phase was an attack between Lake Balaton and Velence, targeting Dunapentele, 70km south of Budapest. Then the units would split so that one part could advance north and another south along the Danube, thus neutralizing Tolbukhin's units on the west bank of the river. The German force consisted of the Sixth Panzer Army under Dietrich and the Sixth Army under Balck. The Sixth Panzer Army consisted of five Panzer divisions, two Schwere Panzer Abteilungen with Tiger II tanks, two infantry and two

German units grouping for the attack. This well camouflaged Panther tank has a full complement of infantrymen on board.

cavalry divisions. The Sixth Army consisted of five Panzer divisions and two infantry divisions. The flanks would be covered in the north by the Third Hungarian Army and in the south by the Second Panzer Army. Attacks from Yugoslavia would be carried out by Heeresgruppe E under Weichs towards Mohacs on the Danube in Hungary. Their aim was to make contact with the units advancing south along the river. Some of the German units would advance to Budapest to retake the city, which had fallen to the Soviets on 28 February. The operation was named *Frühlingserwachen* (spring awakening). The Germans had assembled a formidable force. In total they had 431,000 men, 5,630 pieces of artillery and 877 tanks and assault guns at their disposal, while the Luftwaffe could deploy 850 aircraft.

The build-up of troops on the German side had not gone unnoticed by the Soviets. Tolbukhin postponed his attack on Vienna and awaited the German attack. His idea was to hold and exhaust the Germans, then launch an offensive himself. As at Kursk, the Soviet units built a solid defensive system in depth between Lake Balaton and the Danube. Tolbukhin had 407,000 men, 7,000 pieces of artillery and 407 tanks, while the Soviet Air Force could deploy 965 aircraft.

The weather was not with the Germans. After the cold of January and the thaw of February, a real blizzard raged the day before the offensive, which began on 6 March. The Sixth Army advanced on schedule, but the Sixth Panzer Army struggled to get out of the starting blocks. Only the 1st SS Panzer Corps moved; the 2nd SS Panzer Corps postponed its start until the next day. That day, it also started to thaw and units got stuck in the low-lying areas that were waterlogged and intersected by ditches and channels. However, they persevered, but without the impetus these armoured troops had once shown. Tolbukhin was forced to deploy his reserves but saved the 9th Guards Corps for his own counter-offensive. The 1st SS Panzer Corps reached the Sio Canal on 10 March and managed to establish two bridgeheads on the other side of the canal on 11 March, but failed to break out. In other places, however, the Sixth Panzer Army had gained no more than 10km of ground and had to continue fighting hard until 16 March. On that day the Soviet counter-offensive began, which was in effect the delayed start of the attack on Vienna. Tolbukhin focused on his final objective, attacked the Third Hungarian Army, which promptly fell apart, and advanced on Vienna. On 18 March the Germans were forced to break off their offensive. The Sixth Panzer Army had to fill the vacuum created by the disappearance of the Hungarians as quickly as possible to avoid being cut off and allowing the Soviets to advance rapidly towards Vienna. However, they were too late, and all they could do was fight their way back to friendly lines.

Operation *Frühlingserwachen* cost the Germans more than 500 tanks and assault guns, 300 pieces of artillery and more than 40,000 men. As a result, their units slowly but surely began to disintegrate and the Soviets took the initiative. The morale of the units of the Sixth Panzer Army which had managed to escape was broken, and there was talk of surrender. This was all the more surprising because the core of the Army consisted of Waffen SS units: the fact that they wanted to throw in the towel shows how widespread defeatism had become. On 23 March, Tolbukhin ordered the attack on Vienna, and on 4 April the Soviets crossed the border into Austria. On 7 April they reached Vienna, where the Germans surrendered six days later. Hitler accused Sepp Dietrich, one of his oldest comrades, of allowing his units to make too little effort in the defence of the city and demanded that the Waffen SS men remove their insignia. Sepp Dietrich refused and replied to Hitler that he would rather be shot than carry out this order. The Waffen SS, however, had already made up their minds; men of Leibstandarte Adolf Hitler removed their insignia together with their medals and sent them to Hitler in a bucket.

These events illustrate the hopeless situation in which the German army now found itself. The Wehrmacht was only capable of local counter-offensives, and these were generally stopped quickly by the Soviets. The enemy simply had too many tanks, planes and guns, while the Germans' fuel shortages severely limited

In the spring of 1945 these SU-76 self-propelled artillery pieces are advancing in the Carpathians. Unlike the SU-122 and the JSU-152, the SU-76 was lightly armoured and had the proven 76.2mm howitzer.

their range and meant that they could only reach targets nearby. Tanks, assault guns and tank destroyers could still inflict heavy casualties on the Soviets and temporarily hold back their advance, but in the process the Germans' combat strength was steadily declining. Few reinforcements reached the combat units, and remaining units were combined into ad hoc Panzer Divisions, which were a shadow of their predecessors and only had a limited number of tanks. They were combined into corps and instead of the usual numbers were given exotic names such as Clausewitz, Feldherrenhalle 2, Holstein, Munchberg, Juteborg and Kurmark.

The Soviets approached Graz on 15 April, but then surprisingly halted. They knew what the Germans could only suspect: the battle for Berlin was about to begin, and they did not want to needlessly waste lives just to win more territory.

In the north, meanwhile, the Soviets had focused on capturing Königsberg, the capital of East Prussia. At the beginning of April they drove back the German units into a small area around the city. On 6 April the attack on the city itself began, and on 8 April they reached its outskirts, having isolated the city from the German units in the Samland and from the sea. As a result, evacuation of German troops and civilians was no longer possible. Resistance collapsed in the following days, and on 10 April the Germans surrendered, a total of 27,000 being marched into captivity.

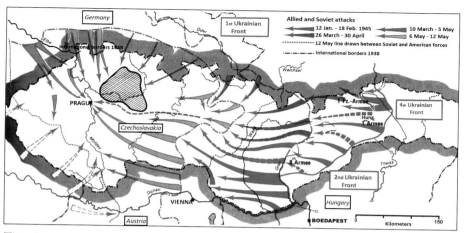

The advance of the Soviets towards Vienna in March/April 1945.

**The end**

Hela was also where the war ended for Horst Krönke. His Abteilung had had no tanks for several weeks and could only wait for the end of the war. While his men searched for food, he went to the harbour of Hela. There he found three *Schnellboote* (speed boats). He asked the guard at the pier if he could speak to the flotilla commander and was allowed through. Krönke had a friendly conversation with Kapitänleutnant Howaldt, who was not much older than himself, and asked if they could leave with him to find safety. That was certainly possible, he was told, and departure would take place within two hours. Krönke was invited to stay on board, but asked if his men could come too. That was not so easy, said Kapitänleutnant Howaldt, with all the refugees who would also want to come along. Krönke then bade farewell to Howaldt and returned to his men. After everything they had been through together, he wanted to stay with his comrades. On 8 May he was captured and taken to a large PoW camp, where he was separated from his men. He never saw them again, and he was not released until June 1948. (22: 129–31)

The last months of the war also saw a slew of new appointments, such as Himmler being given command of Heeresgruppe Weichsel. Guderian, after a number of run-ins with Hitler, was sent on sick leave on 28 March for six weeks. Keitel, who had lost contact with the reality of the battlefield, suggested Bad Liebenstein as a place for Guderian to convalesce, only to be informed that it was already in American hands; and on being offered the alternative of Bad Sachsa in the Harz, Guderian replied that he would prefer somewhere that was not going to be taken by the enemy in the next 48 hours. (41: 228)

## The Battle for Berlin

The Eastern Front had one final act: the battle for Berlin. The situation for the Germans was hopeless, representing exactly what Hitler had warned of in *Mein Kampf*: a war on two fronts which were now rapidly approaching each other. The British and Americans had crossed the Rhine and occupied the coal mines in the Saar. This made it no longer possible to produce Ersatz petrol, the only fuel still available after the loss of the Ploesti fields in Romania and the smaller oilfields in Hungary. Without fuel, the Luftwaffe could not fly and tanks and other vehicles could not move. In addition, the industrial areas of the Ruhr and Silesia had been lost, so that Germany was no longer able to produce ammunition and other war materiel. The entire railway system had collapsed, so troops could no longer be moved. It was clear to everyone that the war was over. The main objective of the units on the Eastern Front, especially those of the Waffen SS, was now to stay out of the hands of the Soviets. They made every effort, especially the units that came from Estonia or Lithuania, to be taken prisoner by the British or Americans. And not without reason: the Soviets showed no mercy in executing German officers and men in key positions on the basis of alleged war crimes – that is, simply fighting for the losing side in a devastating war.

Although the British and Americans reached the Elbe they did not advance further to Berlin. This was in line with the agreements on the future division

The end is near: exhaustion can be read on the face of this German soldier.

of Germany. There was the fear in the background of a 'Werewolf' scenario, in which German units would retreat to the Alpine region and continue the fight, perhaps until 1946. But that did not materialize. The Allies also accepted the fact that the Soviets had a right to exact revenge after the devastation the Germans had inflicted on their country in the preceding years.

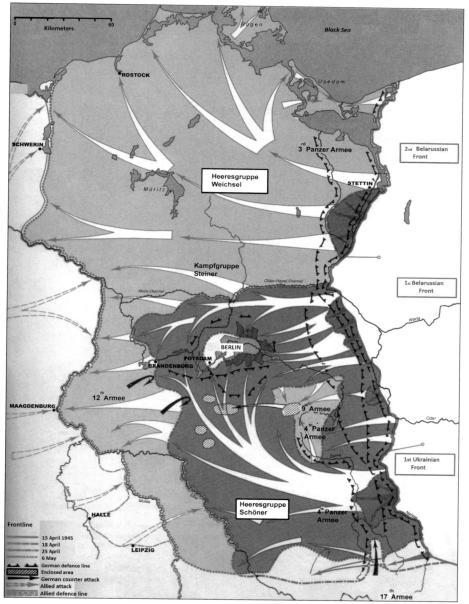

The last Soviet offensives and the encirclement of Berlin in April/May 1945.

Hitler, the author of all this destruction, had arrived in Berlin in January 1945 to personally direct the final stages of the war. It was clear that the Soviets would have little sympathy for him once they conquered the city and he fell into their hands. At the beginning of March, when the Soviets had reached the Oder and the British and Americans were doing their best to level Berlin to the ground from the air, Hitler and his loyalists had retired to his bunker under the Reich Chancellery and remained there until his suicide.

The Soviets had regrouped in the first weeks of April. They set up three fronts on the eastern side of the Oder and Neisse, namely:

- in the north, the 2nd Belorussian Front under Rokossovsky
- in the middle, the 1st Belorussian Front under Zhukov
- in the south, the 1st Ukrainian Front under Konev

There was some friction between the last two commanders about which of them should take Berlin. Given his relationship with Stalin, Zhukov was better placed. Eventually, Konev would focus on an offensive across the Elbe between Dresden and Wittenberg and then advance through Dresden to Prague, while

Soviet units are grouping in the run-up to one of the offensives. A mix of vehicles on display consisting of Soviet trucks, a JSU-152 and US Lend-Lease GMC trucks and a jeep.

to Zhukov was given the honour of taking Berlin. The Soviets could deploy 2,500,000 men and 6,250 tanks, 41,600 artillery pieces and mortars, and 3,255 'Stalin organs', in addition to 7,500 aircraft, for this final offensive of the war. One of the main concerns of the Soviets was the possibility of the British and Americans occupying parts of Germany designated for them. For example, the Americans were at the Elbe in an area that would belong to the Soviets after the war. In response, the Soviets left open the possibility of also advancing into Czechoslovakia. They would advance on a broad front, with Rokossovsky not joining the party until four days into the offensive, as he was still busy repositioning his units from East Prussia and Pomerania.

In early April, Zhukov was given overall command of all units involved in the offensive and he handed command of the 1st Belorussian Front over to Sokolovsky so that he could focus on the main thrust. While the British and Americans did their best to save as many men's lives as possible, Zhukov prepared a classic Soviet offensive en masse, in which the efficient deployment of the units was a secondary consideration. Meanwhile, the German units in the west offered little resistance against the Western allies, with the intent of allowing the British and Americans to advance further into Germany.

## The final preparations

The Germans could do little against the might of the Red Army. Between the 1st Belorussian Front and Berlin was the Ninth Army, consisting of fourteen divisions, none of which was fully equipped. To the north, opposite the thirty-three divisions of the 2nd Belorussian Front, was the Third Panzer Army with eleven divisions, also not fully equipped. The Germans had less than the minimum amount of ammunition at their disposal, while their opponents had more than enough. The defensive Wotan Line, which ran about 15–20km west of the Oder, had been built in a hurry and equipped with flak guns. To make up for the shortage of troops, men from the Luftwaffe and Kriegsmarine had been recruited for service at the front. A total of 35,000 men from these arms were scraped together, none of whom had been trained in fighting a land war. Then there was the Volkssturm, the civilian militia armed with machine guns and Panzerfausten and generally even less well trained than the British Home Guard in 1940.

When it became clear to the Germans that the Allies would divide Germany, Hitler also decided to divide its administrative apparatus. To command the north he appointed Dönitz, the commander-in-chief of the Kriegsmarine, and in the south, Kesselring, an able Luftwaffe officer. On 15 April, Hitler handed over command of the units in the city to Heinrici, the commander of the Heeresgruppe Weichsel, who soon found out that Hitler had made few

A woman accompanies her husband on his way to the front near Stettin. In the spring of 1945, the last reserves of manpower were scraped together.

preparations to defend the city except undermining bridges and buildings. In Hitler's eyes, the German people deserved to lose the war, and the destruction of Berlin was therefore only fitting.

The storm broke on 16 April. The 1st Belorussian Front attacked on a narrow front between the Finow Canal and the area north of Frankfurt on the Oder. The 1st Ukrainian Front attacked between Forst and the area defended by Heeresgruppe Mitte. The attack of the 1st Belorussian Front was held up on the first day by stiff resistance from the Ninth Army of Heeresgruppe Weichsel, but further south, Konev's 1st Ukrainian Front was more successful and managed to advance 10km. Although Heeresgruppe Mitte had two Panzer Divisions in reserve and was not itself attacked, these divisions were not freed by Hitler to come to the aid of Heeresgruppe Weichsel. On 18 April, the Soviets succeeded in slowly but surely pushing back the German resistance but were unable to break through for the time being. The 1st Ukrainian Front managed to cross the River Spree in two places on 19 April, and the same day, the 1st Belorussian Front advanced to Müncheberg, 30km east of Berlin. Almost all the Third Guards Tank Army of the 1st Ukrainian Front managed to cross the Spree on the same day, followed a day later by the Fourth Guards Tank Army. These two armies advanced rapidly on 20 April, Hitler's birthday, reaching a point 15km from Zossen, the headquarters of the Wehrmacht's Supreme Command. The 2nd Belorussian Front, repositioned after its actions in East Prussia and Pomerania, launched its offensive on the same day and had no problem crossing the Oder between Stettin and Schwedt. The Second Guards Tank Army advanced to the north of Berlin, reaching Bernau on the Autobahn Berlin-Stettin. When one of the Soviet spearheads reached Fürstenwalde from the south, the Ninth Army was in danger of being surrounded. Busse, its commander, asked permission to withdraw, a request that Hitler refused. German units had to hold their ground at all times on all fronts; this was still his maxim.

## The fall of Berlin

For a moment an unexpected turn in the battle seemed possible when the Fourth Panzer Army of Heeresgruppe Mitte launched a counter-attack which appeared to have some effect. According to Hitler, the Ninth Army, supported by a newly formed Armee Abteilung Steiner, should now be in the position to attack the Soviet units advancing between the two Heeresgruppen from the flank. But it never happened; the Abteilung that Hitler wanted to deploy only existed on paper, and on 21 April the Twenty-first and Second Guards Tank Armies reached the outer defensive ring of Berlin at Werneuchen, followed a few hours later by the First and Eighth Guards Tank Armies further to the south-east. The Soviets' first priority was now to complete the encirclement of the city and then of the Ninth Army. The latter was accomplished on 23 April, when the lifeline between this Army and Berlin was cut. Hitler ordered the LVI Panzer Corps to withdraw to Berlin to defend the city, but on 25 April the encirclement of Berlin was complete and the battle in the city could begin.

Hitler still believed the situation could be retrieved. He ordered the Twelfth Army to attack from Belzig to Ferch in a north-easterly direction, while the Ninth Army was to launch an offensive to the west. The two Armies were then to advance to Berlin in combination over a broad front. At the same time, the Ninth Army would have to hold the eastern front so that Heeresgruppe Mitte could attack the Soviet units from the south. Meanwhile, Steiner with the 25th Panzergrenadiere Division, the 2nd Kriegsmarine Division and the 7th Panzer Division would have to prevent the 2nd Belorussian Front from breaking out of its bridgeheads on the west bank of the Oder. On 26 April it seemed that the Germans might be able to advance on all fronts, but the next day, all this turned out to be an illusion as the Soviet Third Tank Army managed to break through the German lines and advance west.

Meanwhile, heavy fighting was also taking place in Berlin itself. A

Young and old prepare for the final battle. In the background, a Berlin double-decker bus is still running.

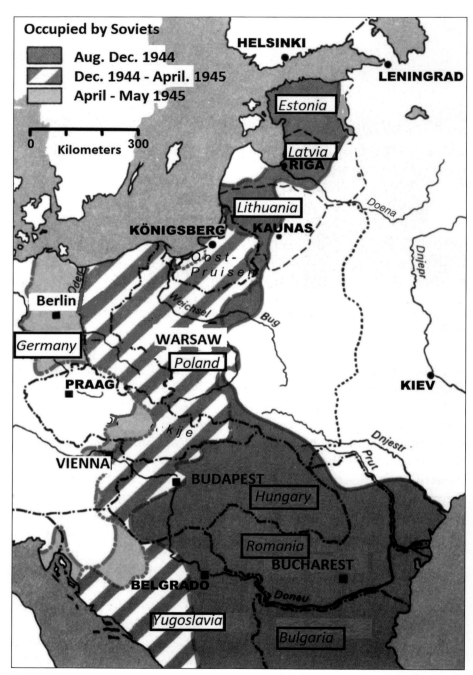

The final course of the front in May 1945.

In Berlin, the Western Allies were confronted by the impressive JS-3 tank. The design of this tank with its 'inverted frying pan' turret would define future generations of tanks in both East and West.

race had broken out between the Soviet units as to which would take the Reichstag building, the ultimate symbol of Nazism. The city was defended in the north by the 11th Fallschirmjäger Division, in the east and north-east by the Müncheberg Panzer Division (scraped together out of training units), in the south-east by the Nordland SS Panzergrenadiere Division, in the west by the 20th Panzergrenadiere Division and in the centre by the 18th Panzer Division. In addition, there were units of the French Charlemagne SS Panzergrenadiere Division. The Soviets' main attacks came from the south-east and north-west. That from the south-east focused on Tempelhof airfield and then the centre of the city, the attack from the north-west was aimed at the Reichstag. On 30 April the Reichstag fell and the Soviets were less than a mile from Hitler's bunker. On the same day, Hitler committed suicide, and on 1 May the German units in Berlin surrendered.

The fall of Berlin marked the end of the war, although fighting continued for another six days before the Germans officially surrendered at Rheims. Dönitz, the new Führer, tried to buy time for German units rushing west to surrender to the British and Americans. But with the fall of Berlin and the death of Hitler, the war in the East was over.

Looking at the Eastern Front, the following picture emerges. In the war as a whole, the Wehrmacht suffered a total of 10,340,000 casualties, including

5,100,000 dead and missing and 5,240,000 wounded. The number of dead and missing on the Eastern Front was 3,800,000, while 3,900,000 were wounded. In addition, approximately 1,000,000 civilians died in eastern Germany during combat operations and the flight to the west. On the Soviet side, the number of dead and missing was estimated at 10,000,000 and the number of wounded at 18,000,000. The real numbers may be considerably higher, because the Soviets always issued underestimates. The number of civilian casualties, on which reliable data is also lacking, will also have run into the tens of millions. But the war was not over yet, as we shall see in the Epilogue.

Epilogue

# Prelude to the Cold War

*After the fighting had ended at the beginning of May, relations between the Soviets and the Western Allies cooled considerably. The chief reason was the attitude of the Soviet Union towards conquered Germany and the German population, resulting in massive flows of refugee and forced deportations, in which more than 2,200,000 Germans died in the period up to 1947. The treks we described in the previous chapter were only a prelude to a much greater displacement of Germans in the closing months of the war and the years immediately thereafter. After the Soviet invasion of East Prussia, between 4,000,000 and 5,000,000 Germans fled from East Prussia, Pomerania, Silesia and East Brandenburg. Approximately 4,000,000 remained, because they delayed or simply did not want to leave their farms, businesses and homes. In addition, millions of Germans lived in the Sudetenland, annexed from Czechoslovakia in 1938, and many more millions of ethnic Germans had lived in Hungary, Poland, Yugoslavia and other eastern European countries since time immemorial. Over the past two years, support had developed within the Allied camp for the transfer of all Germans from the above-mentioned areas to Germany itself, and for the reduction of the total area of Germany by a quarter, by removing the areas historically linked to Germany east of the Oder-Neisse border. This was confirmed at the Potsdam Conference from 17 July to 2 August and enshrined in Article XIII of the Potsdam Protocol. It was partly based on what had been the satisfactory transfer of a total of 2,000,000 civilians between Greece and Turkey in the period 1923–1926 under the direction and coordination of the League of Nations. Hitler himself had played a role in pioneering the forced transfer of civilians: several hundred thousand Germans were moved by him between 1939 and 1941 from the Baltic countries and Bessarabia to western Poland, while at the same time Poles were moved from the west to the east. The aim of this transfer was to allow Germans to re-occupy those areas that had belonged to Germany before the Treaty of Versailles.*

## Deportations before the Potsdam Treaty

Deporting Germans from Poland, Czechoslovakia and other European countries had already been on the agenda at the Yalta Conference of the Allies. But while the Western Allies had pushed from early 1945 for the deportations to be delayed until January 1946, they were already in full swing before and during the Potsdam Conference. The Czechoslovak Minister of State, Ripka, had already indicated in November 1944 that his government wanted to deport all Germans from Czechoslovakia after the end of hostilities. US Secretary of State Stettinius, on 16 January 1945, stressed the need for appropriate international agreements, saying, 'Until such agreements are in place, the United States Government considers that no unilateral action should be taken to relocate large groups of persons.' The British government supported this position, stating that the question of the Germans should be covered by a more comprehensive treaty after the end of the war. Neither the Polish government-in-exile in London nor the Polish communist provisional government raised the question of the *Reichs-* and *Volksdeutsche* (citizens of Germany and ethnic Germans) with the Western Allies. They had apparently already made up their mind on what they considered to be a realistic division of Europe after the war. But the Western Allies had already indicated that these groups of Germans should be covered by further talks and agreements. In reality, the deportations in Poland had begun with the entry of Soviet troops, while in Czechoslovakia they only really got going after the armistice and the disarmament of the Wehrmacht, which still occupied large parts of the areas inhabited by Germans. While the State Department was still considering its position on the future of the Sudetenland, Czech militia and the liberation army under Svoboda were forcing Germans out of their homes and deporting them across the border in increasing numbers. Relatively few articles about the drama that was unfolding appeared in Western newspapers, but the picture they painted was unequivocal. This piece by Rhona Churchill appeared in the *Daily Mail* on 30 May about the deportation of 25,000 Germans from Brünn, now Brno.

> Shortly before 09: 00 they [the Czech militia] marched through the streets, calling on the Germans to be at the door at 09: 00 with a piece of hand luggage, ready to leave the city for good. Women had 10 minutes to wake up, dress themselves and the children, and throw some belongings together in a suitcase. On the street they had to hand over their jewellery, watches, furs and money; only wedding rings were spared. They were then taken to the Austrian border … Arriving at the border, the Austrian

border guards refused to admit the Germans and the Czechs refused to take them back. They were forced to camp in a field between the two borders.

At the time of the article's publication, the Germans had been in the same place for over a month, and hundreds were dying of typhus every day. In the same period, the International Red Cross reported numerous times on the inhumanity of the deportations. One such report read:

> Take the case of the children. On 27 July, a boat arrived in Berlin's western harbor area with a pitiful cargo of 300 children. They came from a children's home in Finkenwalde in Pomerania and were half starved to death. Children from 2 to 14 years old lay in the hold, motionless, their faces gray with hunger, suffering from everything. Their bodies, knees and hands were swollen – a known symptom of starvation.

On the basis of these reports and other information, the Western Allies wanted to sign clear and binding agreements in Potsdam about the movement of large groups of Germans.

## The Potsdam Treaty

The number of Germans to be relocated was unknown at the time of the Potsdam Conference, but on paper it amounted to approximately 15,000,000 civilians, a total that is hard to comprehend. The Soviets had every interest in representing these numbers as being as low as possible. For example, the Poles and Soviets initially indicated at Potsdam that there were just 1,500,000 Germans in the areas east of the Oder-Neisse border. In reality, there were 4,000,000, while another 1,000,000 Germans were on their way back to their homes in those areas after the end of hostilities. They demanded that these Germans be moved to the west.

However, the Western Allies had always assumed there would be only limited transfers of well-defined groups of people. The United States in particular was reluctant to agree to any more. For example, the State Department's Briefing Book Paper of 12 January 1945 stated that the US 'should, whenever possible, express its preference for a limited transfer.' While Churchill declared on 15 December in a heated debate in the House of Commons that 'deportation is a method which, as far as we can see, is the most satisfactory with the longest lasting result', at the Potsdam Conference, partly on the basis of German data, he began to reconsider the possible extent of deportations. He responded to the demands of Poles and Soviets for the forced deportation of all Germans in their assigned areas with the following words: 'The British have very strong moral objections to the displacement of large numbers of people. We can accept a transfer of … say, between 2,000,000 and 3,000,000 people. But a deportation of between 8,000,000 and 9,000,000 people, what the Poles demand, is too much and would be completely wrong.' But in the end, the United States and Great Britain succumbed to pressure from the Soviets and their allies. In Article XIII of the Potsdam Protocol, the signatories committed themselves to a gradual, orderly and humane transfer under proper direction and coordination in order to minimize suffering and death among the deportees. How all this should take place was not elaborated, but was declared to be the joint responsibility of the signatories.

The way in which the Soviets and others interpreted this was an embarrassment to the Western Allies in the early years of peace and helped shape their attitude towards the Soviet Union in the Cold War. Churchill, in his famous address at Westminster College, Fulton on 5 March, 1946, stated that 'the Soviet-dominated Polish government has been encouraged to abuse the position of Germany in a grand and reprehensible manner; at present, mass deportations are taking place in a terrifying manner and on an unprecedented scale.' At that time, to the astonishment of the Western Allies, deportations had indeed begun on an massive scale. Between 3,000,000 and 6,000,000 Germans had been expected, but a massive flood of 15,000,000 deportees had started. Roughly speaking, this was made up of approximately 10,000,000 Germans from the areas occupied by Poland, 3,500,000 from the Sudetenland and 1,500,000 from other areas in Europe. Moreover, the deportations bore no resemblance to the 'gradual, human and orderly transfer' agreed upon at Potsdam.

Article XIII of the Potsdam Protocol instructed the Allied Control Council to record the numbers involved and where the deportees were at that time, and to ensure a balanced distribution across the various occupation zones. The Czechoslovak and Polish governments and the Control Council in Hungary were informed of this and called upon to stop uncoordinated deportations. Through these measures, the Western Allies hoped to gain the necessary space to put everything in place in terms of housing and food supplies for the winter of 1945/46. Mass deaths from starvation, malnutrition and disease were feared.

Stalin paid lip service to this provision, but in a prelude to the Cold War, Soviet propaganda in Poland and Czechoslovakia emphasized the pro-German and pro-fascist attitudes of the Western Allies. Only the Control Council in Hungary suspended the deportations until the beginning of January 1946. Poland supported the temporary cessation of deportations but stated that it wanted to free Stettin and Silesia from Germans, in order to rebuild these industrial areas as quickly as possible. In other words, the deportations continued for a different reason. The Czechoslovaks, in turn, evaded the agreement by pouring as many deportees as possible into the Soviet occupation zone. These refugees then generally cut their losses and tried to reach the American and British occupation zones. The Czechoslovak government claimed that, in line with the Potsdam protocol, these were 'organized transports', while the Americans stated that the treatment of the Germans by the Czechoslovaks was actually the reverse of an 'orderly and humane transfer'. Intelligence reports pointed to widespread abuse of and violence against Germans, who fled for fear of losing their lives. The worst excess was the murder on 31 July 1945 by Czech militia of between 1,000 and 2,700 Germans in Aussig after the blowing up of an ammunition depot. Incidentally, these events prompted the Czechoslovak government to urge the Allies to speed up the deportations, for fear of further sabotage actions by the Germans. This was a bizarre accusation, since most of the German civilian population was already locked up in detention camps or anxiously waiting at home.

This all caused considerable unrest in Great Britain and the United States. Churchill, one of the architects of the deportations, expressed his anxiety in a speech to the House of Commons on 16 August 1945:

I am deeply alarmed at the reports reaching us about the conditions under which the deportation and exodus of the Germans from the new Poland are to take place ... Sparse and tentative accounts of what happened there and is still playing out paint a picture of a tragedy on an unprecedented scale unfolding behind the iron curtain that currently divides Europe in two.

On 15 September 1945, *The Economist* noted:

Despite the Potsdam Declaration demanding an end to the disorganized and inhumane deportation of Germans, the forced expulsion from the provinces of East Prussia, Pomerania, Silesia and parts of Brandenburg continues. These provinces had a population of around 9,000,000 in 1939. Likewise, the deportation of 3,500,000 Sudeten Germans from Czechoslovakia continues. The Council of Foreign Ministers must stop this harrowing tragedy. The wandering millions are almost without food or shelter. The uninhabitable parts of the major urban areas were already overcrowded before the arrival of the refugees, and the rural areas have limited shelter options. The inevitable result will be that millions of them will die of hunger and exhaustion. The Germans, no doubt, have deserved their punishment, but not by torture in this way. If the Poles and Czechs want to be regarded as higher than the Nazis, they must stop the deportations immediately.

Unease was growing in the House of Commons. On 10 October, Foreign Secretary Bevin was asked whether the British government had already protested to the government of Poland about 'the atrocities committed against German women and children in the context of the deportations'. Bevin replied that there had been vigorous protests against these practices, but on 22 October the House of Commons was told by Special Envoy Captain Marples that 'on the basis of the most recent reports from the Red Cross, protests against the disorganized deportation of Germans by the Poles and Czechs did not have had an effect and large numbers of refugees are pouring into Berlin, where thousands are dying in the streets.' On 25 October, a delegation led by Sir William Beveridge comprising seven MPs, four bishops and a other prominent Britons, including several writers, visited Prime Minister Attlee to urge 'negotiations' in view of the imminent starvation of millions by the Russians, Poles and Czechs; the aim was to immediately halt the deportation of Germans from their homes in Eastern Europe during the winter and develop a joint Allied policy in this matter before spring. The Commons devoted the entire following day to discussing conditions on the European continent and concluded that continuing the deportations through the winter was contrary to the Potsdam agreements. But *The Economist* concluded on 10 November that the deportations were continuing despite all the pressure. It was clear that the governments of the Soviet Union, Poland and Czechoslovakia took little notice of the treaty, and the influx of refugees into the British and American zones of occupation continued. At that time, 9,600,000 refugees were in the western zone; the population of Schleswig-Holstein, for example, had increased by 33 per cent due to the arrival of 860,000 refugees.

Bertrand Russell also sounded the alarm in an article in *The Times* of 19 October 1945:

In Eastern Europe, mass deportations are now being carried out on an unprecedented scale by our allies in an apparent attempt to exterminate many millions of Germans, not by gas, but by taking their homes and deprive them of food and let them die a slow starvation.

On 8 December, in an article in the *New Leader*, Russell again protested vehemently against the deportations. He described people being evicted from their homes and put on trains to Berlin:

> The journey to Berlin takes many days and the refugees are not given any food. Many are dead when they reach Berlin; children who die on the way are thrown out of the windows. A member of the American Friends' Ambulance Unit describes the arrival of the trains in Berlin as 'the same as Belsen – carts carry the dead from the platforms' ... British officers compare the condition of people they find in Berlin hospitals to those of concentration camps.

Reports in other newspapers described the journey of 325 orphans and sick children in cattle trucks from Danzig to Berlin in the last week of August. The only food they were given was twenty potatoes and some bread; fifty of them had perished during the 7-day journey, their bodies thrown from the train, and nine died after arriving in Berlin. In the same period, a transport of Sudeten Germans arrived who had completed an 18-day journey in open boxcars. Of the 2.400 who started the journey, 1,050 did not survive. All reports indicated that they had been subjected to robbery, violence and rape throughout the journey to the western zones.

As emotions ran high in newspapers such as the *Daily Herald* and the *News Chronicle*, the Allied Control Council worked out a plan to control the deportations. The pressure for rapid results was heightened by reports from General Eisenhower and Secretary of State Byrnes, both of whom expressed deep concern about the methods of deportation. In addition, increasingly ominous reports reached Byrnes from Czechoslovakia, where anti-Czech sentiment among US military personnel, who were eyewitnesses to the violence against German civilians, was growing rapidly and confrontations loomed. They had already protected women and children against excesses of the Czech militias many times, and the US military authorities feared further escalation.

The plan was finally presented on 20 November. It assumed that there were still 3,500,000 Germans in Poland. Of this number, 2,000,000 would be moved to the Soviet zone and 1,500,000 to the British zone. Of the 2,500,000 Germans in the Sudetenland and other areas in Europe, 1,750,000 would be moved to the American zone and 750,000 to the Soviet zone. Germans from Austria would be moved to the French zone. From December 1945, 10 per cent of these groups would be deported to the relevant zones each month, with the exception of January and February, when 5 per cent would be moved. The general deportation would be completed by August 1946. It was agreed that during extreme weather conditions and if the agreed number of deportees was exceeded, their movement would be temporarily halted. These were very necessary agreements, since in the American and British zones average daily calorie intake had fallen to 1,000, and only 10 to 20 per cent of pre-war housing was habitable.

## Organized deportations

Although the Control Council had now presented a plan, it had neither the administrative nor the logistical organization to carry it out. In practice, therefore, it remained dependent on the benevolence of the Soviets, Poles, Czechs and Hungarians. Both the British government and the International Red Cross tried to control the deportations in the first months of 1946, but without success. Trainloads of refugees continued to arrive in the American and British zones, having not been allowed to take anything more than hand luggage and 500 Reichsmarks. Although most refugees now generally arrived in better condition, some weaker ones did not survive deportation. Many were malnourished, and British and American doctors repeatedly found that women had been victims of rape. Western newspapers now followed the deportations closely, with the *New York Times* reporting in February 1946 that 'the exodus is taking place under conditions reminiscent of a nightmare, without any international supervision and without any pretense of humane treatment. We are responsible for these horrors, which can only be compared to those of the Nazis.' In October the same newspaper wrote that 'the scale of the migration and the conditions under which it is taking place are unprecedented in history. Anyone who has seen the horrors for themselves will conclude that it is a crime against humanity.' As 1946 progressed, however, the situation improved and the number of casualties among the refugees gradually declined. During the winter months, US and UK authorities were able to postpone several deportations to a later date, and the International Red Cross was, to some extent, able to establish workable relations with the Polish Ministry of the Interior. In total, approximately 6,000,000 Germans were moved by means of these organized transports, many more than the Western Allies had planned for. Although the transports rarely met the western minimum standards in the fields of food and medical care, many lives were already being saved by knowing which transports, and of what size, would arrive where and when.

While the American and British authorities focused on sheltering the deportees, the International Red Cross tried to gain access to the internment camps where the Germans were assembled for transportation. It based its request on the fact that these were civilian internees who could be visited at any time. However, the Red Cross was given only limited access, and the situation in the camps it visited was diplomatically described as 'completely inadequate'. This was putting it mildly. For example, the Czechs had used Theresienstadt, the former Nazi concentration camp, to house internees. H.G. Adler, a former Jewish camp inmate, reported that 'the people were appallingly malnourished and mistreated' and that 'the majority of them were children and youths, who were imprisoned only because they were German. Just because they were German …? This sentence sounds terrifyingly familiar, only the word "Jew" has been replaced with "German".' Some camps were particularly notorious. For example, 6,448 (!) of the 8,064 internees in the Lamsdorf camp in Upper Silesia died from malnutrition, illnesses, hard work and physical violence. When the last transports arrived in the western zones in 1947, a final tally could be drawn up. Approximately 12,000,000 refugees from the various areas had fled or been deported to the western zones. Of these, 2,200,000 had died, 1,000,000 of them those who had fled west before the end of the fighting, and the remaining 1,200,000 between May 1945 and May 1947.

## Towards a new confrontation: the beginning of the Cold War

As these tragedies unfolded, Britain and the United States could only watch. They could protest that the extent and manner in which the deportations were being carried out violated the Potsdam Treaty, but they could not intervene. In the first place, the deportations were being carried out by sovereign states exercising their treaty obligations as they saw fit. Secondly, it was all happening in the sphere of influence of the Soviet Union, the only nation that had the power to stop the deportations at any time, or to carry them out as a 'gradual, orderly and human transfer'. However, the Soviet Union had no interest in doing this, and gave countries such as Poland, Czechoslovakia and Hungary free rein to exact revenge against Germans. These countries had, however, overlooked one not insignificant element in their revenge: the deported Germans were generally highly educated people who had played a key role in areas such as administration, agriculture, heavy industry, the chemical and textile industries, shipbuilding, precision mechanics, the optical industry and trade. When these people left for the west, invaluable knowledge and experience left with them. While the Allies still assumed in 1947 that mass emigration of Germans to France and the United States was an option for the overpopulated and malnourished western part of Germany, in 1948 the resources of the Marshall Plan fell on fertile ground and ensured that the population would create the *Wirtschaftswunder*, the economic miracle of West Germany.

The tragedy that unfolded before the eyes of the Western Allies also made a deep impression on a whole generation of soldiers and politicians. It was clear to them that after the victory over Germany they were now confronted by a new opponent with a very different view of freedom, democracy and human rights – and a powerful opponent, moreover, which would pursue its goals in the field of international relations without scruple, using all means at its disposal. In his famous article 'The Sources of Soviet Conduct', George Kennan, then US Ambassador to Moscow, outlined in the July 1947 issue of *Foreign Affairs* magazine under the pseudonym 'X' the concept of what would later become known as the 'Truman Doctrine'. American and British policy towards the Soviet Union was consequently adjusted from 'appeasement' to 'containment', and the war on the Eastern Front gradually turned into the Cold War. However, it was only at the end of the 1980s that the inhabitants of Eastern Europe achieved freedom and democracy; the inhabitants of the former Soviet Union again fell under autocratic rule in the first years of the twenty-first century, and Russia has become an aggressor state which pursues its goals remorselessly, without respect for human rights and making crimes against humanity its trademark. As the Soviet Union did in the Second World War.

# Appendix

# Absolute and Relative Battlefield Performance

The Historical Evaluation and Research Organization (HERO) has built up a database of more than one hundred battles from the First and Second World Wars, supplemented with data from the Korean War and the wars in the Middle East. This database is used to map the combat effectiveness of the various armies. T. N. Dupuy, in his book *A Genius for War. The German Army and the General Staff*, gives a detailed list of the battles in this database. On the basis of this data, he calculated the battlefield performance of the combatants involved

The distinction between absolute and relative battlefield performance is important. The first follows from the calculation of the losses on each side with equal strength; the second takes into account a number of circumstances and links them to a factor. These are the circumstances and factors concerned, in which operating from a defensive posture is the central theme:

- Hurried defence, a factor of 1.2 advantage
- Prepared defence, a factor 1.5 advantage
- Reinforced defence, a factor of 1.6 advantage

All kinds of combinations are of course possible. For instance, fighting initially from a prepared defence line, followed by a hurried defence during a possible retreat. These are further elaborated below. It is striking that the Germans are always in a minority but always have a higher absolute and relative battlefield performance.

## A. Overview of German versus Allied units in World War I (ten encounters)

|  | Allied forces | German forces |
|---|---|---|
| Battle strength of the units involved | 6,896,000 | 5,090,000 |
| Number of casualties | 2,349,000 | 1,866,000 |
| Losses with equal combat strength | 3,241,620 | 1,866,000 |
| Absolute battlefield performance per man | 1.0 | 1.73 |
| Relative battlefield performance per man | 1.0 | 1.44 |

The various encounters involved a total of 6,896,000 men on the Allied side and 5,090,000 men on the German side: a difference factor of 1.36. If there had been as many Germans as Allies, the losses on the Allied side would have been correspondingly higher. The number of losses compared to each other yields the absolute battlefield performance: 1.73. This means that on the Allied side there were 1.73 victims per fallen German. The relative battlefield performance is a factor 1.2 lower because the Germans fought partly from defensive positions and thus had a relative advantage.

## B. Overview of German versus Allied units in World War II (78 encounters)

|  | Allied forces | German forces |
|---|---|---|
| Battle strength of the units involved | 1,783,237 | 940,198 |
| Number of casualties | 47,743 | 48,585 |
| Losses with equal combat strength | 89,838 | 48,585 |
| Absolute battlefield performance per man | 1.0 | 1.84 |
| Relative battlefield performance per man | 1.0 | 1.53 |

The various battles (78 in total) involved a total of 1,783,237 men on the Allied side and 940,198 men on the German side: a difference factor of 1.8. If there had been as many Germans as Allies, the losses on Allied side would have been correspondingly higher (factor 1.8). The number of losses compared to each other yields the absolute battlefield performance: 1.84. This means that on the Allied side there were 1.84 victims per fallen German. The relative battlefield performance is a factor 1.2 lower because the Germans fought partly from defensive positions and thus had a relative advantage. Incidentally, this does not take into account the air superiority and the predominance in materiel on the Allied side. It is unclear what factor should be attributed to this, but it is clear that it should be at least a factor of 1.5, therefore the relative battlefield performance should be 2.25..

## C.  Kursk: Obeyan sector 5–11 July 1943

|  | Soviet forces | German forces |
|---|---|---|
| Battle strength of the units involved | 98,000 | 62,000 |
| Number of casualties | 22,000 | 13,600 |
| Losses with equal combat strength | 34,750 | 13,600 |
| Absolute battlefield performance per man | 1.0 | 2.55 |
| Relative battlefield performance per man | 1.0 | 4.08 |

The Soviets started the fighting at Kursk with 98,000 men versus 62,000 on the German side: a difference factor of 1.58. If there had been as many Germans as Soviets, the losses on the Soviet side would have been correspondingly higher (factor 1.58). The number of losses compared to each other yields the absolute battlefield performance: 2.55. This means that on the Soviet side, there were 2.55 killed per fallen German. The relative battlefield performance is a factor of 1.6 higher because the Soviets were in entrenched positions and thus had a relative advantage – relative battlefield performance 4.08.

## D.  Eastern Front 1944

|  | Soviet forces | German forces |
|---|---|---|
| Battle strength of the units involved | 6,100,000 | 3,500,000 |
| Number of casualties | 5,000,000 | 1,100,000 |
| Losses with equal combat strength | 8,714,000 | 1,100,000 |
| Absolute battlefield performance per man | 1.0 | 7.90 |
| Relative battlefield performance per man | 1.0 | 6.07 |

The Soviets started 1944 with 6,100,000 men versus 3,500,000 on the German side: a difference factor of 1.74. The Soviets, unlike the Germans, were able to maintain their strength during the course of the year through the influx of new units. As a result, the German strength fell to around 2,500,000 men. If there had been as many Germans as Soviets, the losses on the Soviet side would have been correspondingly higher (factor 1.74). The number of losses compared to each other yields the absolute battlefield performance: 7.90. This means that on the Soviet side 7.90 were killed per fallen German. The relative battlefield performance is a factor 1.3 lower because the Germans had the opportunity to build reinforcements and therefore had a relative advantage. This does not take into account the fact that during the course of the year the combat strength on the German side fell from 3,500,000 to 2,500,000. If the average is taken as 3,000,000 men, the ratios are 2.03, 9.22 and 7.09 respectively.

## E.  El Alamein

|  | Allied forces | German/Italian forces |
|---|---|---|
| Battle strength of the units involved | 195,000 | 82,000 |
| Number of casualties | 2,400 | 1,100/1,200 |
| Losses with equal combat strength | 5,520 | 1,100/1,200 |
| Absolute battlefield performance per man | 1.0 | 2.4 |
| Relative battlefield performance per man | 1.0 | 1.6 |

The British started fighting at El Alamein with 195,000 men versus 82,000 on the German/Italian side: a difference factor of 2.3. If there had been as many Germans and Italians as British, the losses on the British side would have been correspondingly higher (factor of 2.3). The number of losses compared with each other provides the absolute battlefield performance: 2.4. This means that on the British side 2.4 men were killed for every fallen German or Italian. The relative battlefield performance is 1.5 times lower because the Germans and Italians were in defensive positions and thus had a comparative advantage. Incidentally, the Axis forces were made up of German and Italian units. The latter had clearly a lower battlefield performance than the Germans. In other words, if only German units had participated in the fighting, the battlefield performance would have been higher.

# Bibliography

1. Adair P. (1994), *Hitler's Greatest Defeat. Disaster on the Eastern Front*. London: Rigel Publications.
2. Alger, J.I. (1982), *The Quest for Victory*. Westport: Greenwood Press.
3. Army Department (1951), *Rear area security in Russia*. Washington: Office of the Chief of Military History.
4. Army Department (1951), *Military improvisation during the Russian Campaign*. Washington: Office of the Chief of Military History.
5. Alvensleben, U. von (1971), *Lauter Abschiede. Tagesbuche im Kriege*. Frankfurt am Main: Verlag Ullstein Gmbh.
6. Auteurs van Command Magazine (1988), *Hitler's Armies; the evolution and structure of German Armed Forces, 1933-1945*, New York: Combined Books, Inc.
7. Broekmeyer M. ( 1999), *Stalin, de Russen en hun oorlog*. Amsterdam: Uitgeverij JanMets.
8. Creveld, M. van (1974), *Fighting Power*. Westport: Greenwood Press.
9. Creveld, M. van (1977), *Supplying War; logistics from Wallenstein to Patton*. Cambridge: Cambridge University Press.
10. Creveld, M. van (1986), 'On learning from the Wehrmacht and other things', in: *Military Review*, January.
11. Dunnigan, I.F. (ed.) (1978), *The Russian Front; Germany's war in the East 1941-1945*. London: Arms and Armour Press.
12. Dupuy, T.N. (1977), *A Genius for War; the German army and the General staff*. London: Macdonald and Jane's.
13. Erickson, J. (2003), *The Road to Stalingrad*. London: Cassell Military Paperbacks.
14. Franz, P. (1984), 'Operational concepts', in *Military Review*, July, pp. 2–15.
15. Garder, M. (1966), *A History of the Soviet Army*. London: Pall Mall Press.
16. Glantz, D.M. (2005), *Colossus Reborn. The Red Army at war, 1941-1943*. Lawrence: University Press of Kansas.
17. Glantz, D.M. and House J. (1995), *When Titans Clashed; how the Red Army stopped Hitler*. Lawrence: University Press of Kansas.
18. Griffith, R. (1992), *Forward into Battle*. Navato (Ca): Presidio Press.
19. Grossjohan, G. (1999), *Five Years, Four Fronts*. New York: Ballantine Books.
20. Guderian, H. (1952/2000), *Panzer Leader*. London: Penguin Group.
21. Hamburger Institut für Sozialforschung (2002), Ausstellungskatalog. Verbrechender Wehrmacht. *Dimensionen des Vernichtungskrieges 1941-1944*. Hamburg: Institutsverlag.
22. Krönke, H. (2004), *The Tiger Project. Schwere Panzer (Tiger) Abteilung 505*. Atglen (PA): Schiffer Military Books.
23. Kurowski, F. (1994), *Infantry Aces. The German soldier in combat in WW II*. Mechanicsburg (PA): Stackpole Books.
24. Laffin, J. (1965), *Jackboot; the story of the German soldier*. New York: Cassell
25. Lewin, R. (ed.) (1984), *The War on Land 1939-1945*. London: Random House

26. Lewis, S.J. (1988), 'Reflections on German military reform' in: *Military Review*, August 1995.
27. Main, S.J. (1997), *The Red Army and the Future War in Europe, 1925-1940*. London: Conflict Studies Research Centre.
28. Messenger, C. (1976), *The Art of Blitzkrieg*. Shepperton (Surrey): Ian Allen Ltd
29. Merridale, C. (2004), *Ivan's War. The Red Army 1939-1945*. London: Faber & Faber.
30. Michulec, R. (2000), *Panzer-Division 1935-1945. The early years 1935-1943*. Hong Kong: Concord Publications.
31. Michulec, R. (2001), *Panzer-Division 1935-1945.The Eastern Front 1941-1941*. Hong Kong: Concord Publications.
32. Millett, A.R. and Murray, W. (eds) (1988), *Military Effectiveness*, volume III, *The Second World War*. Boston: Mershon Centre, The Ohio State University.
33. Milward, A.S. (1979), *War, Economy and Society 1939-1945*. Los Angeles: Universityof California Press.
34. Murray, W. (1990), 'Force strategy, Blitzkrieg strategy and the economic difficulties: Nazi grand strategy in the 1930s' in: Military Review, May.
35. Murray, W. (1992), *German Military Effectiveness*. New York: The Nautical & Aviation Publishing Company of America.
36. Murray, W. and Millet, A.R. (eds) (1996), *Military Innovation in the Interwar Period*. Cambridge: Cambridge University press.
37. O'Balance, E. (1964), *The Red Army*. London: Faber and Faber.
38. Oeting, D.W. (1993), *Auftragstaktik*. Frankfurt am Main/Bonn: Report VerlagGmbH.
39. Ogilvie, R. (1995), Krijgen is een Kunst. Amsterdam: Addison Wesley Publishing Company Inc.
40. Overy, R. (1996), Why the Allies won. New York: W.W. Norton & Company.
41. Perrett, B. (1986/1997), *Knights of the Black Cross*. London: Wordsworth Editions Limited.
42. Piekalkiewicz, J. (1998), *Die Deutsche Reichsbahn im Zweiten Weltkrieg*. Stuttgart: Transpress Verlag.
43. Posen, B.R. (1984), *The Sources of Military Doctrine; France, Britain and Germanybetween the two world wars*. New York: Cornell Studies in Security Affairs.
44. Rees, L. (1999), *War of the Century. When Hitler fought Stalin*. New York: The New Press.
45. Richey, S.W (1984), Review, 'The philosophical basis of the Airland Battle' in: *Military Press*, May, pp 51–2.
46. Rosinski, H. and Craig, G.A. (ed) (1966), *The German Army*. London: Pall Mall
47. Rubbel, A. (2003), *The Tiger Project. Schwere Panzer (Tiger) Abteilung 503*. Atglen (PA): Schiffer Military Books.
48. Samuelson, L. (2000), *Plans for Stalin's War Machine. Tukhachevsky and Military-Economic Planning, 1925–1941*. London: Macmillan Press.
49. Scheiber, H. (1996), *Die 6. Panzer-Division 1937-1945*. Eggolsheim: NebelVerlag Gmbh.
50. Schneider, R., (2003), *Siege. A Novel of the Eastern Front*. New York: Presidio Press.
51. Scott, H.F. and Scott, W.F. (1982), *The Soviet Art of War*. Boulder: Westview Press.
52. Seaton, A. and Seaton, J. (1986), *The Soviet Army 1918 to Present*. New York: New American Library.
53. Shepherd, B. (2004), *War in the Wild East; the German Army and Soviet Partisans*. Cambridge: Harvard University Press.

54. Stoecker, S.W. (1988), *Forging Stalin's Army. Marshal Tukhachevsky and the Politics of Military Innovation*. Boulder: Westview Press.
55. Thorwald, I. (1951), *Defeat in the East*. New York: Ballantine Books Inc.
56. Tsouras, P.G. (2002), *Panzers on the Eastern Front. General Ehrard Raus and his Panzer Divisions in Russia. 1941– 1945*. London: Greenhill Books.
57. Wilbeck, C.W. (2004), *Sledgehammer. Strengths and Flaws of Tiger Tank Battalions in World War II*. Bedford (PA): The Aberjona Press.
58. Wilt, A.F. (1990), *War from the Top. German and British military decision making during World War II*. London: Tauris and Co Publishers.
59. Zayas, A.M. de (1989), *Nemesis at Potsdam. The expulsion of the Germans from the east.* Lincoln: University of Nebraska Press.
60. Ziemke, E.F. (2004), *The Red Army 1918-1941: from vanguard of world revolution to US ally*. London and New York: Frank Cass.

# Index

Dear Reader,

We hope you have enjoyed this book, but why not share your views on social media? You can also follow our pages to see more about our other products: facebook.com/penandswordbooks or follow us on X @penswordbooks

You can also view our products at www.pen-and-sword.co.uk (UK and ROW) or www.penandswordbooks.com (North America).

To keep up to date with our latest releases and online catalogues, please sign up to our newsletter at: www.pen-and-sword.co.uk/newsletter

If you would like a printed catalogue with our latest books, then please email: enquiries@pen-and-sword.co.uk or telephone: 01226 734555 (UK and ROW) or email: uspen-and-sword@casematepublishers.com or telephone: (610) 853-9131 (North America).

We respect your privacy and we will only use personal information to send you information about our products.

Thank you!